KNOWING EMOTIONS

KNOWING EMOTIONS

Truthfulness and Recognition
in Affective Experience

Rick Anthony Furtak

OXFORD
UNIVERSITY PRESS

OXFORD

UNIVERSITY PRESS

Oxford University Press is a department of the University of Oxford. It furthers
the University's objective of excellence in research, scholarship, and education
by publishing worldwide. Oxford is a registered trade mark of Oxford University
Press in the UK and certain other countries.

Published in the United States of America by Oxford University Press
198 Madison Avenue, New York, NY 10016, United States of America.

© Oxford University Press 2018

First issued as an Oxford University Press paperback, 2020

All rights reserved. No part of this publication may be reproduced, stored in
a retrieval system, or transmitted, in any form or by any means, without the
prior permission in writing of Oxford University Press, or as expressly permitted
by law, by license, or under terms agreed with the appropriate reproduction
rights organization. Inquiries concerning reproduction outside the scope of the
above should be sent to the Rights Department, Oxford University Press, at the
address above.

You must not circulate this work in any other form
and you must impose this same condition on any acquirer.

Library of Congress Cataloging-in-Publication Data
Names: Furtak, Rick Anthony, author.
Title: Knowing emotions : truthfulness and recognition in affective
experience / Rick Anthony Furtak.
Description: New York, NY : Oxford University Press,
United States of America, [2018] | Includes bibliographical references and index.
Identifiers: LCCN 2017030834 (print) | LCCN 2017033766 (ebook) |
ISBN 9780190492052 (updf) | ISBN 9780190492069 (online course) |
ISBN 9780190862077 (epub) | ISBN 9780190492045 (cloth : acid-free paper) |
ISBN 9780190099794 (paper : acid-free paper)
Subjects: LCSH: Emotions. | Perception. | Cognition.
Classification: LCC BF723.E6 (ebook) | LCC BF723.E6 F87 2018 (print) |
DDC 152.4–dc23
LC record available at https://lccn.loc.gov/2017030834

*This book is dedicated
to my friends
and family members*

CONTENTS

Acknowledgments   *ix*

PART I
THE RATIONAL AND THE PASSIONATE

1. The Intelligence of Emotions: Differing Schools
   of Thought   3

2. What the Empirical Evidence Suggests   23

PART II
ON REASONABLE FEELINGS AND EMBODIED
COGNITION

3. Feeling Apprehensive   51

4. Emotions as Felt Recognitions   75

CONTENTS

PART III
THE REASONS OF THE HEART

5. On the Emotional *A Priori*   103

6. Love's Knowledge; or, The Significance of What
   We Care About   123

7. Attunement and Perspectival Truth   159

Bibliography   *199*
Index   *225*

ACKNOWLEDGMENTS

These acknowledgments cannot possibly do justice to the many persons upon whom I have depended while writing this book. (One way to have written these pages would have been simply to thank all of the medical doctors who have kept me alive, and to whom I am grateful.) I will inevitably fail to thank adequately those whom I mention, and to say thanks to everyone who deserves this. One must, I'm afraid, be patient and forgiving in order to remain among the friends whom I decided are the most appropriate dedicatees of this text.

For some time, I was planning to have two women whom I admire share the dedication; although I changed my mind about this late in the day, the thought is still worth noting. M. C. N. and K. A. N. have influenced my life and thought profoundly over the past two decades. I thank them both.

This book has been shaped by unusual circumstances, and the writing of these acknowledgments is no exception. When I look back at the acknowledgments page in my first book, I am astonished by the reminder of how many people in my intellectual community at the time had shaped my way of thinking. The only parallel I can draw to that incredibly stimulating environment, in my more recent experience, is the world of ideas that I share with my undergraduate students. Yet to thank individually more than a handful of current and former students would require drawing an inevitably arbitrary line between those named and the rest. So I will say here only a brief word of thanks to all of the Colorado College students who have taken my Philosophy of Emotions course over the past decade or so, for all that they have taught me.

I ought to have admitted earlier a debt to my undergraduate mentors decades ago, Victor Kestenbaum and Christopher Ricks. Their traces are evident in many places here. Those who have helped me most recently, even reading in rapid fashion a draft of the very final chapter, are Ulrika Carlsson, an incisive critic who has led me to clarify a number of things, as well as James D. Reid, a brilliant author and kindred spirit whose judgment I trust almost more than my own, and who is my number one most significant philosophical interlocutor. Sharon Krishek must have been separated from me at birth, although we were born six months apart across the world from each other, because no one else has ever been such a philosophical twin. Heather Churchill, Troy Jollimore, and J. P. Rosensweig provided crucial feedback on some or all of these chapters, aiding my final revisions. Finally, Maria Alexandra Keller has become a friend whose point of view matters more than I could say, and from whom I have learned much. Special thanks to each of them. Other friends with whom I've had critically important discussions related to the themes of this book include Nicole Hassoun, Alyssa Luboff, Madeline Mindich, Willow Mindich, Edward F. Mooney, and Sarah Pessin.

Within the hospitable environment of Colorado College, I am grateful to my discussions with George Butte, Helen Daly, Marion Hourdequin, Jonathan Lee, David Mason, and John Riker.

Individual conversations with philosophers less familiar to me have been crucial, especially when they have taken place when I was taking them from the Denver airport to my campus an hour's drive from there. For this reason I am grateful to Robert Audi, Cheshire Calhoun, Ronald de Sousa, Jesse Prinz, and Matthew Ratcliffe. Innumerable dialogues with Tomi-Ann Roberts have been more significant for this project than those with any other colleague at my home institution, and helped open my eyes to the rich possibilities of doing interdisciplinary research on emotion.

Those were the short lists. Charlotte Allyn, Matthias Barker, Aaron Ben-Ze'ev, the late Ted Cohen, Ben Crowe, Vita Emery, the late Matthew Geiger, Eleanor Helms, Andrew Henscheid, Sara Huizenga, Chad Kidd, Y. Mike Kim, Lior Levy, Teelin Lucero, Kym Maclaren, Jean-Luc Marion, Jennifer McWeeny, Ann V. Murphy, Julie Piering, Robert C. Roberts, Anthony Rudd, Camisha Russell, Shahrzad Safavi, Emma Schiestl, David Stevens, Ella Street, Maria Talero, Iain Thomson, Kate Withy, Dave Young, and Dan Zahavi—have assisted my thinking, in some cases by simply asking a question after a talk. A nameless reader for Oxford University Press also made helpful suggestions, and I am particularly thankful to Lucy Randall for being such an exemplary editor throughout the process of bringing this to birth in its present form.

Cal Poly in San Luis Obispo, the Center for Subjectivity Research in Copenhagen, Colorado College, Northern Arizona University, Ryerson University, Syracuse University, the University of Colorado, Denver; and, the University of Haifa: at each of these institutions some of this text was presented, and in each case there were valuable comments made by members of the audience whose names I have not mentioned and may not know. The same is true of both times that I presented parts of the manuscript-in-progress at the Southwest Seminar in Continental Philosophy, and when I did so twice at the International Society of Research on Emotion.

Let me acknowledge Kate Barnes for her fine, dedicated work in preparing the index, and Colorado College for providing summer funding for the collaborative research grant that enabled Kate to be hired as my assistant.

Chapter 6 incorporates and expands upon my "Love as the Ultimate Ground of Practical Reason," which appeared in *Love, Reason, and Will*, edited by John Davenport and Anthony Rudd (New York: Bloomsbury Academic, 2015).

To end where I began, allow me to express a debt of gratitude in life and work to my family and friends, and let me also thank Martha and Karin.

Denver • Toronto • Copenhagen • Jerusalem

PART I

THE RATIONAL AND
THE PASSIONATE

The Intelligence of Emotions

Differing Schools of Thought

What does emotion have to do with knowing? Quite a bit, as I will argue in this book. Although they tend to involve feelings of somatic agitation, human emotions are not merely physiological disturbances: rather, they are experiences through which we can apprehend important truths about ourselves and about the world. This is not to say that every emotion succeeds at revealing something true—indeed, the question of how emotions could be more or less epistemically reliable is one to which I will devote a fair amount of attention in subsequent chapters. Yet our emotions do *aim* at being truthful, and they embody a kind of understanding that is accessible to us only by means of our affective experience. Specifically, it is only through the emotions that we can perceive meaning in life, and only by feeling emotions that we are capable of recognizing the value or significance of anything whatsoever. Our affective responses and dispositions therefore play a critical role in our apprehension of meaningful truth within human existence: and, for reasons that I shall explain, their felt quality is intimately related to the awareness they provide. In short, affective experience provides a distinct mode of perceptual knowledge and recognition—one that is unavailable to us *except* through our emotions.

An appropriate starting point for my inquiry into this topic is Pascal's statement that the heart has *its* reasons, which are entirely unknown to *mere* reason.[1] What this claim implies is that our dispassionate rational faculty is unacquainted with the reasons of the heart; rationality alone, in other words, is simply not aware of what is disclosed through our emotions. And this does not mean that the insights which are provided by emotion are inconsistent with the conclusions of "cool" reasoning. It means only that our emotions have a reasonableness or a "logic" of their own—that is, they are capable of providing us with knowledge that we could not have acquired in any other way. And if there are some truths that are manifested only through affective experience, then it follows that (*a*) the emotions have intelligible content and may be insightful, and (*b*) they involve a distinctive variety of embodied cognition, which cannot be reduced to or equated with other modes of knowing.[2] They seek to inform us about the world, while whatever truth they might convey is typically brought home to us in an experience of turbulent upheaval. These characteristics of the emotions may lead us to form contrary opinions about whether or not they are trustworthy.[3] Often, we view them as a valuable source of insight due to what they are uniquely able to reveal; on

---

1. Blaise Pascal, *Pensées*, 216. Cf. Max Scheler, "Ordo Amoris," 117.

2. As Peter Goldie notes, our emotional responses "reveal to us what we value, and what we value might not be epistemically accessible to us if we did not have such responses."—*The Emotions*, 48–49. Along the same lines, Philip Fisher points out that what our emotions disclose cannot be known by "other means": *Vehement Passions*, 37–38.

3. Antonio Damasio remarks on "the limits of pure reason" as shown by the diminished emotional capacities of a man with ventromedial prefrontal brain damage, adding that "emotion may be *both* beneficial and pernicious," as this patient's case also shows: *Descartes' Error*, 192–195.

the other hand, we sometimes regard them as unreliable precisely because they differ from other mental processes that do not feel so affectively charged.

This ambivalence about what to make of emotion has chronically plagued our theoretical explanations, no less than our everyday attitudes. In recent decades, there has been a remarkable amount of controversy within the disciplines of philosophy and psychology (among others) about how we ought to understand the cognitive and the bodily aspects of human emotions. Indeed, as one author points out, the question of how to unite "these two equally obvious dimensions of emotional life" in "some effective and plausible way" has been "the difficulty at the heart of emotion theory."[4] On the physiological level of description, emotions are correlated with objectively measurable and subjectively felt patterns of somatic and nervous system activity: fluctuations in blood pressure, respiration, heart rate, muscle tension, and skin temperature (or skin conductance, the ability of the skin to conduct electricity); they are also linked with chemical and electrical changes in the brain.[5] At the same time, emotions are mental states directed toward the world (that is, they have intentionality), whether we conceive of them as appraisals, evaluative judgments, perceptual feelings, or experiences with intentional content which are best described in some other terms. I think we should avoid getting excessively caught up in arguments about terminology; however, the various words we use when speaking about emotions can frame our understanding of affective

4. I cite Peter Redding, *The Logic of Affect*, 2. The persistence of this difficulty in the most recent emotion research is indicated, for instance, by Michelle Maiese's article "How Can Emotions Be Both Cognitive and Bodily?"

5. For an overview see, e.g., Kreibig, "Autonomic Nervous System Activity in Emotion: A Review." In subsequent chapters, I will discuss some of these bodily changes in further detail, referring to specific empirical literature as needed.

experience in different ways, some better than others. This is why debates over how to conceptualize the emotions are not pointless or merely superficial.

Those who place emphasis upon the cognitive or intentional aspect of emotion tend to oppose what has been called the "dumb view" of emotions,[6] according to which our affective feelings are just unintelligent disruptions: pangs, tremors, and meaningless bodily sensations, which bear no inherent relation to the surrounding world. Moreover, some of those who acknowledge that emotions *do* have some kind of intentionality join with advocates of the dumb view in rejecting the idea that the emotions could allow us to know what is actually the case. They argue, for example, that it is "quite wrong" to hold that when we are moved with awe toward something that we "judge, believe, or even think or imagine" that the thing in question is awesome, rejecting the notion that emotions reflect our sense of how the world truly is.[7] This is protesting too much, as we shall see. Before any further discussion of theorists who oppose a cognitive account of emotions, however, let us take a closer look at the views with which they disagree. If I run the risk of surveying for the next several pages literature that is already familiar to some readers, it is for the sake of mapping out this terrain at the outset and clarifying what is at issue.

---

6. It is Alison Jaggar who calls this the "dumb view" of emotion: see "Love and Knowledge," 155–156. Martha C. Nussbaum describes it as "the adversary's view," in contrast to her own cognitive account, and notes that it is frequently based upon "the idea that emotions are 'bodily' rather than 'mental,' as if this were sufficient to make them unintelligent." See *Upheavals of Thought*, 24–25.
7. Christine Tappolet, "Values and Emotions," 129. See also Döring, "Why Be Emotional?," 293. Taking issue with such views, Mikko Salmela explains the sense in which the emotions *do* aim at being truthful in *True Emotions*, 111–116. Tappolet's example is about feeling amused by what (on her account) is felt but *not* thought to be amusing.

ONE SCHOOL OF THOUGHT

Cognitive theorists of emotion argue that each of our emotions is distinguished (from other types of emotion, as well as from non-affective states) by its intentionality: in other words, what allows a certain agitated state to qualify as an episode of fear, and what identifies it *as* fear rather than anger, grief, or another type of emotion, is that it refers to some potential threat or danger. We do not fear what we view as a good thing that might happen, nor do we get afraid of a possible future event that we regard as a desirable prospect. Likewise, the awareness that one has been offended, wronged, or thwarted would constitute anger rather than fear. This intentional directedness is the distinguishing feature of mental phenomena: just as a belief or a perception is directed at whatever is believed or perceived, an emotion is also directed toward an object. We take notice of this, Brentano explains, every time that "we are pleased with or about something, [or] that we feel sorrow or grieve about something."[8] Intentionality is the property of mental states by virtue of which they are directed *at, about, of,* or *toward* persons, things, ideals, places, situations, and so on.[9] Accordingly, as Martha Nussbaum points out, emotions are "defined with reference to particular types of relationship that may obtain between a creature and its world."[10] As Sartre elaborates: "Joy, anguish, melancholy

---

8. Franz Brentano, *Psychology from an Empirical Standpoint*, 88–90. Cf. Edmund Husserl, *Logical Investigations*, 554: "In perception something is perceived, . . . [and] in love something loved."

9. Cf. John Searle, *Intentionality*, 1–2. Fear is among the first examples that Searle mentions, to illustrate what an intentional state is: "If, for example, I have a belief, it must be a belief that such and such is the case; if I have a fear, it must be a fear *of* something or *that* something will occur." My emphasis.

10. Nussbaum, *Upheavals of Thought*, 106–107. Cf. Lazarus, *Emotion and Adaptation*, 30–39. And see also Clore and Ortony, "Cognition in Emotion," 53.

are consciousnesses," and because "all consciousness is conscious-ness *of* something" these emotions are forms of awareness. This, he adds, is why, if we attempt to muster up the "subjective phenomena" of anger without any reference to an "unjust action," then we "can tremble, hammer [our] fists, blush," and so forth, but this alone will not be sufficient to bring about a state of anger.[11] Even if an emo-tion such as anger is characterized by a feeling that one is "boiling up," and by the somatic agitation that accompanies this feeling, a cognitive theorist will argue that this embodied feeling would not amount to *anger* without a sense of some wrongdoing. That is why it would be unreasonable for any of us to get angry at our neighbor for doing something which was not, in fact, our neighbor's doing.

A cognitive appraisal or evaluation is thus a grounding condition of each emotion: when I feel grieved by bad news, my grief could not survive the discovery that the news was false and that no loss has actually occurred. Likewise, I can be disappointed in you only if I feel that you have let me down in some way. Admittedly, my emo-tion could be excessive, unwarranted, or otherwise mistaken. Not only could its object be incorrectly identified or unfairly blamed, but (like any other intentional state) an emotion can be directed toward an object that does not even exist: my anger at the thief who stole my car (when it has not actually been stolen, and there is no such thief), or a child's fear of the boogeyman hiding under the bed. These are cases in which an emotion embodies a *false* impression of what is the case; yet the emotion is capable of being false, *or* true,

---

11. Jean-Paul Sartre, *The Imaginary*, 68–70. As he points out elsewhere, "the man who is afraid is afraid *of* something."—*The Emotions*, 51. Cf. Zahavi, *Husserl's Phenomenology*, 14: "One does not merely love, fear, see, or judge, one loves a beloved, fears something fearful," and so on. In Husserl's terms, there are "intentional feelings" with a "real relation to some-thing objective," i.e., every "joy or sorrow *about* something . . . is a directed act."—*Logical Investigations*, 569–570.

because it refers to the world and presents it as being a certain way. In other words, the emotion asserts *that* something is the case: *that* one has been slighted or harmed, for instance. And it seems obvious that in some instances our emotional impressions are *not* misleading, as when a jealous child is accurately perceiving a potential rival for the attention he or she craves. It is due to the possibility that our emotions might get things *right* that they can also, in some cases, fail to do so. An emotion asserts that the world in some respect *is* the way it seems to us when we are experiencing this emotion. That is why we have a nuanced vocabulary of terms that we apply to emotions and *not* to mere sensations: we routinely describe emotions as being justified or groundless, perceptive or obtuse, reasonable or ridiculous.[12] Whenever we employ such terms, we acknowledge that our emotions are experiences in which we seek to comprehend our surroundings—and that we can by degrees either succeed or fail to apprehend them well, each time we are emotionally moved.

This might seem familiar and obvious enough about our emotions, and maybe it should. Several decades ago, renowned cognitive theorists—such as Magda Arnold and Richard Lazarus in academic psychology, along with Robert Solomon and Anthony Kenny in anglophone philosophy—sought to incorporate this observation about emotion and intentionality into their theoretical accounts.[13] In bringing a cognitive view of emotions out of obscurity and making it well known in their respective disciplines, these

---

12. Cf. Robert C. Solomon, *The Passions*, 162–164 & 172–178. On assessing emotions "as either rational or irrational, 'true' or 'false'," see also Nussbaum, *The Fragility of Goodness*, 383.

13. Prominent works in this school of thought include Arnold, *Emotion and Personality*; Lazarus, "Emotions and Adaptation"; Solomon, "Emotions and Choice" and *The Passions*; and Anthony Kenny, *Action, Emotion and Will*. At the time she was writing, Arnold called for a "return to the common human experience of emotion," or to our familiar "subjective experience," as evidence that must be captured by any theory. See Arnold, *Emotion and Personality*, 1: 11–13.

thinkers were simultaneously renewing a view of emotion that dates back to Aristotle and also relying on more recent insights from the phenomenological tradition.[14] In due course, the cognitive view of emotions would become the leading paradigm in affective science due to its intuitive plausibility. True to the spirit of Aristotle himself, cognitivists have often noted that *some* kind of cognition is involved in emotion without specifying too clearly what sort of cognition this is. (As Richard Sorabji has noted, although Aristotle's discussion of emotions in *De Anima* and the *Rhetoric* is "shot through with cognitive terms,"[15] a variety of terminology is employed in these works and elsewhere to describe what type of mental state a passion or emotion is.) Therefore, we might wonder: does anger involve an articulate *belief* about the intention behind an insulting remark, or is it sufficient for the remark to *seem* like an insult—to "strike us" that way? By the same token, must a fearful person *judge* that she is confronted with danger, or can she be frightened by what appears dangerous even while being convinced that it is harmless? These are questions to which we shall return.

14. Arnold named Aristotle, Aquinas, and Sartre as important antecedents; Solomon acknowledged Sartre as one of his main inspirations; Lazarus pointed back to Aristotle, Heidegger, and Sartre; and Kenny gave credit to Aristotle and Aquinas. See Magda Arnold, "Historical Development of the Concept of Emotion," 147–148 (on Aristotle and Aquinas) and *Emotion and Personality*, 1: 170 (on Sartre); Robert Solomon, *The Passions*, 15 & 131; Richard Lazarus, *Emotion and Adaptation* 131–132 (on Sartre) & 158 (on Heidegger); and Anthony Kenny, *Action, Emotion and Will*, 16. William Lyons credits Arnold with "almost single-handedly" reviving "the cognitive theory of emotions in psychology."—*Emotion*, 44–45. An excellent survey is Rainer Reisenzein, "Arnold's Theory of Emotion in Historical Perspective," 921–925. Lazarus, for his part, spoke as boldly as Heidegger had done half a century earlier when he claimed that our conception of the affects had made no significant improvement since Aristotle's *Rhetoric*: see Richard Lazarus, *Emotion and Adaptation*, 14; Martin Heidegger, *Being and Time*, § 29.

15. Sorabji, *Emotion and Peace of Mind*, 22–23. On how emotional intentionality is "built into" the way things appear, as when a situation is viewed in a certain way, seen *as* a dangerous place to drink water, for instance, see Henry Richardson, "Desire and the Good in *De Anima*," 385.

Ambiguity regarding the problem of how to characterize affective cognition is not always a sign of lamentable imprecision. It may result from the ongoing effort to work out a more adequate formulation. On Arnold's view, a necessary condition of having an emotion is to "perceive or know the object in some way," where this perceptual knowing includes an axiological "appraisal" of value or worth.[16] Lazarus also speaks in terms of cognitive *appraisal*, whereas Solomon and Kenny, among others, use either "belief" or "judgment" to signify the kind of cognition that an emotional response involves.[17] The key idea in any theoretical account of this sort is that to experience fear (for instance) *requires*—or simply *is*—to be conscious of something that appears to be dangerous. The affective experience of fear thus informs us about the alleged danger, and in this sense an emotional response is capable of delivering more or less reliable information about the world. A person who feels anger or disappointment can, in typical cases, tell you what she is angry or disappointed about, and *why* she feels this way. Similarly, if we feel hopeful, then we are aware of an enticing possibility that might be realized. An affective experience therefore points beyond itself, revealing something to us which we recognize by being moved. And this is best accounted for by a theory of emotion that places

16. Magda Arnold, *Emotion and Personality*, 1: 171. On appraisal as the "cognitive determinant of emotion," see Lazarus, *Psychological Stress and the Coping Process*, 52. See also Michael Polanyi, *Personal Knowledge*, 17: the "act of knowing," he says, "includes an appraisal."

17. On "belief" see, e.g., Solomon, "Emotions and Choice," 21–30; Kenny, *Action, Emotion and Will*, 192–193; Gabriele Taylor, *Prime, Shame, and Guilt*, 1–13; and Jack Kelly, "Reason and Emotion," 380. On emotions as judgments see Solomon, *The Passions*, 186–187 and "Emotions, Thoughts, and Feelings," 10–12; Lazarus, *Emotion and Adaptation*, 177–180; Lyons, *Emotion*, 71; Joel Marks, "A Theory of Emotion," 227; George Kerner, "Emotions Are Judgments of Value"; Robert Gordon, *The Structure of Emotions*, 65–70; O. H. Green, *The Emotions*, 31–33 & 77–78; and Nussbaum, "Emotions as Judgments of Value and Importance."

emphasis (not exclusively) on the cognitive or intentional content of emotions.

Later, I will say more about how the cognitive dimension of emotion ought to be understood, and I will argue that the decision by some leading cognitive theorists to call it a "judgment" may have been an unfortunate one (since affective cognition is neither an active nor a reflective process, nor does it require the formulation of statements in language).[18] The term "appraisal" also suggests spontaneous action in the moment of emotional response, so it might be confusing for similar reasons. I shall also explain in more detail below my contention that it has been a mistake on the part of many authors to define the rationality of emotions as unrelated to their bodily character. Right now, however, my aim is simply to point out the main truth which is agreed upon in some form or other by all cognitive theories of emotion, regardless of their differences. Anthony Kenny expresses it well when he points out that "each of the emotions is appropriate—logically, and not just morally appropriate—only to certain restricted objects." He continues:

> If a man says that he is afraid of winning £10,000 in the pools, we want to ask him more: does he believe that money corrupts, or does he expect to lose his friends, or to be annoyed by begging letters, or what? If we can elicit from him only descriptions of the good aspects of the situation, then we cannot understand why he reports his emotion as fear and not as hope.[19]

18. Although these and other unwanted connotations are explicitly disavowed by leading cognitive theorists, some of their preferred terminology seems to invite perpetual misreadings nonetheless, as is shown by the monotonously repeated claims made by their critics, such as that cognitivism would require that emotions involve "cool" reflection, "disembodied" thought, actively endorsed judgments, overtly formulated and consciously affirmed propositions, etc. See Furtak, "Emotion, the Bodily, and the Cognitive," 58.
19. Kenny, *Action, Emotion and Will*, 192–193. Cf. Solomon, *True to Our Feelings*, 161.

The reason why it would not make sense for someone to fear winning the lottery, if he or she can report only good things about winning it, is that an experience of hope is an experience of something under a particular description. One hopes for what seems to be a potential future good, and if winning the lottery is not viewed as a good thing, then the emotion of hope toward this prospect is unintelligible. Likewise, we get afraid of what appears to be significantly dangerous: in other words, what endangers or threatens us is the *formal object* of fear, the sort of thing that fear is about. Another way of making the same point would be to say that the *subjective logic* of fear demands that it be oriented toward an apparent source of harm. It makes sense that we fear what we construe as threatening, and it follows that only a being capable of perceiving itself as threatened can be afraid.[20] If what I fear *is* actually endangering something I hold dear (such as my life and health), in the way that I see it as dangerous, then I am accurately grasping this property of my surroundings *in* being frightened.

This is what I have in mind when I refer to the intelligence of emotions: through our emotions we receive impressions about how the world is, and the content of these experiences is highly specific. Our affective responses give us the sense that things are a certain way, that something *is* a certain way. Anger is not only an inner overheating of the living body, combined with an incidental relation to some external cause; nor is it merely an inclination or appetite that "pushes" us from within.[21] What makes it anger as opposed to fear

20. Cf. Matthew Ratcliffe, *Feelings of Being*, 49. He is echoing Heidegger, *Being and Time*, § 30. I adopt the language of "construal" from Robert C. Roberts, who also points out that every type of emotion has its own "subjective logic." See *Emotions*, 49 & 77. On "formal objects," see Kenny, *Action, Emotion and Will*, 187–192.
21. Cf. Alphonso Lingis, *Dangerous Emotions*, 18. On hunger, for instance, as a "push" from inside rather than a "pull" from the environment, see Nussbaum, *Upheavals of Thought*, 130–131.

or shame is that we *cognize* or apprehend the object of each emotion in a distinct way (one is angry *at* someone, *for* doing some harm). Fear can be described as a "shiver of apprehension" in the face of danger,[22] and shame as the perception that something reflects poorly on me—so if I feel afraid or ashamed of an ashtray, I must view it as a deadly menace, a reminder of my bad habit, or as a shabby decoration. Furthermore, the logic of an emotion entails that we ought to feel other emotions when circumstances change: one's fear that something bad might happen should change to sorrow (or the like) when the bad thing actually does occur, just as one ought to rejoice over the realization of some good outcome that one has been hoping for.[23] By virtue of their cognitive or intentional content, our emotions can provide us with knowledge about significant aspects of the world, showing what matters to us and how things are going—"how we are faring," as one might say.[24] To be in touch with our feelings is thus to be cognizant of the features of the world to which these feelings are responsive. Emotions are epistemically indispensable, because our affective experience is our mode of access to significant truths about what concerns us: in other words, the emotions are embodied affective recognitions that provide us with a crucial vehicle of awareness.

22. Hans-Georg Gadamer, *Truth and Method*, 126. Cf. Nussbaum, *Upheavals of Thought*, 27. The following example is borrowed in part from Jerome Neu: see *Emotion, Thought, and Therapy*, 94. On how the significance of an ashtray *inhabits, animates*, or is *embodied in* the ashtray that we perceive, see also Maurice Merleau-Ponty, *Phenomenology of Perception*, 372–373.

23. Commenting on this need for internal consistency, Alexius Meinong comments that anyone who "feels joy over the existence of something will 'rationally,' one might say, feel sorry regarding its nonexistence."—*On Emotional Presentation*, 111–112.

24. The phrase "how we are faring," in this sense, is employed by Heidegger and appropriated by Prinz: see Martin Heidegger, *Being and Time*, § 29; see also Prinz, "Embodied Emotions," 57 and *Gut Reactions*, 78 & 184–185.

OTHER WAYS OF THINKING ABOUT EMOTIONS

Although numerous philosophers and psychologists have accepted this conception of emotions as cognitive phenomena, which are elicited and differentiated according to what information they take in about the person-environment relationship,[25] others have lamented this emphasis. After all, emotions are quite evidently associated with somatic feelings,[26] and according to some theorists this must be what distinguishes them above all else. And, just as those who focus on cognition or appraisal can find precedent for their view of emotions in the work of such thinkers as Brentano and Aristotle, theorists who dissent from this view often turn to William James for a contrasting model:

> If we fancy some strong emotion, and then try to abstract from our consciousness of it all the feelings of its bodily symptoms, we find we have nothing left behind, no "mind-stuff" out of which the emotion can be constituted, and that a cold and neutral state of intellectual perception is all that remains.[27]

---

25. Cf. Klaus R. Scherer, "The Nature and Study of Appraisal," 369–370. See also Gerald L. Clore, "Why Emotions Require Cognition," 181–182. Nico H. Frijda gives an approving nod to Sartre and Arnold for endorsing a view of emotions as "meaningful perception[s] of the world": see "Emotion Experience," 477. George Downing remarks upon the wide agreement that emotion is a form of cognition: see "Emotion Theory Reconsidered," 246–247. In other words, as Charles Altieri notes, the prevailing assumption is no longer that we must "set irrational, seething emotions against the cool, analytic operations of reason."— The Particulars of Rapture, 4.

26. As Ronald de Sousa points out, emotions involve a "conspicuous participation of the body," and more obviously than "other mental states" do: see The Rationality of Emotion, 153.

27. William James, Psychology: The Briefer Course, 246–247. Among the recent works that oppose theories based on cognition are Prinz's Gut Reactions and Jenefer Robinson's Deeper Than Reason. See also, e.g., Robert Zajonc, "Mere Exposure" and Andrea Scarantino, "Insights and Blindspots of the Cognitivist Theory of Emotions." According to Tappolet, cognitive accounts of emotion are the paradigm to which we quite evidently

Elsewhere, James asserts more firmly that emotions are nothing other than feelings of bodily changes.[28] This claim should not be mistaken for the weaker thesis that most human emotions involve physiological alterations of some kind, such as those that are typical of fear, described here by Antonio Damasio:

> The heart rate changes, and so do the blood pressure, the respiration pattern, and the state of contraction of the gut. The blood vessels in the skin contract. Cortisol is secreted into the blood, changing the metabolic profile of the organism in preparation for extra energy consumption. The muscles in the face move and adopt a characteristic mask of fear.[29]

What James and his followers are arguing is that, without a felt experience of one's own somatic agitation as one undergoes an emotional response, there would *be* no emotion; for, on this view, the emotion simply *is* the phenomenal feeling of those bodily changes. The Jamesian position therefore differs from Aristotle's view, which is that the passions have both mental *and* bodily aspects and that

cannot "go back," for reasons that I will soon consider. See "Ambivalent Emotions and the Perceptual Account of Emotions," 231–232.

28. "My thesis . . . is that *the bodily changes follow directly the* PERCEPTION *of the exciting fact, and that our feeling of the same changes as they occur* IS *the emotion*."—William James, "What Is an Emotion?," 189–190. James Averill suggests that a more apt formulation is "subjective experience dependent upon bodily change": see "Intellectual Emotions," 204.

29. Damasio, *Self Comes to Mind*, 113. The truth of the weaker claims that "emotions are, like all mental processes, bodily," and that some kind of "neurochemical functioning" must be involved in all emotions, is readily conceded by a philosopher such as Nussbaum: see *Upheavals of Thought*, 25; see also Roberts, *Emotions*, 134. Yet this is compatible with emotions being "disembodied" in the sense of which Prinz and other noncognitivists speak (in their criticisms of cognitive theories), as the emotions *would* be if their somatic character were only incidentally related to their felt or phenomenal character, serving as a biological condition but not a constituent part of emotions as experienced: see Prinz, *Gut Reactions*, 25 and *The Emotional Construction of Morals*, 58–59.

these can be jointly captured by two kinds of explanation (one humanistic, one physical); and that, moreover, they can constitute "recognitions of truth."[30] It has more in common with the doctrine put forward in some of Plato's dialogues, which is that emotions or passions are misleading precisely *because* they are of the body: in the *Phaedo*, for example, we are told that fear and other human emotions try to persuade us that "the truth is what the body says it is."[31] Although the disruptive or distorting influence of emotion is not emphasized to the same degree by all Jamesian (or Platonic) theorists, they do tend to regard emotions as "noncognitive" and such notions as "emotional truth" as dubious.[32] In these respects, they both inherit and perpetuate a long legacy of philosophical distrust toward the emotions.

Yet James's acknowledgment of the ways in which our affective life "is knit up with our corporeal frame," which is one of the major claims made in his essay "What Is an Emotion?,"[33] does not entail the conclusion that human emotions are noncognitive interior

30. This last phrase is from Nussbaum, *Upheavals of Thought*, 96. Emotions are described as both embodied and reasonable, for instance, in *De Anima* 403a. See also *Rhetoric* 1378a–1388b, an efficient outline of which is provided by Jon Elster in *Alchemies of the Mind*, 53–75.

31. As Socrates states in *Phaedo* 83b–d (Grube translation); see also Plato, *Phaedo* 66c–d. Variant notions can be found across different Platonic dialogues, yet the *Phaedo*'s account of the physical realm is well deserving of the critique offered by Glen Mazis in *Emotion and Embodiment*, 10–12.

32. For a cognitivist defense of the concept of "emotional truth" see Ronald de Sousa, "Emotions," 70–72; cf. de Sousa, *Emotional Truth*. See also, e.g., Salmela, "True Emotions," and Nussbaum, *Upheavals of Thought*, 46–47. For skeptical opposition to the notion that emotions can be truthful, see inter alia Goldie, "Misleading Emotions," and Paul E. Griffiths, *What Emotions Really Are*. Prinz rightly attributes to David Hume the argument that emotions "do not represent anything": see *Gut Reactions*, 11. Hume's statement that passions contain "not any representative quality" is made in *A Treatise of Human Nature*, 415. On the prevailing (although not universal) bias in Western philosophy against the emotions, see, for instance, Quentin Smith, *The Felt Meanings of the World*, 14–19; Gemma Corradi Fiumara, *The Mind's Affective Life*, 79; and Cheshire Calhoun, "Subjectivity and Emotion," 111–112.

33. James, "What Is an Emotion?," 201.

states which bear only an accidental relation to our surroundings. One valuable upshot of the critique made by neo-Jamesians such as Jesse Prinz and Jenefer Robinson is that they question the assumption that *if* emotions are cognitive or intentional, *then* they cannot be essentially bodily. (I say "essentially" to express the force of James's assertion, cited above, that subtracting feelings of bodily agitation from an emotional experience would leave no emotion at all.) For good reason, cognitivists tend to point out that emotions are unlike "bodily twinges" or "felt churnings," mere sensations that are not *about* anything:[34] itches and cramps are not as important in human existence as loves and fears, and the greater importance of our emotions is *due* to what they reveal to us or what they inform us about. However, we should not assume that the distinctly somatic element in our experience of such emotions as fear, awe, and grief is unrelated to the potentially truth-revealing function of affective experience. A possibility that I will explore further in subsequent chapters is that our emotions can be recognitions of truth precisely by virtue of their bodily character. For now, I simply point out that both of the following propositions *could* be true without implying any contradiction:

(b) that the experience of an emotion such as fear necessarily involves certain feelings of physiological or *bodily* activity; and

(c) that this experience also necessarily involves a *cognitive* impression—which may be accurate or inaccurate, but when accurate is a *recognition*—of something *as* dangerous.

---

34. Mark R. Wynn, *Renewing the Senses*, 27. Cf. Nussbaum, *Upheavals of Thought*, 16; see also Roberts, *Emotions*, 153.

POINTING FORWARD

Even advocates of a Jamesian or "noncognitive" account of emotion generally accept that the intentionality of emotions must somehow be recognized also. This is a sign of considerable agreement that emotions bear a mental relation to what they are about—indeed, few theorists would reject the notion that *some* kind of evaluation or appraisal is necessary for emotional arousal.[35] Most somatic or "feeling" theories differ from cognitive accounts by virtue of insisting on a necessary condition for emotion *other* than intentionality, and by denying that affective intentionality is specifically *cognitive*. In the ensuing chapters, I will examine how we ought to think about the ways in which our emotions can provide us with an apprehension of aspects of the world and of our situation in it, by making us aware of significant matters of concern. This will require doing justice both to embodied affective feelings and to meaningful intentional content, yet *not* simply by coupling these together in a hybrid account. The somatic and the cognitive are not two utterly discrete components of emotion that are mysteriously joined or correlated;[36] rather, they

---

35. The notion of "appraisal" is central to Prinz's "noncognitive" theory as well as Robinson's: see Prinz, *The Emotional Construction of Morals*, 64–65 and Robinson, *Deeper Than Reason*, 26. For instance, Prinz defines emotions as "states that appraise by registering bodily changes," claiming that these bodily changes must themselves have been "reliably caused": this happens when a sign of danger in our environment sets our heart racing, and fear *is* our sense of that racing heartbeat. Thus, our "fears track dangers via heart palpitations."—*Gut Reactions*, 67–78. Of course, reliable causation does not amount to intentionality, because *caused by* does not mean *about*.

36. As Aaron Ben-Ze'ev appears to suggest that they are, their "feeling component" itself lacking intentionality: see *The Subtlety of Emotions*, 64–76. Eva-Maria Düringer also defends a multicomponent account: see *Evaluating Emotions*, 134–135. A related idea, that affects are basically noncognitive but can "sometimes incorporate" a cognitive component, is defended by Brian Leiter in "Moralities are a Sign-Language of the Affects." Despite continual attempts to argue for a blunt and uncompromising version of the noncognitive theory of emotions (see, e.g., Coplan, "Feeling without Thinking," 137–144), the "two theoretical traditions" that Reisenzein and Döring call the "feeling theory" and the "cognitive theory"

are conceptually separable aspects of one unified response. This explains what would be ineffective about the strategy of "grafting" onto a Jamesian account of emotions the added thesis that emotions are *caused by* events in the world (as if causation were tantamount to intentionality), or arguing in some other manner that emotions are "in part noncognitive," while also including something akin to cognition.[37] Any theory that describes emotions as *partially* cognitive, involving a form of intentional world-reference which is deficiently or imperfectly rational, likewise fails to explain why it is that emotions constitute a uniquely truth-revealing mode of embodied understanding for human beings. As I will explain further, affective cognition does not need to prove its epistemic worth by being measured against the standard of some *other* mode of rationality—such as dispassionate judgment, or transparently asserted belief—only to be found wanting according to those (foreign) criteria.

Yet truthfulness *is* at issue in episodes of such emotions as fear, pride, grief, and the like: each of these (and other) emotions aims at disclosing something true. And my account of human emotions would be sadly incomplete if it did not attend to all varieties of affective experience. Moods and affective dispositions, loves and other long-standing concerns, as well as overall features of temperament

have indeed "increasingly moved closer to each other." See "Ten Perspectives on Emotional Experience," 204. I have noted elsewhere that this debate is not a clash between antithetical stances but a critical exchange in which all participants are being forced to refine and modify their positions: Furtak, "Emotion, the Bodily, and the Cognitive," 52.

37. I cite John Deigh's description of "hybrid" theories, then Ronald A. Nash's account of the same: see Deigh, "Concepts of Emotions in Modern Philosophy and Psychology," 32–33; Nash, "Cognitive Theories of Emotion," 481–482. Similar problems exist with what have been called (usually, not by their advocates) "quasi-judgmentalist" accounts, associated with such thinkers as Robert C. Roberts and Patricia Greenspan, among others, according to whom emotions involve a form of intentional awareness that *falls short* of rational cognition. See, e.g., Justin D'Arms and Daniel Jacobson, "The Significance of Recalcitrant Emotion (Or, Anti-quasijudgmentalism)," 130–133.

and perspective, also deserve to be taken seriously as potentially revelatory or truthful states.[38] At each of these levels, our emotions are capable of making known to us what is significant, thereby placing us in touch with whatever matters to us. Furthermore, as we shall see, the phenomenal or "felt" quality of emotional experience (i.e., what it is like) is inherently related to what it is *about*. When our attempts to explain the emotions run up against something in the phenomena which seems ambiguous or intractable, we ought to search for conceptual resources that allow us to form a more adequate understanding. What is needed is not antagonistic conflict between rival theories, but the kind of critical rethinking that can be prompted by weighing both the empirical evidence and the theoretical arguments that have been put forward in favor of one or another account of emotion. Yet this is not to suggest that the position I advocate represents a "middle path" between the cognitive and the noncognitive theorists. Rather, my goal in this book is to explain how our felt recognitions of significance incorporate a sense of what is the case, and therefore how meaningful truth is at stake in our affective experience.

---

38. Cf. Jennifer Hansen, "Affectivity," 36–37: "If depressed states of mind are [or can be] truthful—that is, if they accurately depict or represent states of affairs in the world—then these states of mind are quite crucial for self-understanding." And also for world-understanding. See also, e.g., Heidegger, *Being and Time*, §§ 29–31; Ratcliffe, "Why Mood Matters."

Chapter 2

What the Empirical
Evidence Suggests

It is often hoped that empirical findings will resolve, or at least cast some light upon, a question such as whether (or in what sense) emotions involve cognition. Since the study of emotions has emerged as a thriving field of interdisciplinary research, social psychology and neuroscience have been two of the most influential sources of evidence informing current theoretical accounts. Within the latter domain, disputed issues are rampant—one of which has particular importance for what concerns us at present. In his book *Descartes' Error*, Antonio Damasio argues that emotions are "just as cognitive" as other modes of mental activity, depending on "cerebral-cortex processing" of the kind believed to be associated with sophisticated mental processes.[1] Another neuroscientist, Joseph LeDoux, has popularized the contrary notion that cognition and emotion ought to be classified as separate functions, due to the supposedly "quick and dirty" nature of an affective response such as being startled by a loud noise—this, he claims, is a crude and unintelligent reflex, likely

---

1. Damasio, *Descartes' Error*, xv & 159. For Solomon, this shows that "emotions are necessary to rationality"; or, that they are "forms of intentional awareness."—*True to Our Feelings*, 36 & 166.

to involve only "subcortical pathways."[2] Now, why should it matter to a nonspecialist whether emotions are linked with neural activity in areas such as the orbitofrontal cortex, or in subcortical regions only? Because the prefrontal cortex is the brain area associated with our most complex cognitive processes, such as propositional thought, decision-making, memory, and perceptual awareness. If affective life is made possible by other anatomical structures, which are literally and figuratively "lower" (beneath the cortex, that is, as well as more primitive), this might indicate that emotion and cognition are discrete, and therefore that emotions are noncognitive. And this is the conclusion that LeDoux himself draws[3]—as do other theorists who follow his lead and view his results as definitive.

CONTROVERSIES IN AFFECTIVE SCIENCE

By and large, neuroscientists who emphasize "higher" cortical activity in emotion reject a strict disjunction between emotion and reason, as other cognitive theorists do;[4] meanwhile, those who focus on subcortical activation sound more like Jamesian somatic theorists, claiming, for instance, that "emotional feelings" occur when

2. LeDoux, *The Emotional Brain*, 68–69 & 255. While Damasio states that some emotions involve amygdala activation and others do not, LeDoux regards the amygdala as a crucial brain center for all emotions: see Damasio, *The Feeling of What Happens*, 60–62; LeDoux, *Synaptic Self*, 214–219.

3. Or that he *has* drawn: see LeDoux, "Comment." As this text shows, LeDoux has recently stated that his work is actually in line with "cognitive theories of emotion," rather than with noncognitive theories. Yet his revocation has gone almost entirely unnoticed among philosophers of emotion. (See note 31 below.)

4. See, e.g., Damasio, *The Feeling of What Happens*, 40–41; *Descartes' Error*, 158–160 & 200–201. See also Edmund Rolls, *Emotion Explained*, 35–36; *Neuroculture*, 18–19. Luiz Pessoa claims that "parceling the brain into cognitive and affective regions is inherently problematic, and ultimately untenable."—"On the Relationship between Emotion and Cognition," 148.

we become aware of our own inner physiological perturbations.[5] How could we explain this discrepancy? Some of the divergence may arise from differences in method and orientation, such as we find between the research programs of Damasio and LeDoux. Damasio's research is focused on people whose affective capacities are impaired as a result of brain injury: he has found that neurological damage in certain areas can hinder emotional responses as well as practical reasoning abilities.[6] This seems to warrant the inference that emotion and cognition are integrated, rather than being categorically distinct and independently functioning systems. LeDoux, on the other hand, has focused mainly on the physiology of fear behavior in rats: this research has led him to conclude that an immediate startle response can take place even if only subcortical neural pathways are activated. LeDoux speculates that a similar process can also occur in human beings: when a hiker meets a snake on the trail ahead, for instance, his frightened reaction may involve a "low road to the amygdala" that is triggered prior to any cortical activity.[7] And, once again, "if fear can occur without mediation of the neocortex," as Prinz explains, then "perhaps fear can occur without cognition."[8] According to (what has become) the standard interpretation, this is indeed the upshot of LeDoux's research. It is typical for emotion researchers to cite LeDoux as having proven that "emotions such as

---

5. LeDoux, *The Emotional Brain*, 302. Cf. Jaak Panksepp, "On the Embodied Neural Nature of Core Emotional Affects," 173. LeDoux ought to specify that what he is speaking about is awareness of bodily agitation, not of the *brain* per se: see note 50 below.

6. See Damasio, *Descartes' Error*, 44–51 & 191–194.

7. LeDoux, *The Emotional Brain*, 150–165. On the posited "low road," see also LeDoux, *Synaptic Self*, 121–123. In reply to researchers who reject his claim that human emotions involve merely subcortical processing, he states that "findings from rats should be assumed to apply to humans until they are proven not to."—*Synaptic Self*, 219–220.

8. Prinz, *Gut Reactions*, 34. Jenefer Robinson views LeDoux's results as proof that emotions are "quick and dirty," and hence "noncognitive," reactions: see *Deeper Than Reason*, 47–52 & 58–59.

fear fall into two different 'tracks' of neural response, some involving the cerebral cortex and some . . . more primitive,"[9] the latter of course travelling upon the "low road."

Many philosophical authors give the impression that the existence of subcortical emotions, independent of "higher" cognition, has been decisively established. LeDoux's postulated neural "low road" directly from the thalamus to the amygdala, and the "quick and dirty" travel it is supposed to enable, is baldly embraced by a surprising number of thinkers.[10] LeDoux's work is taken to demonstrate that emotions "are to a large extent isolated from our higher-order cognitive processes," due to the "low road" hypothesis;[11] as another author declares, this "fast pathway"—though admittedly a tiny fraction of a second quicker than the "slow" cortical route, even *if* the "low road" account is true—triggers fear responses "*long* before" we become aware of whatever has frightened us.[12] And the list goes on. In one survey of recent emotion research, intended for a general audience, we find the unequivocal statement that "fear is controlled by two separate pathways in the [human] brain," alongside a diagram of the postulated "high" and "low" routes.[13] Yet this

9. Patricia Greenspan, "Learning Emotions and Ethics," 542. The function of the "low road" is also represented as an empirical fact by Baars and Gage in *Cognition, Brain, and Consciousness*, 428; they do the same, adding diagrams of how fear takes the "low road" in the *human* brain, in their more recent text, *Fundamentals of Cognitive Neuroscience*, 376–379. The same is true of Panksepp and Biven in *The Archaeology of Mind*, 222–236.

10. See, e.g., Jesse Prinz, *The Emotional Construction of Morals*, 57; Paul Griffiths, "Basic Emotions, Complex Emotions, Machiavellian Emotions," 45. "There is a subcortical pathway," Prinz asserts without qualification; and Griffiths assures us in like manner that LeDoux's proposed subcortical route "has been solidly confirmed." Cf. Richard Sorabji, "Emotions and the Psychotherapy of the Ancients," 190: "there are two pathways into the brain," for the emotion of fear in human beings.

11. Tappolet, "Emotions and the Intelligibility of Akratic Action," 109.

12. Berit Brogaard, *On Romantic Love*, 152–153. My emphasis. On the difference of 8 milliseconds (0.008 seconds) between the faster and the "much slower" tracks, see note 32 below.

13. Dylan Evans, *Emotion*, 36–37. In *The Emotional Brain*, LeDoux sets up a parallel, in his illustration of "the road map of fear" (151–152), between the hiker walking up a trail—who

kind of assertion blatantly ignores the ongoing controversy among neuroscientists as to whether LeDoux's conclusions are justified, even regarding the rats that are the primary focus of his research.[14] Damasio, for his part, says that he "cannot endorse" the proposition that the neurological activity associated with human emotions is confined to "the brain's down-under" even in simple cases, since "it is apparent that emotion is played out under the control of both subcortical and neocortical structures."[15] A hiker could not even *see* what appears at first glance to be a snake without some activity in the cerebral cortex. And Edmund Rolls finds it "unlikely that the subcortical route" identified by LeDoux "is generally relevant" for emotion in human beings, since there is good reason to think that any perceptual event more complex than sensing a sudden flash of light or burst of sound—such as hearing a familiar tune, for instance, or perceiving a facial expression—must involve the kind of cognition that "requires cortical processing."[16] As phenomenologists

could perhaps take the high road over the mountain pass or else bypass this higher route in favor of a faster shortcut—and the pathways in the brain, a lower subcortical route and higher cortical trail (163–166). This takes a plausible analogy of efficient travel and extends it by metaphor from a hiker on the trail into the head of the hiker who spies a snake, where personified neural messengers are rushing as fast as they can, conveying messages through the brain.

14. Some neuroscientists have even questioned whether the state identified as "fear" in LeDoux's studies would be more accurately characterized as the "startle" response. See, e.g., Campeau and Davis, "Involvement of the Central Nucleus and Basolateral Complex of the Amygdala in Fear Conditioning Measured with Fear-Potentiated Startle in Rats Trained Concurrently with Auditory and Visual Conditioned Stimuli." As for the question of whether LeDoux's conclusions are relevant to emotions other than fear, see Adam K. Anderson et al., "Neural Correlates of the Automatic Processing of Threat Facial Signals." On the controversy over, and limits of, LeDoux's "low road" hypothesis, see Richard J. Davidson, "Neural Substrates of Affective Style and Value," 74–76.

15. Damasio, *Descartes' Error*, 158–162.

16. Rolls, *Emotion Explained*, 169–170; *Emotion and Decision-Making Explained*, 179–180. And see also Rolls and Grabenhorst, "The Orbitofrontal Cortex and Beyond," 231–238: recent experimental work confirms that the orbitofrontal cortex "is an important brain region for emotion," and that "cognition can descend into the first stage of processing" with respect to perceptions of affective value. As Rolls elaborates, a subcortical route to the amygdala "is

have pointed out,[17] and as our own experience attests, we seldom hear mere "noises" without meaning: ordinarily we perceive sounds with an awareness of *what* we are hearing, such as a particular vehicle approaching from up the street, and the same is true for visual perception. The conclusion drawn in one careful overview of the neural circuitry involved in auditory and visual processing is that LeDoux's subcortical pathway "does not inform us, in any significant way, about the emotion process in humans."[18]

Other neuroscientists have observed that affective responses involve the joint activity of multiple brain areas, none of which should be conceptualized as exclusively affective *or* cognitive.[19] Pessoa, for instance, explains that "cognition and emotion are strongly integrated in the brain," specifically that "brain regions viewed as 'affective' are also involved in cognition" and "brain regions viewed as 'cognitive' are also involved in emotion," which testifies to "a broader cognitive-affective control circuit." Also, some researchers have noted that

unlikely to be involved in most emotions, for which cortical analysis of the stimulus is likely to be required."—*Memory, Attention, and Decision-Making*, 188–190.

17. On how we must adopt a highly artificial attitude in order to hear a "pure noise," see Heidegger, *Being and Time*, § 34. Cf. Heidegger, "The Origin of the Work of Art," 151–152: "We never really first perceive a throng of sensations, e.g., tones and noises," but "we hear the storm whistling in the chimney"; likewise, we "hear the door shut in the house and never hear acoustical sensations or even mere sounds."

18. Gregory Johnson, "LeDoux's Fear Circuit and the Status of Emotion as a Non-cognitive Process," 744–751. This article, well reasoned and thoroughly researched, has been too often overlooked.

19. Pessoa, "On the Relationship between Emotion and Cognition," 148–153. In *Consciousness*, Adam Zeman comments on an array of findings which show that "the brain does not always respect our distinctions" between "thought and emotion": see pages 61–62. Emotions just "*are a kind of information processing*," and "contrasting emotion with cognition is therefore . . . pointless," according to Jonathan Haidt: see *The Righteous Mind*, 52–53. (Haidt, nevertheless, is of two minds about this, endorsing the notion of "two distinct systems" in the brain, one of which is emotional and "automatic" and distinct from the other, which is named "reason" and includes only "conscious" thought involving slow, reflective deliberation: see *Moral Tribes*, 134–138.)

it is rather hasty to make general statements about human emotions based on data concerning initial knee-jerk reactions in rats,[20] which LeDoux himself no longer identifies as the emotion of fear; instead, he now suggests, we ought to refer to the topic of his research as the "innate circuits" implicated in threat "detection and response," and to avoid conflating these with "the feeling of being afraid."[21] He adds that the "phenomenal experience" or "conscious feeling" of fear relies on "cortical areas" that allow us "to cognitively represent the threat as a perceptual event."[22] There is a considerable difference between what is suffered by a rodent startled by a tone that has been paired with shock and the fear experienced by a human being as she enters a doctor's office to learn the result of a biopsy.[23] Although he has not always discouraged readers from making this kind of extrapolation, LeDoux does advise caution, reminding us that even the "crucial" functioning of the amygdala is part of a larger system,[24] which includes an entire living organism in a meaningful environment. Mental functions are seldom "localized" in one neural region, despite what numerous

20. See, e.g., Leslie Brothers, *Mistaken Identity*, 54–55: LeDoux's paradigm, she says, "is probably not even applicable to *fear in general*, let alone to emotion in general." For a concise account of why the subcortical route "is unlikely to be involved in most emotions," see Rolls, *Emotion and Decision-Making Explained*, 165–167.

21. Joseph E. LeDoux, "Comment," 318–319; "Low Roads and Higher Order Thoughts in Emotion," 214–215. Even prior to this revision, LeDoux was guarded enough to state that "fear conditioning may not tell us everything we would like to know about fear, especially human fear."—*Synaptic Self*, 213. His more recent suggestion (in "Comment," 319), that we ought to respect the ordinary-language concept of fear, indirectly responds to a critique made by Brothers in *Mistaken Identity*, 26–27.

22. LeDoux, "Low Roads and Higher Order Thoughts in Emotion," 215. Here, LeDoux also concedes that his views about the experience of emotions have moved closer to those of Rolls.

23. This example is from Richard J. Davidson and Carien van Reekum, "Emotion Is Not One Thing," 16.

24. LeDoux, "Emotion, Memory, and the Brain," 56: "The amygdala is certainly crucial, but we must not lose sight of the fact that its functions exist only by virtue of the system to which it belongs."

popular overviews of emotion research might suggest.[25] For these reasons, it would be judicious to refrain from speaking about a part of the brain as if this were the location where emotions take place, or as if it were a little mind having experiences of its very own—such as fearing, remembering, and getting angry.

Unfortunately, philosophers have not always been cautious about using evidence that is limited and indefinite to justify sweeping conclusions. Thus, we are assured by Robinson that LeDoux's analyses of "conditioned fear in rats" have "wide and important implications for naturally occurring fear—including fear in human beings—as well as for the study of emotion in general."[26] By virtue of this extrapolation, she moves rapidly from startled rats to frightened human beings, then claims that *all* human emotions are "noncognitive," and that our affective life consists of "rough" and "dirty" appraisals that are precipitated without cognition. And others are willing to make the same inference, or generalization, from shocked rodents in a controlled setting to a complete theory of emotions in human beings. So, while neuroscientists such as Rolls and Pessoa bring forward evidence suggesting that a subcortical route to the amygdala "is unlikely to be involved in most emotions," and point out that LeDoux's view "has been challenged" and "is the subject of ongoing debate,"[27] numerous philosophers continue to characterize the contested view as a foregone conclusion, an empirically proven

25. Jaak Panksepp makes note of this fact repeatedly in *Affective Neuroscience*, e.g., on pages 70–76 and 147. See also Sally L. Satel and Scott O. Lilienfeld, *Brainwashed*, 11–16; Adrian Johnston and Catherine Malabou, *Self and Emotional Life*, 175–177.

26. Robinson, *Deeper Than Reason*, 48. On what follows, see *Deeper Than Reason*, 114–115. The "rough" and "dirty" fast track in the brain is endorsed also by Michael Brady in *Emotional Insight*, e.g., 98–101. Johnston and Malabou repeat the same error: see *Self and Emotional Life*, 218.

27. Rolls, *Memory, Attention, and Decision-Making*, 188; see also Luiz Pessoa and Ralph Adolphs, "Emotion Processing and the Amygdala." I quote also Yiend et al., "Attention and Emotion," 104.

and uncontroversial fact. This remains true after LeDoux's own published revocation. For instance, relying on the presumption that human emotions involve only a "low road" in the brain, "isolated from our higher-order cognitive processes," Tappolet dismisses *any* cognitive account of emotions as obviously flawed.[28] Robinson grounds her assertion that affective appraisal is "very fast, . . . bypassing cognition," on this metaphor also.[29] Even Nussbaum, who is hardly a noncognitivist, nonetheless views LeDoux's research as proving that fear is a "primitive emotion," one that "often hijacks thought" entirely.[30] Out of the vast array of empirical research on emotion, a few well-publicized but debatable results have been the focus of an exorbitant amount of attention. This could be due in part to wishful thinking about the promise of using empirical findings to resolve difficult questions about the mind, and partly to the common-sense appeal of the notion that a rapid affective reaction *must* travel on a "fast track" through the brain. LeDoux himself, who has been singled out for critique here largely because of how the consequences of his research are often portrayed, has recently protested that his work has been widely misunderstood, and is actually in line with "cognitive theories of emotion," rather than with noncognitive accounts.[31] Even apart from that claim, it would seem that a reappraisal is overdue.

28. See, e.g., Christine Tappolet, "Emotions and the Intelligibility of Akratic Action," 109–110; see also Tappolet, "Ambivalent Emotions and the Perceptual Account of Emotions," 232.
29. Robinson, *Deeper Than Reason*, 62–63.
30. Martha Nussbaum, *Political Emotions*, 320–322. Such "hijacking" in which the amygdala rushes a message past the "rational mind" altogether is vividly imagined by Daniel Goleman as showing "the power of emotion to overwhelm rationality."—*Emotional Intelligence*, 13–26.
31. LeDoux, "Comment," 318–319. LeDoux has become increasingly circumspect in his discussion of the "low road" and its explanatory power: see, e.g., *Anxious*, 209–217. (See also notes 21 and 22 above.)

Yet even if it *did* turn out to be the case that affective and cognitive processes operated on two segregated levels, one quick and another slow, the more efficient kind of mental processing is no more than "a few milliseconds" faster than the other; this is one of several reasons why, as Mikko Salmela sums up, "recent neuroscientific evidence suggests that the divide between a subcortical 'low road' and a cortical 'high road,'" and the distinction it implies between emotion and reason, is simply misleading.[32] We need to be more patient and cautious when interpreting evidence from empirical psychology: experimental findings can force us to revise our account of what emotions are, but they need to be checked against our best phenomenological accounts of affective experience. It would require quite a bit of elasticity for a noncognitive theory of emotion to explain everything from an instance of reacting to a sudden flash of light or burst of sound to an episode of being moved on behalf of Anna Karenina's predicament; however, this is the range that must be encompassed by any general account of human emotions. Toward one end of the spectrum from lesser to greater cognitive complexity, we find the simple affective reflex of being startled by a fire hydrant that is mistaken for an animal due to its vertical axis of symmetry; at the other end of this continuum, we have the rapid and viscerally disquieting yet intricately thought-informed experience of returning home to find a swastika painted on our neighbor's

---

32. See Salmela, *True Emotions*, 53–55. Cf. Giovanna Colombetti, *The Feeling Body*, 98–101: she surveys the "recent neuroscientific accounts" which "question the view that cognition and emotion are distinct psychological faculties implemented in separate neural areas," concluding that "if it is not true" that the brain is divided into parts that are "either strictly cognitive or strictly emotional," then it is unjustified to distinguish cognition from appraisal: in fact, "cognition in its simplest forms is already a form of appraisal." The difference of 8 milliseconds, between 12 and 20 milliseconds (see Johnson, "LeDoux's Fear Circuit and the Status of Emotion as a Non-cognitive Process," 742), has been inaccurately characterized as that between a rapid, unreflective gut reaction and a slow, reflective evaluation of that initial response—as it is, e.g., by Robinson, *Deeper Than Reason*, 53.

door. In the latter case, our affective response activates a set of intelligent attitudes and beliefs, but it involves a felt sense of bodily agitation just as much as the former case does. At the same time, the simpler emotion (like the more complex one) incorporates a kind of perceptual recognition, an intake of meaningful information from the world.[33] Each instance of fear, then, "aims toward truth," toward getting something right, and this is precisely why it can be mistaken, as it is when we momentarily misconstrue an inanimate object as a creature facing us.[34] Our prehistoric ancestors may have been more likely to get angry upon receiving a blow to the head, as James says, while we more often become angered by such offenses as getting cut off in traffic.[35] However, both the primitive episode of anger and the more "civilized" one have the same kind of intentional content: in both cases, an embodied human being is upset or agitated by what is perceived as a nontrivial wrongdoing. And it seems plausible that

33. Responding to Robinson's paper on "Startle," Nussbaum writes: "To call an emotion cognitive does not, of course, entail that it is either conscious or reflective; it is just to say that it involves processing of information," plus at least a "rudimentary appraisal of the situation."—*Upheavals of Thought*, 115. Cf. Robinson, *Deeper Than Reason*, 43: "non-cognitive" appraisals can function as "information-processing devices." Robinson therefore admits that emotions do involve cognition as Nussbaum defines it. Empirical reasons for doubting whether the startle response even ought to qualify as an emotion are given by Ekman et al. in "Is the Startle Reaction an Emotion?" See also Keith Oatley, *Best Laid Schemes*, 19: in summary, he explains that "startle is not an emotion" but rather a "reflex reaction" that "can be triggered reliably" by "a loud, sharp sound." Ekman and his colleagues also note that its physical characteristics are dissimilar to those of an emotion such as surprise, with which it might otherwise seem continuous.

34. That emotions simply *do not* aim at revealing the truth is flatly asserted by Döring in "Why Be Emotional?," 293–294; see also Tappolet, "Values and Emotions," 129–130. On the contrary, it seems that even a brief shudder of fright is one of the phenomena which, as Merleau-Ponty states, "have a significance, even though they are not yet thematized."—*Phenomenology of Perception*, 319–320. About the evolutionary advantage of being able to detect vertically symmetrical objects, see Daniel Dennett, *Consciousness Explained*, 179–180.

35. See William James, "What Is an Emotion?," 195–196.

the two episodes of anger, like the more and less rudimentary cases of fear, may involve similar patterns of somatic agitation.

We should bear in mind Aristotle's observation that passions or emotions ought to be attributed to the *person* who is experiencing the emotion, and not to some part of that person.[36] Thus, we rightly say, "I made a decision" or "I had an idea," since it is we ourselves who think and decide, not an organ or another part of our anatomy doing its own thing. Likewise, it is *you* who sees, not your eyes, although your eyes are involved in your seeing.[37] And by the same token, when you feel pity or fear, it is *you* who feels these emotions—not just your mind, your brain, or your sympathetic nervous system. Whatever we might find out from studying the conditions under which the amygdala is activated, we certainly do not learn that the amygdala *itself* is capable of apprehending danger. People with brains have emotions, but brains (or parts of brains) do not have emotions of their own.[38] To think that they do is to make a category mistake, ascribing to part of a living organism a state that can only be meaningfully ascribed to the whole organism.[39] It is "not my brain but I myself" that warmly recognizes my grandmother, and not my brain but I myself (a human being *with* a brain) that

---

36. Aristotle, *De Anima* 408b. See also *Nicomachean Ethics* 1149a. On the former, see Heidegger, *Basic Concepts of Aristotelian Philosophy*, 132–133.

37. Just as the eye alone does not have any visual experience, the brain itself "knows nothing and understands nothing," as John McDowell points out: "The Content of Perceptual Experience," 201. Cf. Aristotle, *De Anima* 412b. On the "person-environment relationship," see Lazarus, *Emotion and Adaptation*, 89–92.

38. Following LeDoux, who suggests that the amygdala is on the lookout for danger, Robinson describes it as the place in the brain "where the emotional significance of threat is registered." See *Synaptic Self*, 214; *Deeper Than Reason*, 49. Cf. Pinker, *How the Mind Works*, 371–372.

39. On the notion of a "category mistake," see Gilbert Ryle, *The Concept of Mind*, 16–23. See also Per Holth, "The Persistence of Category Mistakes in Psychology," 210. A similar kind of mistake, unfortunately, is made by cognitive theorists when they speak of fear *itself* as perceiving a threat: see Nussbaum, *Upheavals of Thought*, 27.

is ontologically the kind of thing that can experience emotions.[40] This is an elementary theoretical point, yet it is frequently ignored in interdisciplinary research on emotions. So readers of prominent texts in this field will be told, with an air of scientific authority, that "emotions reside in perceptual systems of the brain," that there is a place "where desires can be found in the brain," that "our brains can often decide in seconds" how to respond to a stimulus, and that "the prefrontal cortex acts as an efficient manager of emotion."[41] This may be harmless enough *if* understood as shorthand for the well-founded claim than an author intends to be making (provided that he or she does not actually mean to imply that our heads are full of "homunculi" who are experiencing emotions). But it is nonetheless a misleading way to speak, and it can lead philosophers to such conceptual confusions as the notion that oxytocin is "not itself an emotion, but apparently an element of love and related emotions such as trust."[42] Should anyone so much as *entertain* the ontological possibility that oxytocin could be an emotion? By even considering the notion that a chemical in the brain could itself qualify *as*

40. Robert Sokolowski, *Phenomenology of the Human Person*, 193. See also Solomon, *True to Our Feelings*, 146–147: we should not forget, he says, that the brain is "part of an organism" existing in "an environment."

41. I cite, respectively, Prinz, *Gut Reactions*, 205; Schroeder, *Three Faces of Desire*, 29; Damasio, *Descartes' Error*, 172–173; and Goleman, *Emotional Intelligence*, 26–28. Robinson states that the amygdala "computes the affective significance" of stimuli and "defends against" anything deemed threatening: *Deeper Than Reason*, 49–61. LeDoux's willingness to adopt this manner of speaking is partly to blame, because Robinson clearly follows his lead: for his personification of parts of the brain, see, for instance, *The Emotional Brain*, 163–165. Prinz likewise refers to the prefrontal cortex as "weighing one emotion against another"—*Beyond Human Nature*, 297.

42. Greenspan, "Learning Emotions and Ethics," 542. A more sensible assessment of the research to which Greenspan refers is provided by Ronald de Sousa in *Emotional Truth*, 162–169. The risks of overlooking such ontological questions as whether a chemical in the brain, deprived of context and meaning, could in itself qualify as an emotional state, are explained by John Dupré in *Human Nature and the Limits of Science*, 1–6. Cf. Marilynne Robinson, *The Givenness of Things*, 6–8.

an emotion, the author making this claim evinces an absurd belief about what human emotions are.

In order to exercise good judgment in appealing to scientific findings, we must bear in mind that emotions do not take place in a private interior realm, enclosed within the skull. Rather, they arise from our engagement with the world, as we are provoked by actions, events, and situations; and they have their identity by virtue of much that is external to the living organism. An investigation of "fear behavior" could not get started unless we could specify the conditions under which fear would arise: e.g., in creatures who are disturbed by a sudden noise (which may indicate threat). This does not mean that a physiological analysis of fear cannot inform us of anything other than what we already knew about this emotion; it does, however, set boundaries to the investigation. We must be able to distinguish *instances* of fear in order to measure the neurological activity that is characteristic of fear, and for this reason it is impossible for us to find out from such measurements that fear is something radically unlike what we thought it was in the first place.[43] Damasio rightly points out that research on "the brain's emotional apparatus" can provide us with knowledge that is ethically relevant, by helping us to understand emotions such as fear and grief, and more protracted mood states as well;[44] what it *cannot* show us is that fear, grief, and anxiety are merely "in the head." From the vantage point of a grieving or frightened person, one's affective state is outwardly oriented: it is *about* some aspect of the world. Likewise, when I become angry, "the location of my anger" is not only within me, but (as we might say) in the space between myself and the

---

43. This point is made by Nussbaum, *Upheavals of Thought*, 58–59; see also Roberts, *Emotions*, 48.
44. Damasio, "Neuroscience and Ethics," 6.

person at whom this emotion is directed.[45] The emotions we feel, then, "are part of our cognitive engagement with the world," and "integral to our ability to grasp the meaning of a situation." What goes on in the brain of an emotional person, therefore, is just one part of a larger story.

Ideally, the relationship between conceptual explanation and empirical research ought to be a symbiotic one. In the absence of careful philosophical analysis of mood and emotion, as Owen Flanagan observes, "the neuroscientists don't know what they are looking for."[46] Phenomenological observations and explanations should also be informed and even (when appropriate) revised by research from the human and natural sciences.

However, the balance between empirical work and theoretical explanation, in which each is able to learn from the other, is lost when philosophers limit their role to that of simply reporting upon experimental findings. Instead of selectively citing the latest study that appears to support our own preferred view, as if this "resolved" the matter once and for all,[47] we should attempt to make sense of disagreements between leading researchers, and to figure out how the phenomena can support such variant views. The discrepancy between LeDoux's account of emotion and Damasio's is

---

45. Merleau-Ponty, *The World of Perception*, 84. Regarding what follows, see Mark Johnson, *The Meaning of the Body*, 66–68.

46. Flanagan, "Neuro-Eudaimonics," 595–597. A comparable point is made by Francisco Varela, in "Neurophenomenology"; see also Ratcliffe, *Feelings of Being*, 123 and Zahavi, "Naturalized Phenomenology," 35–36. Speaking for the neuroscientists themselves, LeDoux remarks that one reason why "brain researchers" have "disagreements about how emotion is instantiated in the brain" is that "we don't agree about what we are looking for." See "Low Roads and Higher Order Thoughts in Emotion," 214.

47. As LeDoux appears to do, for example, in *Synaptic Self*, 219–220. Robinson contends that her view of emotions is *the one* that is supported by "*the currently available evidence*": see *Deeper Than Reason*, 3. Zajonc also argues that "the facts" are consistent only with his theoretical position, and not with those of his rivals: see "On the Primacy of Affect," 117–121. Cf. Delancey, *Passionate Engines*, 31–37.

an instructive case. It could be that the *impersonal* cognitive abilities that are intact in Damasio's patients, who suffer from an impairment of emotional reasoning pertaining to personal matters, are the same cognitive abilities that LeDoux has often described as not essential to affective arousal.[48] If this is the case, as I believe it is, it would suggest that modes of cognitive functioning which are relevant to thinking about matters of personal significance require emotion, whereas other modes of cognition (those associated with impersonal reflection) may by comparison be affectively flat and neutral.[49] This, in turn, may help us to specify what type of cognitive activity *is* (and is not) involved in most human emotions.

Even if we could define a certain type of emotion in terms of a characteristic pattern of brain activity—and the fact of neural plasticity may prevent us from doing this too strictly—we still would not have identified the characteristic somatic agitation that is typically part of our affective experience. That is, the "feeling of bodily changes" emphasized by William James does not include any felt sense of our own *brain* activity as such.[50] This is agreed upon not only by phenomenologists, but also by naturalists of the most

---

48. See Damasio, *The Feeling of What Happens*, 41–42; *Looking for Spinoza*, 143–144. Cf. LeDoux, *The Emotional Brain*, 176; *Synaptic Self*, 24. This is also consistent with Ratcliffe's interpretation of the Capgras delusion: diminished affective response is "likely to play a more significant role" in hindering the "perception of those to whom a person is close." See *Feelings of Being*, 145.

49. Patients with damage to the ventromedial sector of the prefrontal cortex, for instance, show a pronounced impairment in their ability to think about "matters pertaining to their own lives," even while their capacity for quantitative reasoning remains unchanged: see Bechara et al., "Emotion, Decision Making, and the Orbitofrontal Cortex," 295. Cf. Paul Thagard, *Hot Thought*, 127–128.

50. LeDoux is certainly wrong to claim that affective feelings occur "when we become consciously aware that an emotion system of the brain is active," since this *never* happens: see LeDoux, *The Emotional Brain*, 302. Roberts provides a rebuttal of LeDoux's statement on page 43 of *Emotions*, while Johnston and Malabou (surprisingly) endorse it: *Self and Emotional Life*, 188–189.

reductive sort.[51] Our experience of being emotionally moved does, however, incorporate some awareness of the muscle contractions associated with our own facial expressions and postural changes (such as flinching or cowering), and we can also feel such bodily changes as increased heart rate and sweat gland activity (which is correlated with heightened electrical conductivity in the skin), as well as interoceptive (colloquially, "gut") feelings.[52] Somatic feelings such as these play "a prominent and vital role" in our affective experience, and when emotion researchers focus on what is distinctly *somatic* about human emotions, what they have in mind are our characteristic feelings of bodily upheaval.[53] What concerns us, however, as Goldie clarifies, is "the phenomenology or the qualitative nature of our personal experience of these changes rather than . . . the impersonally observable, and quantitatively measurable, changes themselves."[54] Yet the tendency to speak about felt bodily changes as if they must be *about* nothing other than one's own physical state (still perpetuated by Prinz and other theorists)[55] can

51. See, e.g., McGinn, *The Problem of Consciousness*, 8; Dan Zahavi, *Husserl's Phenomenology*, 13; and Paul Churchland, *Matter and Consciousness*, 26. As McGinn puts it, "Introspection does not present conscious states as depending on the brain in [any] intelligible way."

52. For a summary of various aspects of physiological change in emotional experience see Frijda, *The Emotions*, 133–135; and Ben-Ze'ev, *The Subtlety of Emotions*, 10. See also Frijda, *The Laws of Emotion*, 154; and Robinson, *Deeper Than Reason*, 30–31.

53. David Pugmire, *Sound Sentiments*, 14. Even if we understand emotions as mental phenomena, James says, we still ought to accept that, "to a great extent at any rate, they are simultaneously affections of the body."—*Essays in Radical Empiricism*, 142. Even "guilt pangs" involve "somatic signals" that can be felt, according to Jesse Prinz: see *The Emotional Construction of Morals*, 59–60. Jon Elster holds that "each emotion has a unique quale or feel to it."—*Alchemies of the Mind*, 248. On how affective feelings can enter "into the intellectual content of the emotion," see Wynn, *Renewing the Senses*, 28–29. Cf. Nussbaum, *Political Emotions*, 400: "What feels wrenching and visceral about emotions is often not independent of their cognitive dimension."

54. Peter Goldie, *The Emotions*, 52. On how these changes *may* be interpersonally available, see Joel Krueger, "Empathy and the Extended Mind." Cf. Max Scheler, *The Nature of Sympathy*, 260.

55. Jesse Prinz, *Beyond Human Nature*, 294: Emotions "are perceptions of changes in the body."

lead us to assume that, if our emotions have any intentional content, this must be *despite* their bodily nature. It is a mistake to assume that our embodied affective feelings are an extraneous aspect of emotions, unrelated to their intentionality. So, after reviewing some additional empirical evidence—which supports the view that our feeling of being in a certain emotional state *does* typically include a sense of the embodied upheaval associated with that emotion[56]—I will explain how the somatic agitation we feel when we are affectively moved might actually *contribute* to the way that the emotions inform us about how things are going in our world of concern.

LOOKING BEYOND THE BRAIN
(TO THE LIVING BODY)

When we look to other aspects of our physiology, we encounter more directly the characteristic somatic agitation that is part of our affective experience. Since emotions involve bodily agitation, we should expect to find a strong correlation between somatic states and felt emotions. Studies on facial and somatic feedback have indeed uncovered such a correlation. When the musculature of the face is indirectly manipulated so that a person is unwittingly opening the mouth in something like a smile, he or she is likely to experience more positive affects.[57] People have reported feeling more

---

56. For a concise account of these, see Levenson, "Autonomic Nervous System Differences among Emotions"; Redding, *The Logic of Affect*, 17–21.

57. Specifically, people find the same comic strip more amusing, and the same literary narrative more agreeable, if they are holding a pen in their open mouth or pronouncing the name "Peter," rather than holding their lips closed or saying the name "Jürgen." In each case, the latter induces an expression more similar to a frown, the former something more akin to a smile. The "pen in the mouth" study is Strack, Martin, and Stepper, "Inhibiting and Facilitating Conditions of the Human Smile"; the other one is Zajonc, Murphy, and Inglehart, "Feeling and Facial Efference." For an unsuccessful attempt to replicate the results

warmly disposed toward someone they met while holding a warm cup of coffee, and more excited about someone they encountered on a high, narrow bridge.[58] Admittedly, other studies have been inconclusive, prompting one social psychologist to declare that "the contribution of [somatic] feedback to emotional experience is less than convincing."[59] Even if adopting a sad or angry facial expression is not *sufficient* for inducing a state of sadness or anger, as the evidence indicates it is not, someone who is inadvertently making either type of expression *is* likely to be more susceptible to experiencing the corresponding emotion. And this goes for somatic feedback of other kinds, including proprioceptive awareness: adopting an upright posture does not *create* pride, but it may help to facilitate feelings of pride, perhaps by lowering the threshold of what seems like a reason to feel proud.[60] When other bodily states are subjectively experienced, they *can* have an impact on our dispositions toward emotion: if I receive a shot of epinephrine, this will not be sufficient to *induce* anger, but it may very well make me feel agitated

---

of Strack, Martin, and Stepper's study, see Wagenmakers et al., "Registered Replication Report." While it is emphasized that this result does "not invalidate the more general facial feedback hypothesis" (page 924), it does undermine strong versions of this hypothesis, such as numerous philosophers defend.

58. See, respectively, Lawrence Williams and John Bargh, "Experiencing Physical Warmth Promotes Interpersonal Warmth"; Donald Dutton and Arthur Aron, "Some Evidence for Heightened Sexual Attraction under Conditions of High Anxiety."

59. Matsumoto, "The Role of Facial Response in the Experience of Emotion," 773. On the existence of emotion in subjects with facial paralysis, see Alan Fridlund, *Human Facial Expression*, 176–178. Contrary to what Prinz maintains (see *Beyond Human Nature*, 247), just being in a certain bodily state is *not* sufficient for an emotional response to occur: see, e.g., Roberts and Arefi-Afshar, "Not All Who Stand Tall Are Proud," 715. The data from numerous studies appear to support the thesis that bodily feedback influences emotion but is not sufficient to bring it about.

60. Stepper and Strack, "Proprioceptive Determinants of Emotional and Nonemotional Feelings," 215–216. As these authors point out, the grounds for having a "full-blown emotional experience" of pride would include an awareness of some accomplishment.

"as if" I were angry,[61] thus leaving me more irascible—more prone to anger—as a result.

Aristotle long ago remarked on this phenomenon: namely, that a person can be angered by a slight provocation when the body is in a state similar to that of an angry person.[62] Now, the notion of a physical state *resembling* that of an angry person would be unintelligible unless anger is distinguished by a distinctive pattern of physiological agitation. And some recent evidence suggests that it is: research on facial expressions indicates that anger, fear, and disgust are each roughly linked with a specific pattern of autonomic nervous system arousal.[63] Admittedly, only modest and somewhat "coarse" differences have been found between the physiological contours of one type of emotion and those of another.[64] Moreover, these results are based on simulated affects in an artificial setting, and they do not imply that all episodes of anger, fear, or disgust must necessarily involve the same pattern of bodily changes.[65] Fear might be more

61. Gordon, *The Structure of Emotions*, 94–96. Cf. Randolph Cornelius, "Gregorio Marañon's Two-Factor Theory of Emotion"; Jesse J. Prinz, *Gut Reactions*, 70. See also Dolf Zillmann, "Sequential Dependencies in Emotional Experience and Behavior," 263–264.

62. See *De Anima* 403a, where Aristotle adds that the bodily agitation characteristic of fear can on some occasions be felt in the absence of anything frightening.

63. The distinctive somatic markers for anger, fear, and disgust involve the conjunction of heart rate, diastolic blood pressure, and skin temperature or conductance. See Levenson, "The Search for Autonomic Specificity," 255; Paul Ekman, R. W. Levenson, and W. V. Friesen, "Autonomic Nervous System Activity Distinguishes between Emotions," 1209; and A. F. Ax, "The Physiological Differentiation between Fear and Anger in Humans." Cf. Prinz, *Gut Reactions*, 72–74 and *Beyond Human Nature*, 245–246. On the respiratory changes involved in different emotions, see Pierre Philippot et al., "Respiratory Feedback in the Generation of Emotion."

64. Rolls describes these differences as "coarse," while Levenson admits that they are "small": see *The Brain and Emotion*, 72; *Neuroculture*, 18–19; and "Autonomic Nervous System Differences among Emotions," 26.

65. Noting some inconsistency across various studies, as well as variation in different individuals or situations (even for different instances of the same type of emotion), Richard Davidson concludes that "the evidence does not support the idea that different discrete emotions have unique and invariant autonomic signatures." See "Parsing Affective Space," 467–468. The specificity of the observed autonomic differences, and their magnitude, are

reliably correlated with apparently frightful objects in our environment than it is with a spike in heart rate and a drop in skin temperature. Moreover, in order for our somatic feelings to be *emotional*, they must be experienced as being about significant features of the world. And, furthermore, our sense of being emotionally stirred is not always aligned with measurable physiological arousal;[66] some emotions seem to occur with only subtle or minimal feelings of somatic agitation.

Yet even after all of these qualifications have been made, the evidence—from social psychology, especially—is still too significant to be ignored: in many cases, the feeling of being in a particular affective state *does* include a sense of whatever visceral changes are associated with that emotion.[67] It may be true that I cannot be angry at you unless I am convinced that you have slighted, harmed, or thwarted me—as the cognitive theorists have shown with their own set of canonical studies, which illustrate that beliefs and appraisals can have a powerful effect on our emotions.[68] But if my pulse

hardly enough to justify the claim that each emotion has a uniquely identifying physiological profile. This is acknowledged by Robinson, "Emotion," 31. Cf. Levenson, Ekman, and Friesen, "Voluntary Facial Action Generates Emotion-Specific Autonomic Nervous System Activity," 379–381.

66. On the correlation between physiological indicators and subjective reports, see P. J. Lang, "The Three-System Approach to Emotion," 18. See also A. D. Craig, "How Do You Feel?" On the lack of noteworthy somatic activity for some emotions, see Frijda, *The Emotions*, 172–173 and Buck, *The Communication of Emotion*, 48.

67. See, e.g., Michael Tye, *Ten Problems of Consciousness*, 125–127; see also Paul Redding, *The Logic of Affect*, 17–21 and William E. Lyons, *Emotion*, 60. On what distinguishes interoceptive, proprioceptive, and kinaesthetic feelings, see Dan Zahavi, *Self-Awareness and Alterity*, 94–103.

68. See, e.g., Richard Lazarus and Elizabeth Alfert, "Short-Circuiting of Threat by Experimentally Altering Cognitive Appraisal"; Craig Smith and Phoebe Ellsworth, "Patterns of Cognitive Appraisal in Emotion." See also Klaus Scherer and Grazia Ceschi, "Lost Luggage: A Field Study of Emotion-Antecedent Appraisal"; Matthias Siemer, Iris Mauss, and James J. Gross, "Same Situation—Different Emotions." Cf. Paul Rozin and April Fallon, "A Perspective on Disgust," 24; Martha C. Nussbaum, *Hiding from Humanity*, 88; Ira J. Roseman, "Cognitive Determinants of Emotion" and "Appraisal Determinants of Discrete Emotions";

is racing and my skin is flushed, then I am already in a bodily state resembling that of an angry person, and as a result I am likely to find myself more easily angered. This is why Benvolio, in *Romeo and Juliet*, worries that his friends are apt to be provoked into fighting with their rivals on a warm summer afternoon:[69]

> The day is hot, the Capulets abroad,
> And if we meet, we shall not 'scape a brawl;
> For now, these hot days, is the mad blood stirring.

If I become angry and then discover that I have not been wronged after all, my anger may still take a little while to dissipate completely, because the physiological commotion associated with anger has a momentum of its own which does not subside instantly—contrary to what has been argued by leading cognitivists.[70] And we need not stipulate that every type of emotion can be linked with a universal and invariant physiological signature in order to observe that there is "something it's like" to be angry, something that it feels like to be afraid, and likewise for other emotions. Furthermore, it makes sense to accept that there is a correspondence between these differences in experienced affective feeling and some of the "coarse"

Ivan E. de Araujo et al., "Cognitive Modulation of Olfactory Processing"; and Klaus Scherer, "Studying the Emotion-Antecedent Appraisal Process." Finally, for a review of recent research along these lines, see also Agnes Moors et al., "Appraisal Theories of Emotion."

69. William Shakespeare, *Romeo and Juliet*, III.i.2–4.

70. Solomon, *The Passions*, 178–179: when I discover that my car has not been stolen, my anger at John for stealing it "vanishes in an instant." This appears to be mistaken, even if Solomon is right to claim that anger has a certain kind of cognition as its necessary condition. Robinson says that "I can still 'be angry'" after discovering I haven't been wronged," since my "physiological reactions may still keep going after the relevant evaluation has been rejected."—*Deeper Than Reason*, 78–79. Again, see Aristotle, *De Anima* 403a–b. The source of the phrase "what it is like," as a way to denote the "subjective character of experience," is of course Nagel, in *Mortal Questions*, 166–168.

differences in neural and somatic activity that have been observed with respect to specific emotions. James appears to be right when he claims that "the bodily sounding-board" is typically active in our affective responses, and more regularly than we tend to recognize,[71] especially if we have laid stress mainly on the cognitive aspect of emotions as *opposed* to the somatic.

When Solomon and Nussbaum, among others, claim that embodied feelings are inessential factors that cannot reveal the identity of an emotion, they are overstating the case for cognitivism.[72] The somatic feelings involved in affective experience can hardly be dismissed as extraneous phenomena that just incidentally happen to accompany our emotions themselves. This is because those feelings are not merely blind sensations devoid of intentional content: when we undergo an emotion, our somatic feelings carry significant information about the surrounding world. We can perceive things *about* the world *through* our feelings, in other words; unfortunately, this crucial feature of affective experience has been left out of most accounts.[73] As Merleau-Ponty remarks, the body is palpably involved in our perceptual "comprehension" of the world, and this is

---

71. James, "What Is an Emotion?," 202. See also Ratcliffe, *Feelings of Being*, 229.

72. Nussbaum argues that we cannot distinguish what type of emotion we are undergoing from the "feeling of agitation all by itself," since "judgment alone" distinguishes emotions: see *Upheavals of Thought*, 29 & 196; on page 25, she submits that emotions are "bodily" just in the way that "other mental processes" are. Cf. Solomon, *The Passions*, 179–180.

73. Ben-Ze'ev, for example, claims that "the feeling dimension" of our affective experience "has no significant cognitive content."—"Emotion as a Subtle Mental Mode," 252–253. Ratcliffe counters that bodily feelings "are part of the structure of intentionality," and that such feelings "can be *in* the body but *of* something outside the body."—"The Feeling of Being," 44. He writes that many "bodily feelings" are "not solely perceptions of our bodily states, distinct from the perception of our surroundings."—*Feelings of Being*, 77. See also *Experiences of Depression*, 34–41. Cf. Gilbert and Lennon, *The World, the Flesh and the Subject*, 108: affective feelings "must be experienced not just as bodily sensations which affect one, as in physical illness, but as sensory states through which I discern features of the world that matter to me." Goldie agrees: "there are emotional feelings of a kind that can be directed" toward the world. See "Getting Feelings into Emotional Experience in the Right Way," 232.

especially true of affective experience.[74] Not every feeling of bodily agitation delivers intentional content, and—as the cognitivists have correctly maintained—emotions *do* refer to the world and therefore have intentionality.[75] Nevertheless, the role of the living body in our affective experience does not seem to be merely random or accidental. Just as surely as the person who is experiencing fear feels afraid *of* something, he or she also *feels* afraid—with a sense of bodily agitation, whether subtle or pronounced. To leave this out of an account of emotion would be to neglect a prominent feature of our affective life, one that we acknowledge every time we describe ourselves as being shaken, disturbed, or upset. In experiencing a "shiver of apprehension," to use the phrase by Gadamer that I cited above, one receives meaningful information about the world; yet the shiver is also something that one *feels*. It is through our "living, feeling bodies" that we emotionally recognize significant aspects of the situations in which we find ourselves.[76] Our affective responses involve

74. See Merleau-Ponty, *Phenomenology of Perception*, 273: "my body is the fabric into which all objects are woven, and it is, at least in relation to the perceived world, the general instrument of my 'comprehension.'" Cf. Zahavi, *Self-Awareness and Alterity*, 123: we perceive external things by means of the lived body.

75. See Roberts, *Emotions*, 339: "a person who is really fearful fears *something*," even if the bodily feelings aroused by simulated fear might make a person feel "as if" he is afraid. On perceiving danger by perceiving our bodies, see Prinz, "Response to D'Arms and Hills," 731–732: he ought to have said that we perceive danger *through* our embodied responses. Husserl notes that "not all experiences are intentional," as is demonstrated by the existence of mere sensations: see *Logical Investigations*, 556.

76. Ratcliffe, *Feelings of Being*, 28. Michael Stocker reminds us that only emotions with "a distinct bodily expression" were said by James to be embraced by his theory; yet, even if some emotions involve less palpable somatic agitation, I don't think we need to accept Stocker's claim that many embodied "feelings" do not "require any bodily feeling" at all. See *Valuing Emotions*, 19; see also "Intellectual and Other Nonstandard Emotions," 404–407. There are, as Armon-Jones points out, nonemotional bodily feelings: see *Varieties of Affect*, 7. Yet we shouldn't presume that somatic feelings must be merely "nonintentional bodily movements," as Nussbaum does: see *Upheavals of Thought*, 25. I explain why she *ought* to make more room for feelings in her theoretical account in "Martha C. Nussbaum's *Political Emotions*," 646–649. In his later work, Solomon realizes that bodily feelings can actually

somatic changes *and* they are intentionally directed toward persons, circumstances, and ideals. The bodily aspect of an emotion does not simply cause the mental, either: it is a mistake to argue that emotions are mysteriously evoked states of physiological turbulence which are followed by subsequent cognition, incorporating intelligence only after the fact.[77] Emotions must, rather, be understood as *feelings* through which we *apprehend* what matters to us. The embodied phenomenology of emotions is linked with the revelation of value or significance: this, as I shall explain further, is precisely what we are made aware of through our affective feelings.

be "perceptions of the world": *True to Our Feelings*, 140–141. See also Gadamer, *Truth and Method*, 126.

77. The sense that a menacing animal is threatening is not *subsequent* to a mysteriously "triggered" bodily disturbance, as Harré appears to imply in his description of fear: "Emotions as Cognitive-Affective-Somatic Hybrids," 295 & 299–300. Robinson makes the same error throughout *Deeper Than Reason*—see, e.g., pages 59–61. On the explanatory inadequacy of "hybrid" theories, see also Kristjánsson, "Some Remaining Problems in Cognitive Theories of Emotion," 400–401. As I will spell out in the following chapters, emotions are unified experiences and *not* combinations of bodily agitation *plus* intentionality. Prinz inaccurately reduces the theoretical alternatives available to two, which he characterizes in the following *either/or* disjunction: "Embodiment theorists think that appraisal judgments often trigger emotions, but aren't essential, and appraisal [cognitive] theorists say that bodily feelings are often triggered by emotions, but aren't essential. One view emphasizes thought, and the other feelings."—*Beyond Human Nature*, 244–246.

PART II

ON REASONABLE
FEELINGS AND
EMBODIED COGNITION

Chapter 3

Feeling Apprehensive

As we have just seen, evidence suggests that *some* affective responses may be elicited without intricate cognitive processing;[1] yet this is unlikely to be true for most human emotions. Simple acts such as deciding what to do, or recognizing a close friend, can be severely impaired in the absence of emotion. This is demonstrated by subjects with a variety of abnormal conditions,[2] and it appears to indicate that certain modes of practical reasoning require affective arousal. Those who assert that human emotions are largely or entirely independent of "higher" brain activity, or that they can be elicited through mere facial feedback or chemical induction,[3] are making exaggerated claims. It does seem to be the case, however, that our bodily states can affect our susceptibility toward emotional arousal, because we are more readily disposed toward specific types of emotion when we are in similar bodily conditions. And, as I observed in the previous chapter, empirical research also suggests

1. Cf. Zajonc, "Mere Exposure," 226.
2. Examples of cognitive impairment related to flat or neutral affect are noted by Ronald de Sousa, "Emotions," 67–68; Jon Elster, *Alchemies of the Mind*, 292–293; Simon Blackburn, *Ruling Passions*, 129–131; Matthew Ratcliffe, *Feelings of Being*, 143–147; Glen Mazis, *Emotion and Embodiment*, 32; and Maurice Merleau-Ponty, *Phenomenology of Perception*, 182.
3. See, e.g., Jenefer Robinson, *Deeper Than Reason*, 45; Jesse Prinz, *Gut Reactions*, 39–40; and Michael Brady, *Emotional Insight*, 98. Cf. Christine Tappolet, "Emotions and the Intelligibility of Akratic Action," 109.

that discrete patterns of somatic upheaval can indeed be identified, at least for a few "basic" emotions. Such findings correspond with the observation that there is something it's like to feel a particular emotion: that, in other words, the experience of emotion has a distinct subjective character. Moreover, these differences in our subjective feelings, from one affective experience to another, constitute different embodied ways of experiencing significant features of the world.

A better appreciation of how the living body is involved in affective experience should therefore help us to understand the distinctive kind of cognition that emotional responses involve. Rather than assuming that bodily feelings are nothing but physical disturbances devoid of intentionality, we should acknowledge that they can be feelings *about* our surroundings,[4] which have intentional content and are therefore capable of conveying significant information. The somatic agitation we feel when we are trembling with fear, for example, is not a mere sensation but a felt apprehension of danger. And to feel pangs of guilt is to undergo what might be called a thoughtful bodily agitation.[5] That is how emotions involve the living body in referring to persons, ideals, memories, possibilities, events, and so on. This demands an account of human emotions, not as hybrids of rational judgment somehow conjoined with irrational corporeal commotion, but as feelings through which we apprehend what is significant to us.

---

4. On the way in which "bodily feelings" can be "themselves world-directed, or at least intimately caught up into a world-directed state of mind," see Mark Wynn, *Renewing the Senses*, 31–32.

5. Contra Prinz's contention that only a "non-cognitive theory of the emotions" can explain why a "bodily disruption" would be involved in feeling guilt, his own formulation in an informal study asks subjects to imagine "the feeling you have *when you think about* the fact that you haven't written back" to an old friend: see *The Emotional Construction of Morals*, 55–60. My emphasis.

If this is correct, and our emotions are a mode of experience through which we become aware of whatever appears to be meaningful, then when reliable they can place us in touch with axiologically salient aspects of the world. Furthermore, the emotions constitute a mode of apprehension that cannot be classified as *either* cognitive *or* bodily because it is both at once. An episode of fear, or of any other easily nameable emotion, should not be regarded as a mindless bodily state or as a disembodied mental state—for neither of these alone would be sufficient for the emotion to exist. Without a sense of some apparent danger, we would not experience fear; yet we also could not be afraid without feeling a shiver of fright.[6] This implies that the state of fear has an intentional content which is accessible through an embodied affective response of a particular sort, *and* which (as I noted in chapter 1) is inferentially related to other emotions: there is a logical need for consistency between my fear at one moment of a potential harm that is immediately threatening and my subsequent relief once the threat has been averted.[7] More generally, human emotions are experiences by means of which we can potentially recognize or apprehend significant truths about self and world. Thus, as William James says, our emotions remind us of "how much our mental life is knit up with our corporeal frame."[8] On my account, however, somatic feeling and cognition are elements of

---

6. Cf. Linda Zagzebski, "Emotion and Moral Judgment," 117: "it is possible that there are psychic states that are both cognitive and affective," in such a manner that "the cognitive aspect of the state cannot exist apart from the affective aspect," and vice versa. Along similar lines, Bennett Helm argues that our feelings can be "rich and complex states" with refined intentional content: see *Emotional Reason*, 155. David Pugmire notes that "feeling is the key to 'grasping' the worth one realizes something to have."—*Sound Sentiments*, 17.

7. Cf. Jan Slaby, "Emotional Rationality and Feelings of Being," 61–62. See also, again, Meinong's *Emotional Presentation*, 111–112.

8. William James, "What Is an Emotion?," 201.

one unified affective experience in which the way an emotion *feels* is intrinsically related to what it is *about*.

NOTHING TO FEAR? PHOBIAS AND OTHER (SO-CALLED) RECALCITRANT EMOTIONS

Nevertheless, any view that emphasizes the intentionality of affective feeling must be able to explain cases in which bodily turbulence *without* intentional content is apparently sufficient to generate an emotional response. If we could become frightened while knowing full well that no danger is near, simply by virtue of our bodily state, then this would suggest that fear need not involve cognitive awareness of an apparent danger or threat. And James argues that this is in fact the case: that stage fright, for example, is "wholly irrational"—because it can be experienced by a person who is "inwardly convinced" that the audience's opinion of him or her is "of no practical account."[9] With this thought experiment, he introduces an alleged counterexample of a type that has been repeatedly employed by other theorists. Robinson, for instance, refers to the case of a person who once had a car accident after skidding in a blizzard, and who now fears skidding on snowy roads "whether or not she is really in danger."[10] Goldie also reports that one can plausibly feel that a situation is dangerous while sincerely believing that it is not at all dangerous: he cites Hume's example of a man "hung out from a high tower in a cage of iron," who is afraid of falling although he supposedly "knows himself to be perfectly secure."[11] Acrophobics can experience "intense fear" of heights, Roberts

---

9. James, "What Is an Emotion?," 195.
10. Robinson, "Emotion," 41–42; see also *Deeper Than Reason*, 19–22. She traces the example to Patricia Greenspan: see Greenspan, *Emotions and Reasons*, 17–26.
11. Peter Goldie, *The Emotions*, 22–37 & 76–78; David Hume, *A Treatise of Human Nature*, 148.

contends, although they do not actually think that their well-being is threatened; and Stocker adds that passengers in an airplane could be frightened by the prospect of crashing even without regarding a crash as likely to occur.[12] In similar fashion, Prinz claims that one can fear something despite regarding it as harmless, and others have endorsed analogous views: for instance, that a person who "believes firmly that this spider is not dangerous" could still be "terribly frightened" by it.[13] In each of these cases, a person's felt emotions are at odds with the beliefs that he or she consciously affirms. Examples of this kind are intended to demonstrate that we can feel fear while being convinced that there is no good reason for us to be afraid—and, by implication, that our emotions are liable to conflict with our better judgment. This is often described as the problem of "recalcitrant" emotions. Those who believe that it *is* a problem see the emotions in question as proof that emotions are utterly *un*reasonable, or that they *sometimes* don't listen to reason, or that they are only *somewhat* rational.

---

12. Roberts, *Emotions*, 90; he refers to Barbara O. Rothbaum et al., "Effectiveness of Computer-Generated (Virtual Reality) Graded Exposure in the Treatment of Acrophobia." See also Stocker, *Valuing Emotions*, 38–39. These examples provoke Richard Sorabji to make the following category mistake: denying that "a height is dangerous does not automatically calm the amygdala," he says. See *Emotion and Peace of Mind*, 6 & 146–147. Yet the amygdala *itself* is not the sort of thing that can be emotionally upset. Robinson makes the same mistake: see, e.g., "Emotion," 35–36.

13. Prinz, *Gut Reactions*, 23; see also John Morreall, "Fear without Belief," 360. The passage about fear of spiders is from Julien Deonna and Fabrice Teroni, *The Emotions*, 54. Altered emotions "do not [always] follow changes in belief," Amélie Rorty claims in "Explaining Emotions," 103. See also Justin D'Arms and Daniel Jacobson, "The Significance of Recalcitrant Emotion," 129–130 & 140–143. As we saw in chapter 2, arguments of this kind are frequently connected with dubious appeals to evidence from neuroscientific research: see, e.g., Craig DeLancey, *Passionate Engines*, 41–46. As Gregory Johnson explains, however, it is neurologically "not possible for a response generated by [the] thalamo-amygdala pathways to be a response to any type of complete object, and certainly not" a reaction to a "meaningful stimulus that might signal danger. . . . For example, in the simple case of a fear response caused by seeing a spider, this process presumably includes cells that can respond to a spider qua spider, and these cells will be located in the cortex."— "LeDoux's Fear Circuit and the Status of Emotion as a Non-cognitive Process," 750.

Because phobic fear is so frequently cited as evidence of an alleged discrepancy between emotion and cognition, it merits special attention. Understanding the way that affect and cognition are interrelated in cases of apparently irrational fear might provide us with a key to understanding what distinguishes affective cognition in other cases as well.[14] I am reluctant to view these simply as instances of emotion without cognition or intelligence. It seems that the examples listed above have been too hastily identified as evidence of affective experience being hermetically sealed from reason, and as proving that fear can persist in a person who is *convinced* that he or she has nothing to be afraid of. My contention is that people who are shaken with fear, which is directed toward a particular object, are *not* entirely convinced that this object is harmless. Those who are frightened *don't* simply "know" that there's nothing to fear: the fearless person is more unequivocally aware that there is no reason to be afraid.

When we study the language used by theorists who put forward such examples, it betrays that they are half-aware of protesting too much. Clearly, someone driving a car in wintry conditions cannot be accurately characterized as knowing "perfectly well" that he or

14. The only type of ostensibly noncognitive fear that I will set aside is the peculiar variety of nonconscious "fear" elicited in some empirical studies, which can be identified as fear only by third-person measures such as amygdala activation and is provoked by "masked" stimuli of which the subject is unaware. Nico Frijda describes this condition as "affective blindsight," observing that people afflicted by it are "deeply handicapped," because they are unmoved to avoid danger, feeling "no reason" to do so since they have not experientially registered any significant threat. Frijda, *The Laws of Emotion*, 218–219. See also Jason M. Armfield, "Cognitive Vulnerability." Prominent studies of this kind include, e.g., Öhman and Soares, "'Unconscious Anxiety'"; and "Emotional Conditioning to Masked Stimuli." See also, e.g., Paul J. Whalen et al., "Masked Presentations of Emotional Facial Expressions Modulate Amygdala Activity without Explicit Knowledge." Andrea Scarantino refers to this as "blindfright": see "Insights and Blindspots of the Cognitivist Theory of Emotions," 734–738: as he concedes, this might be the *only* exception to the rule that emotions involve cognition (if it does indeed qualify as a counterexample).

she is in a safe situation, because there *are* evident risks involved.[15] Now, a person who feels terrified of driving may be exaggerating these dangers, but such a case is poorly described as one in which we know that we are safe and yet we're nonetheless experiencing a fear which persists *despite* this knowledge. Ordinarily, *when* a person is afraid, she is acutely conscious of whatever it is that frightens her, and she is aware of it *as* a danger or a possible source of harm. Empirical studies have confirmed that those who fear flying in airplanes tend to hold unrealistic beliefs about the statistical likelihood of crashing, that height phobics report believing that they are likely to fall—and that arachnophobics, compared to other subjects, view a spider bite as much more liable to occur and to cause serious harm.[16] So are these emotional responses just isolated from rational processing, or do they involve flawed rationality? Rather than assuming that phobic fear must necessarily be noncognitive and irrational, we ought to accept the evidence which suggests that those who suffer from irrational fear often have cognitive attitudes or beliefs that are in accordance with the fear they tend to experience. That a person feels a certain emotion is *not* epistemically insignificant: it provides evidence, if not the only kind of evidence

---

15. On knowing "perfectly well," see Greenspan, *Emotions and Reasons*, 23 and Roberts, *Emotions*, 89–91. On the evidence indicating that phobics often hold "idiosyncratic cognitions" or beliefs, see Susan Thorpe and Paul Salkovskis, "Phobic Beliefs," 805.

16. See André T. Miller et al., "Irrational Cognitions and the Fear of Flying"; Bethany A. Teachman et al., "A New Mode of Fear Expression"; Mukul Bhalla and Dennis R. Proffitt, "Visual-Motor Recalibration in Geographical Slant Perception"; and Mairwen K. Jones and Ross G. Menzies, "Danger Expectancies, Self-Efficacy and Insight in Spider Phobia." It seems that Cheshire Calhoun is right to find problematic the alleged "belief that spiders are harmless" in someone who fears spiders: "Cognitive Emotions?," 335. Cf. Michael Brady, "The Irrationality of Recalcitrant Emotions," 414. Philosophers of emotion continue to trot out this example, however, as if it were utterly decisive: see, e.g., Deonna and Teroni, *The Emotions*, 54–56 & 67–69. The experimental literature showing that phobias involve an increased expectancy of harm is surveyed in Stefan Hofmann's "Cognitive Processes during Fear Acquisition and Extinction in Animals and Humans."

available, about what he or she believes and how he or she views and interprets the world. One cannot fear something *while* viewing it as harmless, because one does not regard it as harmless in the moment of being afraid.

When we turn to examples in which something of greater moral consequence is at stake, it becomes easier to discern what is problematic about the presumption that a person's fears reveal nothing about the attitudes and convictions that he actually holds. In order to illustrate "an emotion contingent upon a belief I held in childhood, but have since rejected," Roberts invites us to imagine "that I grew up in a region of the United States where [African-American] people were regarded as sub-human. . . . I believed that their being elevated to a status of equality was unjustifiable and threatened the very fabric of white civilization," and therefore "my emotions toward black people were then a mixture of fear, resentment, and contempt." Years later, after he has become convinced that his earlier beliefs were false and has modified them accordingly, all the same "in certain situations I find my former emotions returning," e.g., "when my sister's date turns out to be a beautiful burly fellow as black as pitch, my immediate response is that old revulsion and anxiety." How should we account for this? Roberts suggests that, in this example, he *does* truly believe that black people are his equals: yet "they appear to me, in certain lights, not to be equal."[17] And Robinson presents the following parallel scenario: consider a man, she says,

who for deep reasons going back to his childhood and his relationship with his mother, resents Esther, his female boss. But

---

17. Roberts, "What an Emotion Is," 195–197. On the "cognitive aspect" *of* our perceptual and affective experience, and on its phenomenology, see Bahlul, "Emotion as Patheception," 118.

he does not judge or believe that Esther is unfair and dictatorial: indeed he sincerely denies that she is.[18]

It only *seems* to this man that his female boss *is* harsh and unkind: he *feels that* she is this way. In this hypothetical instance, Robinson assures us, the sexist man's *beliefs* are perfectly in order: he simply tends to focus on women's behavior "as domineering or hostile," and this attitude is on her view irrelevant to his cognitive framework. Although he "believes" that women are capable of being fairminded, he *experiences* them as overbearing and unjust. He feels that this is how women are—to him, this is how they seem to be—yet, despite the fact that he resents them for this, he sincerely believes otherwise? This is what we are told by philosophers who argue that a person's emotions are divorced from his or her beliefs in such cases as these.

What is it to hold a belief sincerely? According to Roberts, "To assent to p is to be disposed to say 'yes' to the question 'p?' or 'Is p true?'," so if one is asked, "Is it true that black people are equal?," and one answers by saying, "Yes, they are," then one is therefore unequivocally convinced of their equality.[19] And Robinson obviously makes a similar assumption about the nature of belief: while her noncognitive view of emotions differs from Roberts's conception of emotions as "construals" which are not as sharply contrasted with cognitions, both agree that a person's emotions need not show us what he or she believes. Others share their intuition,[20]

18. Jenefer Robinson, *Deeper Than Reason*, 23. She traces the example to Amélie O. Rorty: see Rorty, "Explaining Emotions," 112.

19. Roberts, *Emotions*, 84–85. By contrast, Ratcliffe notes that "being able both to put a tick next to a sentence [on a survey] and to define the relevant words . . . does not [amount] to a capacity for genuine assent."—*Experiences of Depression*, 142.

20. See, e.g., Döring, "Why Recalcitrant Emotions Are Not Irrational," 125: she can see no reason why anyone would hold "that the judgment which supposedly defines the emotion

but I think it ought to be rejected, for it refuses to acknowledge the intentional or intelligent content of the emotions. If I were the female colleague of the man in Robinson's example, or the sister's boyfriend in the case that Roberts depicts, I would question any theory which insisted that the flagrantly sexist or racist emotions felt *toward me* by a specific person were *not* indicative of that person's cognitive attitudes. Even if I were charitable enough to grant that their avowed opinions about my race or gender showed me *something* about what they thought, I would know that these professed beliefs did not reveal the whole truth about how they view things—for something *else* is disclosed by their emotions. And if we altered the example to make *me* the one under scrutiny, we could say that my visceral convictions about race became enlightened after years of living in an ethnically mixed neighborhood, even if my articulate views were perfectly decent when I first moved there. Calhoun has noted that "our cognitive life is not limited to clear, fully conceptualized, articulated beliefs," since it also includes those "dark" cognitions which constitute a large part of our "unarticulated framework for interpreting the world." [21] This whole complex background, including but not limited to our consciously affirmed beliefs, forms our affective outlook: and all of our convictions, not only the articulate ones, influence how we respond emotionally.

In many cases, it appears that a person's irrational emotions reflect his or her unreasonable beliefs. Rather than viewing the

is somehow unconsciously held and thus not acknowledged by the subject," in cases where conscious beliefs conflict with one's emotional response. On the complexities of believing and not believing which are often involved in cases such as this, see Fingarette, *Self-Deception*, 12–32.

21. Calhoun, "Cognitive Emotions?," 338. Cf. Nussbaum, *Upheavals of Thought*, 36: "The mind has a complex archaeology, and false beliefs, especially about matters of value, are hard to shake."

distorted emotions as the *result* or the *cause* of the inaccurate beliefs, we ought to note instead that affect and cognition are aligned just as we should expect them to be. The actor or public speaker suffering from stage fright may honestly believe that the audience members and their opinion pose no *threat* to him, and yet still be quite rationally afraid of the possibility that he will perform badly, granted that he does care about performing well. And to those who fear spiders or mice it may seem likely, if not that these creatures will cause serious injury, that they might run up one's arms or legs, or get into one's clothing—prospects that may qualify as awful.[22] If so, these cases would no longer seem to show that fear can exist without *any* idea of something bad that could happen. If the person who becomes afraid while driving on an icy road is telling herself that she is perfectly safe, it may be that her fear is appropriate while her overtly stated belief is false.[23] If her emotion is responsive to the actual dangers of her situation, then what she *thinks* she knows (namely, that she is in no danger whatsoever), ought to be revised by the insight which is embodied in her affective response. When we rely upon a composed judgment (such as, "I shouldn't be afraid, I know there's no danger here") in order to dismiss an emotional response, we risk being oblivious to the emotion's content, which can be intricately nuanced and highly specific even if it has not yet

22. Cf. Alex Neill, "Fear and Belief," 97–98. Robinson argues straightforwardly that "a belief that I am in danger is neither necessary nor sufficient for fear": see *Deeper Than Reason*, 98. Yet see, e.g., Armfield, "Manipulating Perceptions of Spider Characteristics and Predicted Spider Fear," as well as Thorpe and Salkovskis, "Phobic Beliefs."

23. Perhaps, as Christine Tappolet suggests, "the fear [is] appropriate and the judgment that there is no danger utterly wrong."—"Emotions and the Intelligibility of Akratic Action," 112. A similar point is made by Döring in "The Logic of Emotional Experience," 241. See Calhoun, "Subjectivity and Emotion," 121: it would be a mistake to assume "that in emotion-belief conflicts it must be one's emotions, not one's beliefs, that are irrational."

been put into words.[24] In short, cool reasoning is not always more intelligent than emotion. If I am an unusually calm driver, this is not because I "know perfectly well" that driving is safe (in fact, it is not) but because I am unaware of its risks at the moment, since my affective attention is oriented rather toward the beauty of the open road, the worth of what I will be doing after I arrive at my destination, or something else altogether.

The characters in the examples offered by Roberts and Robinson would be more accurately understood as experiencing a conflict, not between reason and feeling, but between the (cognitive-affective) attitudes they want to endorse and those that govern how things appear to them. Now, such a person could be only paying lip service to nonracist or nonsexist beliefs; however, he may also have good intentions to form a less perniciously biased perspective. Yet, in the event that the latter is true, it's clear that his more tolerant beliefs have not thoroughly "sunk in"; insofar as they haven't, though, he does not wholeheartedly believe what he claims to believe, and it would be false to say that he does.[25] Believing is not a binary one-or-zero matter, as if one either simply does believe a proposition or simply doesn't. Many beliefs are held with lower degrees of conviction that fall short of "full blooded believing," and a person cannot legitimately be said to *know* that X is true (e.g., that not only Caucasian people are trustworthy) if she experiences the world as if X were

---

24. Eugene Gendlin has observed that embodied "felt meanings," or affective feelings, can be quite precise: they are "not indeterminate," only "capable of further symbolization." See *Experiencing and the Creation of Meaning*, 145–146.

25. On the different kinds of "knowing" involved in propositional thoughts versus intentional states such as inarticulate convictions, see Ratcliffe, *Rethinking Commonsense Psychology*, 198–203. In *Nicomachean Ethics* 1147a, Aristotle notes that those who have just learned something can "say the words" without knowing what they mean, since this knowledge must develop over time. The point is that believing or knowing admits of varying degrees. Cf. Ratcliffe, *Feelings of Being*, 184: "Accepting a proposition . . . is not sufficient for a sense of conviction."

false (e.g., by habitually feeling distrust toward nonwhites).[26] By the same token, someone qualifies as being afraid of spiders because, in the presence of a spider, he *feels that* the creature is threatening or takes it to *be* a threat. It is therefore disingenuous to claim that he knows perfectly well that spiders are harmless just because he has explicitly affirmed the truth of a statement to that effect. A more complete account of this case would take stock of the sense in which he has the knowledge that spiders are harmless, as well as the sense in which he doesn't: for he sometimes endorses propositional beliefs according to which spiders are harmless, and yet his intentional attitudes reveal that spiders *do* at other times seem dangerous to him. This is demonstrated by the fear he experiences, for this emotion contains a sense *that* spiders are threatening—which is precisely why the emotion is capable of being at odds with his articulate belief that spiders are harmless.

We should not assume that affective feeling is an "extra," without which cognition remains just the same. The explicit propositional belief that danger is near, minus a felt sense of being threatened, is deficient;[27] and what it lacks is epistemically relevant. For a person who *is* convinced that danger is near, this conviction incorporates a

---

26. The phrase "full blooded belief" is from Michael Stocker, "Emotional Thoughts," 59–60. As he points out, some instances of fear involve *uncertainty*, or the thought that something *might* be a threat. See also Nussbaum, *Upheavals of Thought*, 40–41: a person for whom the significance of a loved one's death "sink[s] in" will feel "disturbed"; thus, not to feel moved would be a sign that this death has not entirely registered in one's awareness.

27. Again, consider Damasio's patients with brain damage, who are cognitively impaired precisely *because* they reason without feeling: see, e.g., *Descartes' Error*, 46–51. Roskies equates the beliefs of patients with damage to the ventromedial cortex (who tend to suffer from emotional impairment) with the moral beliefs of other human beings, and then cites the former as empirical "proof" that people don't feel moved to act in accord with their beliefs! By taking it for granted that emotionally deficient beliefs are like any other beliefs, she leaves aside the possibility that *unemotional* moral thoughts are those that fail to motivate. See Roskies, "Are Ethical Judgments Intrinsically Motivational?" Helm is on the right track when he observes that, when you feel fear, "the badness of the threat is thrust upon you,

feeling of being threatened. It would be inconsistent *not* to feel motivated as if to get away from an apparent danger, since we are moved with an awareness that it may be threatening *in* apprehending it as fearsome. If we had ancestors who could dispassionately judge that they were facing something dangerous *without* feeling moved to avoid it, then they were afflicted by a kind of practical irrationality which probably rendered them unfit to survive. Our somatic turbulence, when we experience fear, contains an intentional reference toward the possible source of harm from which we are recoiling.[28] The feeling of being disturbed by fear is our way of taking *in* this urgent news about the world, of recognizing a potential threat as such. The person who feels afraid is not undergoing a blind agitation, but responding to an object that is apprehended as a potential danger.[29] In the absence of this bodily affective upheaval, he or she would not be recognizing the significance of that particular fact. To believe wholeheartedly that one is threatened, it is not sufficient to endorse an overtly formulated statement about being in the presence of danger: and, likewise, to feel *that* something *is* harmful is evidently to be not entirely convinced that it is harmless. The affective feeling of being threatened by an object that one regards (*when one is not afraid*) as innocuous is also problematic. If nothing else,

---

grabbing your attention and moving you—literally—to respond." See Helm, "Emotions as Evaluative Feelings," 253.

28. This is what distinguishes "the emotional commotion of real fear" from dispassionate acceptance of the fact that danger looms, as Richard Shusterman points out in *Body Consciousness*, 149. On the intentionality of bodily feeling in such cases, see Richard Wollheim, *On the Emotions*, 117–118. See also Goldie, *The Emotions*, 58–60: he describes this in terms of "feeling towards."

29. This apprehension, which is inherent in the feeling of fear, refutes the claim that someone can feel afraid while being convinced that the feared object is "completely harmless," as Paul Griffiths and Andrea Scarantino insist: see "Emotions in the Wild," 441. Cf. Ronald de Sousa, *Emotional Truth*, 60: affective valence, he rightly notes, cannot be dissociated from qualitative experience.

this "recalcitrant" emotion demonstrates that one has ambivalent cognitions about the frightful thing. One's emotions are evidence of conflicting opinions about what is truly the case. When Othello says, "I think my wife be honest, and think she is not,"[30] he is giving voice to his own painfully contrary affective experiences of jealous suspicion and calm trust toward Desdemona—*each* of which seems to him well grounded when he is in the grip of that particular feeling.

Far from showing that emotion and cognition are categorically discrete, phobias ought to remind us that emotional cognition is typically an experience in which one *does*, at least tentatively, accept that things truly are as they appear to be.[31] Acknowledging this allows us to grasp the difference between the belief that spiders are nothing to fear, in a person who is *not* afraid of spiders, and the explicitly stated belief that spiders are harmless in another person who fears them nonetheless. If a person is afraid, then she must find the world threatening in some respect, at least while she is experiencing fear. For the fearsome *seems* dangerous to us, and insofar as we fear it, we feel that it *is* a danger. Why should this be viewed as irrelevant to our cognitive attitudes about what might endanger us? Again, assenting to a proposition is not sufficient evidence that one is convinced of its truth, just as denying the truth of a proposition is not sufficient proof that one is persuaded of its falsity. As a matter of fact, studies have shown that those who regard themselves

---

30. Shakespeare, *Othello*, III.iii.384.

31. Cf. Luca Barlassina and Albert Newen, "The Role of Bodily Perception in Emotion," 23–25. As these authors observe, "in emotional experiences, bodily feelings, feelings towards and cognitive phenomenology are *phenomenally integrated*," in "a complex, integrated conscious experience." See Calhoun, "Cognitive Emotions?," 342: through a person's emotions, the world appears a certain way. "To the acrophobic," for example, "heights [must] appear dizzyingly treacherous." Furthermore, "ordinarily we believe that things are as they seem." As E. M. Adams agrees, "in perceiving that the rose is yellow," usually "I think that the rose is yellow."—*Ethical Naturalism and the Modern World-View*, 188. See also Pugmire, *Rediscovering Emotion*, 116–117.

as invulnerable to emotional bias are *more* likely than others to be swayed by tacit cognitive prejudices that clash with their avowed beliefs.[32] If we take all of this evidence into account, we will no longer view phobias as proof that the "fear system" is impervious to our cognitions, nor will we misunderstand recalcitrant emotions in general as showing that beliefs per se are divorced from emotional responses.[33] The fact that people tend to exaggerate the dangers of air travel, and to believe that airplane crashes are much more common than they actually are, is seldom cited as evidence that our beliefs as such are irrational and likely to mislead us. Emotions such as phobic fear can involve faulty rationality without being unreasonable in the sense of not answering to reason or lying wholly outside the realm of rationality.[34] Unlike in the case of certain perceptual illusions, which continue to appear the same way to us even once we know that the appearance is illusory, "successful therapy of phobic fears" can eliminate false beliefs about the object *and* make it no longer seem dangerous.[35] After this change, a person no longer finds his or her attention intensely drawn to the formerly feared thing as it was before. We will be closer to understanding affective cognition if we cease to assume that the person afflicted by phobic fear has

---

32. See, e.g., Eric Luis Uhlmann and Geoffrey L. Cohen, "I Think It, Therefore It's True." For a discussion of similar evidence, see also Jennifer Saul, "Implicit Bias, Stereotype Threat, and Women in Philosophy," 43–44.

33. As Paul E. Griffiths suggests they are, following Zajonc: see *What Emotions Really Are*, 92–93.

34. Quite sensibly, LeDoux makes the observation that "phobic objects" such as "snakes, spiders, heights," and so on, "are often legitimately threatening, but not to the extent believed by the phobic person."—*The Emotional Brain*, 130.

35. See Reisenzein, "Emotional Experience in the Computational Belief-Desire Theory of Emotion," 220, with references. See also, e.g., Armfield and Mattiske, "Vulnerability Representation"; and Bernstein, "A Time-Saving Technique for the Treatment of Simple Phobias." In this regard, see also Starkey, "Emotion and Full Understanding," 131–135.

exactly the same convictions about the frightful object as do people who *feel* completely unafraid of it.

We will misconstrue these cases if we locate either the dawning apprehension of danger, or any other variety of affective recognition, in a dispassionate judgment which occurs *before* (and could occur *without*) any felt emotion. Theorists of emotion have too often made the error of depicting an appraisal or evaluative judgment as an antecedent, precipitating condition of an affective response.[36] And it is also inaccurate to describe emotional cognition as following *after* an agitated feeling has arisen, since it is not as though we first notice a bodily disturbance and then conclude that someone must have died, since our somatic agitation has a grief-like "feel" to it. According to Prinz, because anger simply *is* a perception of certain bodily sensations, it makes sense to reason as follows: "if you experience your body preparing for aggression, then chances are you have encountered something offensive," yet the somatic changes which constitute anger carry no information about what the offense might have been.[37] But this is false. To perceive the loss of a beloved person just *is* to feel the emotion of grief, with its specific intentional content. Likewise, an object appears frightening insofar as I feel afraid of it, and I feel afraid to the degree that it seems frightening

36. Lazarus, for instance, stipulates that "certain patterns of appraisal *cause* particular emotions": see *Emotion and Adaptation*, 172–173. William Lyons makes a similarly misleading claim, viz., that an emotional state involves "an evaluation which causes abnormal physiological changes." See *Emotion*, 57–58 & 88. Prinz concedes that "a judgment [that] one's lover has been unfaithful" may provoke the "embodied appraisal" of jealousy: see *Gut Reactions*, 98–99. Yet typically, he thinks, the causal sequence is the other way around, and cognitions occur *after* feelings of bodily responses. He assumes that one or the other must come first. So does Robinson, who argues that "cognitive monitoring and labelling of emotions occurs subsequent to an initial gut reaction," which itself involves only "non-cognitive" physiological changes. See *Deeper Than Reason*, 414.

37. See "Sensational Judgmentalism," 8. On "attributing irritability [or] edginess" to a sensation in the chest or gut, although such states are "attributable to a *whole* person" only, not to parts of a body, see Bahlul's instructive analysis: "Emotion as Patheception," 106–107.

to me.[38] Consequently, we must accept that a form of belief is inherent in affective perception, even if this amounts to nothing more than a tacit perceptual acceptance of what appears to be true. In feeling *that* X is Y, that the bear is threatening, we take this creature *to be* dangerous—that is, we apprehend it *as* a potential source of harm and respond to it in this light. Examples such as this illustrate the sense in which there is "a believing inherent in perceiving," as Husserl notes.[39] In this case, our embodied affective feeling of being afraid is the mode of experience through which we recognize the bear as a potential threat.

One recognizes (or misconstrues) a situation *as* threatening, not by making subsequent judgments or interpretations derived from initially unintelligent sense data, but by responding to an aspect of one's surroundings in a specific manner. When I am suddenly confronted with an animal in my path, and feel that it is likely to harm me, I am aware of it as a threat and I feel afraid. In this unified experience of apprehending apparent danger, I implicitly think that the animal *is* dangerous: the cognitive process of emotional apprehension or recognition can take place quickly and tacitly, and can enable me to know something, prior to any reflective act of judgment. A perceptual experience is capable of revealing something true *although* I do not formulate a thought such as, "Here is a creature that might hurt me." Overtly affirming a proposition is not sufficient, nor is it even necessary, for the emotion of fear to involve cognition: prior to

38. John Dewey says that an episode of fear "may be described equally well as 'that terrible bear,' or 'Oh, how frightened I am.'" In other words, "the frightful object and the emotion of fear are two names for the same [unified] experience."—"The Theory of Emotion," 174–176.

39. See *Analyses Concerning Passive and Active Synthesis*, 66–68. This is echoed in Wittgenstein's claim that seeing aspects involves the "echo of a thought in sight": *Philosophical Investigations*, 212. On the ways in which human emotions involve "cognitive interpretation" or "seeing-as," see also Nussbaum, *Upheavals of Thought*, 5 & 127–129. Cf. Roberts, *Emotions*, 87–88. Also, on the sense in which "feeling may itself be the vehicle of thought," see Wynn, *Emotional Experience and Religious Understanding*, 91–93.

any direct formulation, this affective experience allows a person to apprehend an imminent danger.

Explicitly affirmed beliefs of which the subject is transparently aware should not be regarded as the definitive standard for cognition, by comparison with which any other mental state somehow falls short of qualifying as cognitive.[40] Those who uphold this standard take for granted a view of human reasoning toward which I will direct further scrutiny in later chapters. For the time being, I will point out only that by artificially narrowing the realm of the cognitive, some philosophers are led to the conclusion that our beliefs play "a far smaller role" in human existence than we tend to assume.[41] For the sake of appreciating the cognitive attitudes that actually govern our practical outlook and our way of understanding the world, we need to appreciate the distinct contribution that affective experience can make to our knowledge. Emotional upheavals manifest a person's deepest convictions about reality and value; they allow significant recognitions to "hit home" in a way that is powerfully felt. Some time after his grandmother's death, the narrator of Proust's novel returns to a vacation spot where he had formerly stayed in a room adjoining hers. Making a familiar corporeal gesture, he leans forward and starts removing his boots: then, all of a sudden, he is inundated with emotion:

> I was shaken with sobs, tears streamed from my eyes. . . . It was only at that moment—more than a year after her burial, because

40. Cf. Norman Malcolm, "Thoughtless Brutes," 19–20: "It is the prejudice of philosophers that only propositional thoughts belong to consciousness." He invites us to "suppose that as you pass an acquaintance he says 'Hello' to you, and you respond in kind. Did you think to yourself, 'He said, "Hello" '? Suppose you did not. Would it be true, therefore, that you were not conscious of his greeting? Of course not." For an analogous critique of common philosophical conceptions of the transparency of reason, see also Quassim Cassam, *Self-Knowledge for Humans*, 2–10 & 58–70.
41. Tamar Gendler, "Alief and Belief," 663.

of the anachronism which so often prevents the calendar of facts from corresponding to the calendar of feelings—that I became conscious that she was dead. . . . I had only just [now] learned that I had lost her for ever. . . . I clung to this pain, cruel as it was . . . and I longed for the nails that riveted her to my consciousness to be driven yet deeper. . . . I knew that if I ever did extract some truth from life, it could only be from such an impression.[42]

The painful truth that he recognizes, and the way it feels to recognize this, are aspects of a single experience of apprehensive feeling, or emotional knowing. Although in one sense the narrator already knew of his grandmother's death, he did *not* know it perfectly well. The full significance of her death does not register in his awareness until this later moment. It is only now, "a year after her burial," that "he learns that she is dead," as Samuel Beckett comments.[43] "For the first time since her death he knows that she is dead, [and] he knows *who* is dead." The upheaval of grief *is* this recognition. To do justice to such an episode of grief, we must reject any theoretical account which insists that Marcel already knew "perfectly well" that his grandmother had passed away, and that he therefore learns nothing with any cognitive content in this later experience of overwhelming emotion. Nonetheless, as we have seen, that is how many philosophers would be compelled (by their own theoretical positions) to interpret Marcel's experience.

---

42. Marcel Proust, *Cities of the Plain*, 783–787.
43. Beckett, *Proust*, 26–28. Cf. Nussbaum, *Upheavals of Thought*, 44–45. On the mental and bodily "emotional disturbance" during profound grief, see also Murray Parkes and Richard Brown, "Health after Bereavement."

NEITHER MERE FEELINGS NOR
MERE JUDGMENTS

Intellectual activity divorced from corresponding affective feeling is profoundly lacking—not only in its qualitative feel, but also in its epistemic import, or its ability to inform us about matters of significance. The new knowledge introduced to Marcel in the experience described above is axiological: he learns what it *means* to him personally that his beloved grandmother is gone forever. William James is right to say that "fear" minus the feeling of upheaval would not be fear, but it is also true that fear would not be the emotion that it is without any sense of danger. An elevated pulse rate and tingling skin would not qualify as fear if they were induced mechanically, but those same symptoms *could* be an intrinsic part of one's emotional response if they arose with the awareness that one is (or might be) threatened with harm.[44] By now it ought to be clear that we need not choose to focus *either* on somatic feeling *or* on intentional content, because a feeling of bodily agitation can be intentionally directed toward something in the world to which one is responding. The body "is not just an object perceived," as Ratcliffe notes, "but also that through which we perceive," and the embodied feelings characteristic of fear are integral to the experience in which we perceive an apparent threat.[45] A similar kind of embodied perception occurs when I grasp a cold glass of beer. I do not merely feel that my hand is becoming cold; rather, through my hand I feel the coldness of the

---

44. Cf. Oliver Letwin, *Ethics, Emotion, and the Unity of the Self*, 86–87.

45. Ratcliffe, *Feelings of Being*, 132. Following James, Prinz argues that emotions are perceptions of "bodily states" that are "reliably caused" by things in the environment: see *Gut Reactions*, 68–69 and "Embodied Emotions," 56–57. Yet again, however, reliable causation does not amount to intentionality. A state that is *caused* need not carry any information about what has caused it.

glass. Accordingly, to claim that the somatic disturbance involved in fear is just *caused* by something outside one's own body does not capture the way that one's living body is involved in apprehending the fearful object as such. We are physically moved when we recognize an apparent danger and appreciate its significance, and the turbulent feeling of being shaken by fear *is* our way of recognizing a looming threat. In this manner, our embodied affective feelings are *about* features of the surrounding world, and they can reveal these features to us in their significance.

To argue that emotions have intentionality, therefore, is not to deny that feelings play a palpable role in affective experience. In order to capture what is distinctive about affectivity, we must acknowledge that "what it is like" to undergo an emotion is to feel *that* the world (or some aspect of it) is threatening, offensive, or whatever the case may be. To account for the qualitative feeling, we must realize that the felt sense in question is directed toward one's surroundings in a specific way.[46] Usually, a person is not self-consciously aware of his or her affective state itself to the exclusion of any awareness of what he or she is upset *about*: when you ask someone to tell you more about his anger, he doesn't *only* describe his physiological sensations—"I'm boiling up!" or, "My heart is racing!"—instead, he talks mainly about the intentional content of his emotion, or about *why* he is angry.[47] Nevertheless, his feelings of somatic agitation are *intrinsic to* this very emotion, and without the experiential sense of "boiling up" over Z's remark he may not have noticed that Z had

46. Cf. Solomon, *True to Our Feelings*, 233–234. See also Goldie, *The Emotions*, 57–58: "the bodily feeling is thoroughly infused with the intentionality of the emotion." An apt example is offered by Robin May Schott in *Cognition and Eros*, 109–110: if a friend "gives me something" as a gift, then "my feelings of warmth and appreciation" constitute an experience of what I would call affective recognition.
47. See Roberts, *Emotions in the Moral Life*, 72. Uncharacteristically, Ronald de Sousa gets this wrong: see *Emotional Truth*, 29–31.

ridiculed him, or that his own insecurity about the trait that Z had belittled rendered him vulnerable to reacting in this way.[48] And, in the same experience in which I feel anger for some reason, I "feel myself feeling" this emotion.[49] This is not because emotion is cognitive and *also* bodily, as if these were discrete and conjoined parts, but because affective cognition is tangibly embodied, such that to be convinced that one's circumstances are disappointing *is* to feel disappointed. As Sartre observes, "a knowing consciousness that is at the same time an affective consciousness does not have *one part* knowledge and *one part* feeling."[50] Emotions embody the felt recognition of states of affairs that include significant loss, threat, achievement, and so on. What it means to have lost a beloved person—this particular disturbing truth—registers in our awareness in an experience of turbulent upheaval. Our *feelings about* that loss are both somatic ("feelings") and intentional ("about"). Moreover, there is no good reason for us to assume that this emotional episode must be either a mental event with physiological effects or a bodily process followed by reasoning. Rather, the somatic and the cognitive are integrated in a unified experience of a particular living person who is meaningfully engaged in the world.

At this point we can see why it would be false to claim that emotions are outside the cognitive realm altogether, *or* to argue that

---

48. In *The Mind's Affective Life*, 79–80, Fiumara writes that, if we had not realized this before, "we learn from anger that someone has offended us, and we even learn about [our] vulnerability" too: this, in her view, shows that "affective states are cognitive" and that "emotions are an important source of knowledge about ourselves." See Jorge Arregui, "On the Intentionality of Moods," 401.

49. Samuel Todes, *Body and World*, 266–267: this shows how "the sense of our body is inextricably involved in our thought." See also Zagzebski, "Emotion and Moral Judgment," 115.

50. Jean-Paul Sartre, *The Imaginary*, 72–73. Cf. Ratcliffe, *Feelings of Being*, 27: typically, one's feeling of somatic agitation "*is* the emotional apprehension of a situation; the intentionality and bodily nature of the emotion are entangled." See also Paul Redding, *The Logic of Affect*, 43.

emotions can simply be identified with intellectual judgments. Either alternative is inadequate *because* emotions constitute a distinctive means of apprehension, in which something comes to be realized or perceived that could not have come to be known in any other way. It is only through grief that we sense the significance of a personal loss, and only through fear that we can apprehend the threat of danger.[51] More remains to be said about how a perceived loss or danger must impinge upon one's concerns in order to be affectively moving, but at present my point is that a dispassionate "thought" of loss or danger, without any feeling of grief or fear, is cognitively defective. In our affective experience, sensibility and understanding are inextricably bound together. In order for us to acknowledge that human emotions are not irrational disturbances, but potentially truth-revealing phenomena, our account of cognition may need to be broadened.[52] However, without such conceptual widening we will not appreciate the kind of insights (*or* misconceptions) that are embodied in our felt apprehensions of meaning. The cognitive awareness that an emotion incorporates is inherent in its phenomenal character, in the phenomenology of the affective experience. Furthermore, because what we recognize through our emotions could not be adequately grasped by another means, affective experience gives us a distinctly valuable mode of apprehension. One sense in which the heart has reasons of its own, along with its own form of intelligence, is that what our emotions disclose would be otherwise inaccessible to us.

---

51. Cf. Sue Cataldi, *Emotion, Depth, and Flesh*, 113–115. See also David E. Cooper, *Existentialism*, 86–87 and Robert E. Wood's introduction to Stephan Strasser, *Phenomenology of Feeling*, 19–20.

52. Others addressing this topic have argued for a broader, more inclusive notion of cognition. See Jerome Neu, *Emotion, Thought, and Therapy*, 36–37; Elizabeth Grosz, "Philosophy"; and Fiumara, *The Mind's Affective Life*, 75–76. Cf. Furtak, *Wisdom in Love*, 12–14.

Chapter 4

Emotions as Felt Recognitions

Like other varieties of affective upheaval, the feeling of fear thus·
underpins this more general claim: namely, that it is through our
emotions that we are able to discern whatever has meaning or significance for us. Additionally, we have good reason to think that our
capacity for emotional apprehension is embodied in quite specific
ways. People with diminished amygdala function can sometimes
learn to make intellectual inferences about nearby danger *without*
feeling afraid, but this is a poor substitute for the affective capacity
to respond that most of us depend upon.[1] In order to characterize
that ability more adequately, we must acknowledge that the emotion of fear contains "an intrinsic intentionality"—in other words,
that *how* it feels to be afraid is related to *what* fear is about.[2] The
prospect of a hailstorm qualifies as a danger for someone who cares

1. See, e.g., Phelps and LeDoux, "Contributions of the Amygdala to Emotion Processing."
On states in which amygdala damage has left a person with "no feeling of apprehension"
when threatened, see Patricia Churchland, *Brain-Wise*, 349. Cf. Damasio, *The Feeling of What
Happens*, 63–67. In *Emotional Insight*, on page 22, Brady notes "evidence that the emotions
of *normal* subjects can draw or shift attention" to "important objects and events, and can
thereby have epistemic value," citing "Fear and the Focus of Attention" by Faucher and
Tappolet, 119–120.
2. Hanna Pickard, "Emotions and the Problem of Other Minds," 97. See also Roberts,
Emotions, 83.

about her tomato garden, and when she becomes afraid, her affective feeling *is* a sense of that imminent danger. The experience of fear is a felt agitation of the living body, by virtue of which one recognizes an apparent danger as such. To become passionately agitated, in this way *or* in another way (with a different emotion), is to have one's attention drawn to something that is experienced as axiologically prominent, and to be moved to respond accordingly. Emotions are best understood as constituting a distinct mode of embodied cognition, which alerts us to what has meaning or value,[3] as far as we are concerned, and which brings to light matters of significance that we care about. Once again, we see how the phenomenal character of emotion is intimately linked with what it reveals.[4]

How can embodied feelings contribute to the intentionality of emotions? When we detect a potential threat in our environment, or a sign of danger, our body mobilizes its resources to respond. In some cases the best response is to turn and run away, but in other cases "doing something" when frightened could mean pressing the brake pedal, or reaching for the phone to make an urgent call. The feeling of fear involves a sense of our somatic response, and of having our attention focused on the danger as "something to be avoided" or escaped.[5] To be frightened is thus to have an experience in which an apparent danger is recognized in a keenly compelling manner. This intentional content is made available to us *in* and *through* the

---

3. Far from being "noncognitive," Mark Johnson says, "emotion and feeling lie at the heart of our capacity to experience meaning," and thus "emotions are a primary means for our being in touch with [the] world."—*The Meaning of the Body*, 53 & 65.

4. This is why "the phenomenology of emotions," that is, "their essentially affective character," is best "explained in terms of their intentionality."—Helm, "Emotions as Evaluative Feelings," 253. Cf. Colin McGinn, *The Problem of Consciousness*, 29: "what the experience is like is a function of what it is of, and what it is of is a function of what it is like."

5. Aurel Kolnai also notes that taking flight from a "threatening object . . . need not literally mean running away," since it can take the form of "*averting* an impending danger rather than fleeing a presence."—"The Standard Modes of Aversion," 584–585.

visceral feelings of being shaken with fear.[6] These are inherent elements of what it's like to be afraid, and James is correct when he says that "a cold and neutral state of intellectual perception" would be all that remained if we were to eliminate all phenomenal feelings from the experience of fear.[7] The cold and neutral state of mind in which I have the abstract opinion that something might be dangerous, but not in such a way as to pose a real, immediate threat to anyone whom I care about, differs from the feeling of being afraid of a pertinent, urgent danger. In the former instance, my awareness of the situation is lacking *because* I am not emotionally upset—and the difference between a "cool opinion" and the "hot cognition" involved in feeling afraid is *not* epiphenomenal. We do not know what it *means* that danger is at hand if we are unmoved by this information: a neutral observer coolly considering some potential threat is in a different cognitive state than a person who is emotionally aware of that same danger.[8] The latter is taking the risk seriously as a significant threat to a person whose life and well-being he or she values. The mental state of someone who feels afraid thus has a different intentional

---

6. This is *not* to reduce emotions to mere bodily sensations, but to view our lived body as allowing us to understand the world "and find significance in it." See Merleau-Ponty, *Phenomenology of Perception*, 275. Nussbaum, drawing on Aristotle, calls emotion an "acknowledgment" of salient "features of the situation," i.e., "a *recognition* of the particular."—*The Fragility of Goodness*, 309. A person who "noted the fact" that a loved one had died "but was devoid of passional response," she explains, would "not really *see, take in, recognize* what had happened."

7. "What Is an Emotion?," 193 & 199. As Prinz points out, James made note of the possibility that the bodily changes we feel could sometimes be more "virtual" than actual: see *Gut Reactions*, 5–6. Cf. Damasio, *Descartes' Error*, 155–158; Damasio, *The Feeling of What Happens*, 288. On modes of somatic awareness, and individual variations in the accuracy of bodily self-awareness, see also Giovanna Colombetti, *The Feeling Body*, 164–169.

8. As Heidegger points out, "pure beholding" could never discover anything *as* a threat: see *Being and Time*, §§ 29 & 30. On how things appear from "involved" versus "detached" standpoints, see P. F. Strawson, *Skepticism and Naturalism*, 36–37. Richard Lazarus distinguishes "hot" emotional cognition from "cold" thought processes in *Emotion and Adaptation*, 130–132. A similar distinction is made by Thagard in *Hot Thought*, 158–159. Cf. Michael Stocker, "Emotional Thoughts," 63–64.

content from that of someone who is merely contemplating a possible danger: this difference in affective feeling delivers or discloses a different sense of the world.

THE TRUTH ABOUT MORTALITY: A MODIFIED COGNITIVE ACCOUNT

Let's examine a case in which the news about someone's death "hasn't sunk in yet," and we haven't yet been emotionally moved by the realization that this person is deceased: we might find ourselves saying that we "can't believe" she is dead. Our opinion that this person has died, without the deeply upsetting feeling of grief, is akin to a tentative hypothesis that we have scarcely begun to acknowledge—it does not carry the force of a profound conviction, or of a vivid perceptual impression.[9] If I have heard just now that someone I care about has passed away, I may be intellectually accepting the truth of this report without being fully aware of what it means. It is reasonable to conclude that I don't fully *know* about this person's death, because the thought of her death minus the feeling of passionate upheaval is not the same thought. When I am not emotionally agitated in the appropriate way, my understanding of what has taken place, *in* its significance, is deficient or incomplete. In such a case, intellectual ratiocination without emotion falls short of "full rational judgment."[10] I could dispassionately *judge* "that I have suffered a loss

---

9. I quote Matthew Ratcliffe, *Rethinking Commonsense Psychology*, 203. Nussbaum also points out the relevance of cases in which a distressing truth has "not yet sunk in" emotionally: *Upheavals of Thought*, 40–41; see *The Therapy of Desire*, 376. Troy Jollimore speaks of instances in which an unpleasant emotion such as grief has epistemic value as a "cognitive response" to a circumstance in the world in "Meaningless Happiness and Meaningful Suffering," 336–340.
10. Stephen Mulhall, "Can There Be an Epistemology of Moods?," 192. Without "access to one's grief," he adds, a complete "understanding of what has [occurred] is not possible."

without being sad, sorrowful, or grieved," but this does not prove that emotion and cognition are simply divorced from one another.[11] Rather, what it indicates is the cognitive inadequacy of unemotional reason, which lacks the intense awareness of the event's reality and value which would be conveyed to us through an emotional response. Indeed, before I start to experience grief, I have hardly begun to apprehend the meaning of this death as a significant loss, and in that sense I am not fully aware of what has happened. We should not be surprised that it takes time for this awareness to "sink in," and for us to appreciate by degrees what it means that a person whom we love has died. The extreme transformation that such a loss implies, the way that its impact shakes us up and reverberates through our world of concern,[12] becomes realized continually throughout the open-ended process of grieving.

If to *know* something adequately is to recognize and appreciate its meaning or significance, then emotions have a distinct role to play in human cognition. There may be some rational capacities that remain intact in a human being with an impaired ability to become passionately moved, but there are also truths—personal, significant truths—that he or she has no way of knowing, without emotions. Something is made known to us in the experience of being emotionally troubled, for instance by grief, which is not apparent when we just apathetically have an opinion about human mortality without any sense of its personal significance. Likewise, we can accurately assert the fact that all human beings are mortal, and then draw the inference that we ourselves must die one day, while remaining

Patricia S. Greenspan argues that emotions "are based on reactions to particular facts, as they come into consciousness": see "A Case of Mixed Feelings," 237.

11. Robinson, *Deeper Than Reason*, 14: she views this as proof that emotions are "noncognitive."
12. As others have noted: see, e.g., Nussbaum, *Upheavals of Thought*, 80–81; Goldie, *The Mess Within*, 56–57. See also Kym Maclaren, "Emotional Clichés and Authentic Passions," 59–62.

largely unconscious of what we claim to know. Or we can feel powerfully affected by the significance of this fact, emotionally agitated by the thought of our own mortality:

> Suppose I assent to the proposition "I will die one day." I could "believe" it in quite different ways. I might dispassionately affirm it. Alternatively, I might be filled with a sense of existential dread and helplessness when envisaging the all-too-real prospect of my nonbeing. Do I really *believe* it in the former case?[13]

In the former case, I am either not wholly convinced, or not entirely aware, of what it means that I am a mortal being. The emotional mode of apprehension, on the other hand, embodies *more* awareness than *mere* reason. At those times when a person is gripped by the affective recognition of what it means to be finite, she is experiencing what I would call *emotional knowing*. By comparison, we can see what must be lacking in a more dispassionate judgment about such existentially significant matters as one's own mortality or the death of a loved one.[14]

What I am suggesting is not that we must be perpetually upset in order to have any knowledge about human mortality, but that if

13. Ratcliffe, *Feelings of Being*, 160. He observes that the term "belief" can denote "a range of different kinds of conviction." Frankish makes a similar claim in *Mind and Supermind*, 1–2: "belief" can name "an episodic thought or a long-held opinion," a "speculative hypothesis" or an "item of profound faith." Cf. Husserl, *The Crisis of European Sciences and Transcendental Phenomenology*, 82–83: each "act of believing" has its own "mode of certainty": e.g., "straightforward certainty, surmise, holding-to-be-probable, doubting, etc." My example above alludes to Leo Tolstoy, *The Death of Ivan Ilyich*, 93–94.

14. I am indebted to Nussbaum's powerful account of how acknowledging a loved one's death, not merely as a neutral fact, but with a recognition of what it means to have lost this beloved person, demands that one be "disturbed"—in a way that is incompatible with preserving equanimity. Yet feeling disturbed in the relevant manner *does*, I think, require somatic agitation such as a change in one's pulse rate, as Nussbaum claims it does not. See, e.g., "Emotions as Judgments of Value and Importance," 192–195. As Susan Dunston notes,

we *never* felt emotionally agitated by the awareness of what it means to be finite, if we had never been upset at the thought of possibly or actually losing someone whom we love, then what we *know* about death would be less than what we *do* know after experiencing these emotions, and what we are most intensely conscious of when we *are* emotionally moved. What is true of these emotions is also true (as has been noted) of a simple episode of fear: for instance, when a momentary scare on the highway makes us recognize that driving on icy roads can be dangerous.[15] Just before we became afraid, this fact about the dangers of winter driving may have been available to us somewhere in our stock of knowledge, but—to employ a forced phrase that expresses the point well—we *were not knowing* this at the moment. We were unaware of those dangers. To be completely unmoved by any of these facts would be to regard bodily harm or death as insignificant matters that are of no concern, or not to acknowledge them as genuinely possible for us. Affective experience has an "informational value" which we misinterpret if we think that emotions "do not involve any complex information processing," or that there is no *epistemic* difference between dispassionate reflective thought and emotional knowing.[16] On the contrary, we ought to view

speaking about acute grief, "this is not an experience to be understood 'from the neck up.'" See "Philosophy and Personal Loss," 162.

15. In his account of a related example, Prinz gets this right: when I feel emotionally outraged by gender discrimination, I recognize its wrongness. Then, I may continue to think it is wrong once I've recognized this, even if I am most fully aware that it's wrong only when I feel outraged. See "The Emotional Basis of Moral Judgments," 37–38. According to classical Stoic epistemology, what it means to believe or know something is to be actively *believing* or *knowing* it. As Tad Brennan explains, "their term 'belief' applies only to thoughts you are having right [now], things that are really on your mind."—*The Stoic Life*, 64.

16. Robinson is the source of the cited denial that emotions are informative: *Deeper Than Reason*, 45. Norbert Schwarz and Gerald L. Clore discuss the "informational value" of emotions, moods, and other affective experiences in "Feelings and Phenomenal Experiences." See also Nussbaum, *Upheavals of Thought*, 19–23. The epistemic difference between dispassionate reasoning and emotional knowing is implicitly denied by anyone who claims

human emotions as a potentially truth-disclosing mode of embodied cognition—as experiences in which we apprehend or perceive significant aspects of our existence. This is why I have defined emotions as "perceptions of significance," and my present aim is to modify and expand upon this definition.[17] In feeling grief, or fear, or embarrassment, or gratitude, or any other felt recognition, we are affected by something meaningful that registers in our awareness. In every experience of affective recognition, an embodied emotional feeling reveals a significant truth—or else a significant misconception—and the phenomenal character of the emotion is inextricably related to what it informs us about. Affective feeling, then, is intertwined with intentionality. When a human being becomes emotional, she is being receptive to qualitative properties of the world, which matter to her in ways that she recognizes through her affective responses.

EMOTIONAL KNOWING: VARIETIES OF AFFECTIVE RECOGNITION

When we experience an emotion and thereby become aware of how something is meaningful or significant to us, we are not deliberately making appraisals or judgments about it—nor are we actively

that wholehearted belief requires nothing more than propositional assent: i.e., that a person who judges or believes that *p* is simply one who says "yes" when asked if *p* is true. See, e.g., Roberts, *Emotions*, 84; and Stephen Stich, "Beliefs and Subdoxastic States," 504. As I explained in chapter 3, an affirmative answer in reply to a question about whether one is going to die someday does not, in my view, constitute sufficient proof that one is wholeheartedly convinced or fully aware of what this means. Finally, I owe the phrase "emotional knowing" to Jennifer McWeeny, "Freedom in Feeling."

17. Furtak, *Wisdom in Love*, 6. I follow Ronald de Sousa in considering perception to be "a form of cognition" that is discernibly somatic and which can be more or less conscious: "Emotions," 62–65.

endowing it with value. Rather, we are being receptive to significant features of the world, which already matter to us (as I shall explain further in the next chapter). In such an experience of affective cognition, something is intelligibly disclosed to us through a phenomenal feeling: in fear, as we have seen, an aspect of our surroundings strikes us as dangerous. Our fear, then, is either an emotional awareness of that actual danger, or a false sense that something *is* dangerous when it is not. The experience is therefore capable of being evaluated in terms of its truthfulness. In the same way, an emotion such as gratitude or grief has an intentional content: when we are moved by a specific emotion, the intentional object of the emotion registers in our awareness in a particular light. In this experience of affective recognition, we *take* that event or state of affairs, whatever has provoked the emotion, *in* a certain way; that is, we feel aware of it either as a fortunate gift or as a profound loss. In either case, the affective tone of our experience is related to *how* we are apprehending the object. And it is not as though our appraisal of loss is a disembodied thought added onto our somatic feeling, making it into a cognitive state of grief—rather, the recognition of this specific loss is contained within our experience of that emotion. In similar fashion, when we feel "a joy *in* [a certain] state of affairs," our emotion of joy is the felt sense of what we find good in this state of affairs.[18] As emotional beings, "creatures to whom things matter," that is,[19] we do not encounter brute stimuli that impinge upon

18. Edmund Husserl, *Logical Investigations*, 581. See also Zahavi, *Husserl's Phenomenology*, 22–27: "the core of intentionality consists of the interpretation of something *as* something." Heidegger cautions us against assuming that we initially encounter "something that is free of meaning, and then a meaning gets attached to it."—*Logic*, 121. About our "incarnate" sense of a meaning or significance which is "external" to us, and *not* imposed upon neutral data, see Merleau-Ponty, *Phenomenology of Perception*, 190–192.

19. In Frankfurt's apt phrase: see *The Importance of What We Care About*, 80.

us causally, but rather we sense that things are meaningful: what we feel emotions *about* is perceived in a certain light, with a felt axiological valence. What we apprehend emotionally seems to *be* a certain way (the stray dog is a threat, the orange clouds at sunset are awesome). By feeling emotions, we perceive the world in its rich and varied significance.

Once we have recognized that neuroscientific research does *not* provide strong evidence in favor of the thesis that human emotions are typically "subcortical" and thus noncognitive, we must reopen the question as to whether emotions involve a form of cognition. As you will remember, Prinz argued that "if fear can occur without mediation of the neocortex, then perhaps fear can occur without cognition."[20] Aside from the fact that this "perhaps" advises a caution that has seldom been maintained by philosophers, it appears—as I have explained above—that fear in human beings *cannot* usually, and may not *ever*, take place without cortical activity. If it does not, then perhaps it cannot occur without cognition. The question depends, of course, on how "cognition" is defined, but we have good reason to classify the "recognition of personal meanings," through an affective experience in which one apprehends, grasps, or *cognizes* those meanings, as a cognitive process.[21] Recognition of a spider is impossible without cortical activity in the brain;[22] thus, because recognition is a form of cognition, *when* we feel afraid (whether to a rationally appropriate or to an irrationally excessive degree) of a spider that suddenly runs across our table,

20. Jesse Prinz, *Gut Reactions*, 34. Prinz adds that this last term is ambiguous, since "cognitive science has not settled on a definition of cognition."—*Gut Reactions*, 41.

21. Mikko Salmela, *True Emotions*, 19. Cf. Ronald de Sousa, "Emotions," 62. See also Peter Goldie, "Seeing What Is the Kind Thing to Do."

22. Again, see Johnson, "LeDoux's Fear Circuit and the Status of Emotion as a Non-cognitive Process," 749–751. See also Rolls, *Emotion and Decision-Making Explained*, 180.

we *must* be having a cognitive experience. Affective knowledge, or emotional knowing, is well described as the attainment of a "recognitional vision," an experience through which we are in touch with an aspect of the world, via the distinctly embodied mode of cognition of which our living bodies are capable.[23] It is through this kind of somatic affectivity that our sense of reality takes shape and gets sustained over time, both informing our discrete experiences of emotion and being reshaped by each of those episodes. Emotional feeling has a "cognitive function," as Scheler notes,[24] due to the specific kind of intentionality that distinguishes it. When, for instance, we are moved by the beauty of a place, our affective experience can reveal actual "qualitative characteristics" of the world. What it is like to perceive, emotionally, *that* the place is beautiful—or that an animal is potentially harmful, or that a remark was unkind—is to see X *as* Y precisely in feeling that X *is* Y. An emotion thus has a propositional structure, which is why it is susceptible to being evaluated as true or false, accurate or inaccurate, in various ways and to varying degrees.

The phenomenal contours of our emotions are linked with the conditions of our physical embodiment, such that the intentional content of an affective experience cannot be disentangled from how it feels. What agitates us is the valence of something we are perceiving in its significance, and we sense this significance through the

---

23. See Henry Pietersma, *Phenomenological Epistemology*, 41 & 136: "the body is truly cognitive," he adds, since "the cognitive powers of embodied percipience" reveal "the distinctiveness of the body-subject," that is, "its distinctive cognitivity." On the "somatic affectivity" through which our "sense of being" takes shape, see Robert D. Stolorow, *Trauma and Human Existence*, 30.

24. Max Scheler, *Formalism in Ethics and Non-formal Ethics of Values*, 257–258. He is speaking in this passage of the relation between affective feeling and the axiological qualities or values which are felt. On the way that "I appraise the meaning of a situation *through* . . . the specific state of my body," see Colombetti, *The Feeling Body*, 155–156.

feeling of being agitated. Actually *feeling* self-respect "has a cognitive function of providing us with an experiential . . . understanding of our worth," an understanding that we do not possess if we are torn between the reflective thought that we are worthy of respect and, on the other hand, emotions of loathing and abhorrence toward ourselves.[25] In this case, our cognitive view of our own worth is indeterminate, at best: we are internally conflicted. Speaking of a woman with such a conflict, and of the "emotional work" that she might still need to do, Calhoun explains:

> Because what we feel is tied to how we interpret situations, helping others to get the right moral perspective cannot be detached from working to correct their emotional attitudes. I think of times, for example, when after a class on sexual harassment, a student has come to me with her story about a teacher or employer. Her emotional reaction to harassment concerns her. Even though intellectually she condemns harassment, she doesn't know how to feel its wrongness in her experience. She doesn't know how to feel angry, or if she does, she doesn't know how to accept the legitimacy of her anger.[26]

The "emotional work" that this student ought to do, as Calhoun sums up, might enable her to *feel* the truth of what (in some sense) she has already admitted must be true, yet so far without being fully convinced. To feel that one is legitimately angry, in this case, *is* at

---

25. Salmela, *True Emotions*, 79–81. Ratcliffe observes that perception has a "conceptual structure," and that affective experience is hence "not wholly distinct from conceptual understanding" but "an indispensable ingredient of that understanding."—*Rethinking Commonsense Psychology*, 172.

26. Calhoun, *Moral Aims*, 217–218. I admittedly simplify the example, which in any particular case will have further complexities beyond what I'm considering.

once to recognize that harassment is wrong and that one has been harassed—in Calhoun's terms, to *feel* its wrongness. Presumably, this is the cognitive achievement that the person described above has not yet attained.

The subjective character of affective experience is thus related to what it reveals about the world. When we wholeheartedly undergo an emotion, we do not suffer blind physiological agitation devoid of meaning, nor do we have intellectual activity without passion: rather, in affective cognition we encounter "the inseparability of consciousness and embodiment."[27] Emotional apprehension is a kind of embodied, somatic knowing—not to be equated with dispassionate propositional judgment, but not to be denounced for "falling short" of it, either.[28] In other words, emotional cognition does not need to prove its cognitive worth by being measured against the standard of some *other* mode of rationality: indeed, the distinctiveness of affectivity is a good thing! That we can feel endangered, for instance, "without consciously judging that" we are in danger, without explicitly affirming the truth of sentences deliberately formulated, and without making inferences *based* on our perceptual awareness,[29] ought to be recognized as evidence of

27. Dillon, *Merleau-Ponty's Ontology*, 139. Cf. Merleau-Ponty, *The Phenomenology of Perception*, 142. See also Linda Zagzebski, "Emotion and Moral Judgment," 109–110: "an emotion is a unitary psychic state that is both cognitive and affective."

28. D'Arms and Jacobson claim that emotions incorporate intentional attitudes that fall "short of belief": see "The Significance of Recalcitrant Emotion (or, Anti-quasijudgmentalism)," 131. See also, e.g., Price, *Emotion*, 138–139. As Armon-Jones points out, even if "affective feelings are not beliefs," it "does not follow that they are" distinct from "any kind of cognitive process."—*Varieties of Affect*, 28–29. They could, she suggests, involve "imagination-based thought." Cf. Nussbaum, *Upheavals of Thought*, 65–67.

29. Robinson, *Deeper Than Reason*, 22. Zajonc, who is correct that the conscious, reflective making of inferences is not required for affective cognition, nonetheless draws a faulty inference from this insight: see "Feeling and Thinking," 151. That emotions must be nonpropositional, and that they involve nothing akin to thought, belief, or imagination, is asserted by Tappolet: see "Values and Emotions," 129–130. Emotions are portrayed as nonconceptual,

what is distinctly valuable about emotional cognition, rather than as proof that emotions are noncognitive. To become afraid is to sense a potential threat, and to get angry is to be aware of something as injurious, obstructing, or offensive: when we feel that the thing to which we are reacting has these qualities, we are relying on a mode of cognition which is discerning and highly specified.[30] We can get annoyed without formulating any explicit thoughts about what is annoying us, yet the texture of our affective awareness has a distinct *feel* to it; and when we try to specify what we are feeling, our articulation may capture this felt sense more or less adequately. Our "nonthetic consciousness," as numerous phenomenologists would say, operates implicitly with a particular content that can always be spelled out in more explicit detail.[31] That an emotion incorporates a prereflective mode of reason does not entail that it is nonrational, or that it is in any other way *less* than rationality.

We apprehend and make sense of the world not only through overtly formulated statements, but also through tacit responses that orient our attention toward situations. Emotions are embodied and thoughtful modes of intentional experience, which have the immediate felt quality of sensory perception and reveal the world

---

or not "mediated by conceptual thought," also by Griffiths and Scarantino: see "Emotions in the Wild," 437 & 450.

30. The specificity of affective feeling is noted by Eugene Gendlin in *Experiencing and the Creation of Meaning*, 54–55. On the highly nuanced understanding that is "embodied in the comportments of everyday life," see Reid, "Ethical Criticism in Heidegger's Early Freiberg Lectures," 48.

31. Merleau-Ponty describes "non-thetic" experience or consciousness, in which nothing is explicitly posited or linguistically thematized, throughout *Phenomenology of Perception*: see, e.g., 281, 301, 319–320, & 327. Cf. Sartre, *Being and Nothingness*, 13. Lawrence Hass claims, rightly it seems to me, that "Merleau-Ponty is really a cognitivist," provided that "cognition be understood" as both "embodied and situated."—*Merleau-Ponty's Philosophy*, 84–85. On not-yet-thematized cognition, "wordless" and "somatic" knowledge, see Christopher Bollas, *The Shadow of the Object*, 281–282.

to a particular subject. Affective experience may involve nonconceptual awareness, as long as it enables us to *take in* aspects of our
surroundings. And it can involve thoughts that are less than fully
conscious, although only by degrees: we are not totally unconscious
of our emotions in the same way that we would be unconscious after
fainting.[32] For instance, as Charles Taylor observes, there are cases in
which "when I finally allow myself to recognize that what has been
making me uncomfortable in [a] situation is that I'm feeling jealous,"
I realize at the same time that "in a sense I wasn't totally ignorant
of this before."[33] And while our affective cognition *can* incorporate
reflective or conceptual thought, oftentimes it does not—however,
it can be intelligently discerning without being either deliberate or
linguistically thematized.[34]

As we have seen, there is no good reason to classify emotions
as neurologically confined to a specific region or hemisphere of
the brain, and we certainly ought to avoid regarding them as "judgments" that are "deliberately" made: emotions are answerable to
what is the case, and are therefore not subject to our voluntary control.[35] Whether accurately or not, we discern a potential threat when

32. On the topic of "unconscious knowing," Linda Brakel shows that "one can indeed
know without knowing one knows": see "Knowledge and Belief," 464. Cf. Schwitzgebel,
"In-Between Believing."

33. Taylor, "Merleau-Ponty and the Epistemological Picture," 35. In this example, his jealousy was not something of which he was *completely* unconscious as he would be if he had
received a blow to the head, but more like the tacit awareness of one's own bodily posture.
Cf. Gendlin, "Thinking beyond Patterns." Freud's account of what is "capable of becoming
conscious" is also relevant to this case: see "Consciousness and What Is Unconscious," 4–6.

34. Speaking about unformulated forms of awareness, Merleau-Ponty writes that "the awareness of the amputated arm as present," in a person suffering from phantom limb syndrome,
"is not of the kind: 'I think that. . . .'" See *Phenomenology of Perception*, 94.

35. As Elster says, "it is precisely because people cannot 'decide to believe' that they cannot decide
which emotions to have."—*Alchemies of the Mind*, 308. Robinson takes herself to be refuting
the cognitive theorists when she points out that emotions "are not directly under our control,"
and are not " 'judgments' that we consciously and deliberately make."—"Emotion," 43. Against
"narrow views" of cognition, cognitive theorists have generally maintained that "the appraisal

we experience fear, and our sense of why this object might be dangerous can vary greatly in complexity. It may have been instilled in us through an experience from our prelinguistic infancy, or it may depend on an elaborate process of study and reflection, such as our recent analysis of the financial markets or the medical literature on various causes of cancer. Both the simple emotion and the more complex one qualify as felt perceptions of significance: they are feelings of being threatened. An account of emotions as embodied, felt recognitions can span the common ground underlying a wide spectrum of affective states, from simple and brief responses to more abiding passions. It must emphasize that affective cognition requires feeling, not incidentally but crucially. Moreover, it can never lose sight of the fact that affective feelings are *about* something, or that they have intentional content.

The account I am articulating here will not find baffling or inexplicable instances of mixed emotions which arise when we are responding to two "different *aspects*" of a situation, as when a friend receives an award for which we ourselves were overlooked (to borrow an example),[36] and we feel proud yet also disappointed. Or, since instances of mixed emotions are often much more complicated, a modified cognitivism such as I am proposing should also be theoretically adequate to explain the intelligent attitudes and apprehensions of meaning involved in more complex cases. For

process can and often does proceed automatically," as Agnes Moors notes: "Automatic Constructive Appraisal as a Candidate Cause of Emotion," 140 & 155–156. Gerald Clore and Andrew Ortony observe that affective cognition need not be "explicit" or "deliberative": see "Cognition in Emotion," 39–42.

36. I cite Salmela, *True Emotions*, 115. Those who are overly impressed by such examples, as if they showed that emotions cannot involve cognition, include Robinson: see *Deeper Than Reason*, 19–20. Cf. Greenspan, "A Case of Mixed Feelings." Helm points out that an emotion "implicitly endorses or assents to the view of the world the emotion presents" in *Emotional Reason*, 64.

example, when a son attending the funeral of an estranged parent feels profoundly ambivalent about this loss: "His entire body began to tremble and quake, and it looked as though he were on the edge of violently regurgitating. He was overcome with a feeling for his father that wasn't antagonism but that his antagonism denied him the means to release. When he opened his mouth, nothing emerged except a series of grotesque gasps."[37] This, after all, is the sort of thing we wish to understand, when we are trying to understand human emotions. So, to mention one more desideratum for now, a theory of emotions as felt recognitions of significance should be able (as I hope to have shown) to account for the ambiguities of "not *fully* believing" involved in cases of phobic fear, conflicting attitudes about race or gender, and the like.[38] In each type of case, it is possible to grant *in some sense*—in the abstract, on further reflection, with one's consciously endorsed beliefs, or to a certain degree— that, for instance, a fall from this height is unlikely or that the guy dating one's sister is unlikely to harm her. This is why a person can affirm a belief that there's no danger here, while feeling afraid nonetheless.[39] Yet when his or her emotions are inconsistent with this professed belief ("There's no danger here"), he or she does not *know* this wholeheartedly, or univocally, in its significance. And the same is true of the person who is partly aware, yet not quite convinced, of her or his own worth—who can acknowledge while speaking to a therapist that she or he is *not* utterly worthless, but who still tends to feel worthless nevertheless.

---

37. Philip Roth, *Everyman*, 13.
38. Maura Tumulty, "Managing Mismatch between Belief and Behavior," 267–268.
39. I differ from Goldie, then, on the question of how to interpret an utterance such as "I feel afraid of the ice, yet [I know that] it is not dangerous."—*The Emotions*, 74–75. Cf. Price, *Emotion*, 95.

DEGREES OF AWARENESS IN THE FELT PHENOMENOLOGY OF EMOTIONS

In a strict sense, we can "perceive" only what is in front of us, or what impinges right now on one or more of our faculties for sensory perception. The reason for viewing emotions as involving perceptual awareness *more broadly defined* is that, when we are passionately moved, something impinges on us in such a way that we feel immediately aware of it—palpably *confronted* with it, one might say. Through our emotions we experience the world in a certain way; they involve apprehending something, as it were, under a certain description. This is similar to what other cognitive theorists have argued when they have defined emotions as ways of seeing whatever moves us personally, or as perceptual impressions or construals. It also accommodates the points made against the standard cognitive accounts, that affective responses are (often, if not always) rapid, uncontrolled, and not dependent on deliberative reasoning.[40] Intentional content cannot be divorced from phenomenal feeling, because it is through felt affective experience that our living body is

---

40. Nussbaum speaks of emotions on the model of "seeing-as" or "seeing X as Y," in *Upheavals of Thought*, 5 & 127–129. "Concern-based construals" is the phrase used by Roberts: see *Emotions*, 49, 64–65, 79, and 91–92. Solomon claims that emotions involve corporeal "judgments" that are often not "fully conscious" in *True to Our Feelings*, 196 & 204–206. Kinesthetic "judgments of the body" is another phrase he uses: see, e.g., *Not Passion's Slave*, 190–191. Heidegger's notion of "nonreflective understanding" is cited by Lazarus as the "way of knowing" most important for human emotions in *Emotion and Adaptation*, 152. Cf. Heidegger, *Being and Time*, § 32. We can find in Arnold's work a portrayal of what moves us emotionally as "known in a particular way," as "affecting me personally," with an embodied intelligence similar to that of an athlete: see *Emotion and Personality*, 1: 171–175. Cf. Samuel Todes, *Body and World*, 47. The view that I am arguing against maintains that a criterion of truthfulness is irrelevant to emotions: see, e.g., Greenspan, "A Case of Mixed Feelings," 236. To state that an emotion is "a *cognition*," then, is to claim that it *can* be reasonably assessed as more or less veridical or mistaken: Broad asserts this in "Emotion and Sentiment," 203–205.

related to the world. An "experience of salience" and a "phenomenal feel" are inextricably "bound together," as Wynn agrees,[41] such that a thing's axiological salience and its experiential feel are aspects of a single unified apprehension in which its significance registers in our awareness.

Furthermore, the emotions are not merely embodied in the minimal sense that all mental states are, by virtue of involving bodily processes: rather, they are charged with a somatic agitation that we ourselves feel. This is why judging something as beautiful is by no means equivalent to *feeling* aware of its beauty. As we find in Coleridge's ode on dejection, one can appreciate that something is lacking in the emotionally "blank" eye of the beholder when we watch a colorful dusk giving way to a night sky full of stars, and we "see, not feel, how beautiful they are!"[42] The lack of what Husserl calls an "affective pull" from our surroundings plunges us into a blank world, in which nothing affords us any sense of meaning or any motive to respond: in the absence of any emotional feeling of significance, we could perhaps identify objects, but they would seem flat and lifeless, devoid of value.[43] Likewise, if we were incapable of feeling amused, we could not (try as we might) find anything amusing. It is a theoretical error, as Heidegger makes clear, to presume "that objects are at first present as bare realities, as objects in

---

41. Wynn, *Renewing the Senses*, 35–36.

42. Samuel Taylor Coleridge, "Dejection: An Ode," from lines 27–38, in Coleridge, *Poems*, 280–281. Damasio characterizes the predicament of one utterly dispassionate patient as that of *seeing* what would (for others) be "emotionally charged visual stimuli" but *not feeling* any emotional response: see *Descartes' Error*, 44–45; see also Johnston and Malabou, *Self and Emotional Life*, 59.

43. Husserl, *Analyses Concerning Passive and Active Synthesis*, 98 & 215–220. See also Ratcliffe, *Experiences of Depression*, 166 & 186–187. Cf. Deonna and Teroni, *The Emotions*, 122–123; and Blackburn, *Ruling Passions*, 8–9. Regarding what follows, see Claire Armon-Jones, *Varieties of Affect*, 32; and Bernard Williams, *Ethics and the Limits of Philosophy*, 129.

some sort of natural state, and that they then . . . receive the garb of a value-character, so they do not have to run around naked."[44] To take our emotions seriously as feelings through which we recognize meaning or significance, we need to reject the notion that the world is a value-neutral screen onto which we project nonexistent qualities. Instead, we must think about the human world as having properties that cannot be identified apart from our affective responses. I will have more to say about this in later chapters.

By now, it ought to be evident that our emotions *do* aim at truth: although they are not infallible in attaining this goal, even their failures to get things right are evidence that they contain an embodied mode of understanding through which the world seems to us to *be* a particular way. The fact that this distinctive kind of awareness is unavailable to us except through affective experience is the main reason why our emotions ought to be understood as a type of felt cognition. We gain very little by preserving an artificially restricted notion of what constitutes the cognitive realm: in actual practice, we speak as though there are degrees of believing or knowing, and there is philosophical precedent for this as well. Aristotle, for instance, writes in Book VII of the *Nicomachean Ethics* of "ways of knowing" that include perceptual recognition, either employing or not using our knowledge of a general truth which is relevant to a particular case, or having merely the superficial ability to state true opinions without knowing what we mean because these opinions have not yet "become part of" us.[45] We should also admit into the cognitive realm

---

44. Martin Heidegger, *Phenomenological Interpretations of Aristotle*, 68–69. Cf. McDowell, *Mind, Value, and Reality*, 113–130. Pertinently, Maclaren remarks that "we are not subjects *thinking* about a world beyond us, *judging* its meaning," and then "*actively* choosing how to act; we are, rather, beings perceptually caught up in, and *moved by*, an immediately meaningful world."—"Emotional Metamorphoses," 27.
45. See *Nicomachean Ethics*, 1146b–1147b. On degrees of conscious awareness within affective experience, see also Damasio, *The Feeling of What Happens*, 36–37.

such cases of impure cognition as when a person partially "knows" something of which he or she is not currently thinking, or something which has not yet "sunk in," or that he or she has not grasped in its personal significance. An emotion is a perceptual recognition in which we are aware of the world in a specific way; we feel that a situation or state of affairs *is* a certain way, that a road is unsafe, a remark is hostile, or a recent achievement is grounds for pride. What these examples have in common is in each case a felt recognition of significance, one which is susceptible to being more or less accurate. Such an emotion reveals how things seem to be, and what meaning they hold from our concerned vantage point.[46] Although they are biologically and culturally conditioned, the emotions are *especially* revelatory of a person's own distinctive point of view—which is shaped by our temperament, our biographical experience, and our whole conception of existence. Indeed, it is *through* our emotions most of all that we *have* a sense of reality and an understanding of what life means. They are an indispensable way of gaining insight about ourselves and about our surroundings at the same time.

According to Merleau-Ponty, we do not fully comprehend the death of a friend "until the time comes when we expect a reply from him and when we realize that we shall never again receive one."[47] In this moment of recognition, we feel more acutely a loss of which we were already *partially* aware: the personal *significance* of this loss now

---

46. Cf. Calhoun, "Cognitive Emotions?," 342: we can "infer from a person's emotions" that things "must *appear* to them [to be] a certain way." See also Gardner, *Irrationality and the Philosophy of Psychoanalysis*, 96–97. On how, in a perceptual experience, the world seems to be a certain way, and we perceive *that* something appears to be the case, see Christopher Peacocke, "Scenarios, Concepts, and Perception," 107; Searle, *Intentionality*, 40–41. See also Green, *The Emotions*, 40. As Ratcliffe points out, "when I see a cup in front of me, the content 'there is a cup in front of me' is part of the experience. In 'believing that there is a cup in front of me,' there is no second stage where I infer that the contents of my experience are veridical and therefore adopt the belief that the cup is really there."—*Feelings of Being*, 147.

47. *Phenomenology of Perception*, 93.

inundates us in an experience of passionate upheaval. Now we know what it means to have lost him forever—for instance, how extraordinarily sad it is that we will not again be able to communicate with our friend. To feel this overwhelming sadness is to know how much our friend has meant to us, and therefore to know the meaning of his loss: it is to be aware of this, not only as a fact mentioned in a newspaper obituary, but as the painful and permanent absence of this person whom we have loved and valued so much. All of this is part of what we apprehend in the experience of emotionally knowing that a loved one has passed away—for Marcel, that his beloved grandmother is gone forever. "Knowing can be violent," as Nussbaum points out, when such painful a truth is coming to be known: the upheaval we experience *is* the "full recognition of that terrible event."[48]

What we thereby recognize, or become cognizant of, "hits home" with us in and through the experience of being shaken. Something similar, if less intricately complex, is taking place when the winter driver shudders with fear as her vehicle begins to skid across the icy road. The potential dangers of driving on snow or ice, and the concern for avoiding bodily harm, immediately become present to mind—they suddenly loom large in her perceptual consciousness, commanding heightened attention in an intensively somatic manner and preventing her from thinking about anything else at the moment. Just like the person who is pained

---

48. *Upheavals of Thought*, 45. Cf. Nussbaum, *The Therapy of Desire*, 376–381. With regard to this, and to what follows, see Deonna and Teroni, *The Emotions*, 16–17: "It is noteworthy that the term 'unconscious' covers several distinct kinds of phenomena." For instance, "something may [rightly] be called unconscious merely in virtue of the fact that one's attention is not at the present time directed towards it." On how a state of mind, such as an affective feeling, can be less than fully conscious—because we lack higher-order awareness of it, for instance—yet nonetheless actual, see Gardner, *Irrationality and the Philosophy of Psychoanalysis*, 207–214. It is untrue, he notes, that "for any mental state" there must be "a conscious self-ascriptive belief about that state."

by sadness and grief, she is recognizing a significant matter of concern, and apprehending it with a viscerally charged feeling of emotional awareness. Each of these people, in becoming agitated with emotion, is feeling aware of a truth that had not previously been brought to his or her attention. Their affective feelings are not discrete from the intentional and rational content of their emotions, and conversely their felt cognitions are not independent of but intrinsic to their sense of bodily agitation.[49] They each exemplify a distinctly emotional mode of knowing.

It is not only the imagined human beings that populate our thought experiments who would be deprived of possibly knowing significant truths if they lacked the capacity to become passionate, after all: it is we who deprive ourselves of this possibility when we disregard the meaning of our emotions. Classifying emotions as "rough" and "dirty" physiological responses, calling them "blind" and "noncognitive," or claiming that the experience of an emotion is as free-floating a phenomenon as "seeing an afterimage," and no more susceptible to being true or false:[50] all of these arguments have the effect of trivializing our emotions, by encouraging us not to take

49. See, e.g., Wynn, *Renewing the Senses*, 28–29; Goldie, *The Emotions*, 59–60. On belief as, in some sense, inherently contained within perceptual experience, see also Slote, *A Sentimentalist Theory of the Mind*, 25–26. Again, see also Wittgenstein's *Philosophical Investigations*, 212, on perception incorporating an "echo of a thought"; and Husserl's *Analyses Concerning Passive and Active Synthesis*, 66 & 70–72, on belief inherent in perception and on "perceptual apprehension." That embodied affective states "constitute" our "intelligent access to the world" is also noted by Rebekka Hufendiek in *Embodied Emotions*, 13–14.

50. Robinson labels the emotions as "rough," "dirty," and "non-cognitive" throughout *Deeper Than Reason*: see, e.g., 54–56, 58–62, 70, 98, & 157–163. Prinz claims that feeling an emotion is akin to seeing an afterimage: *Gut Reactions*, 240. On emotions as blind, see also Kant, *Anthropology from a Pragmatic Point of View*, §§ 74 & 75. According to McDowell, if "an experience is *not* blind" then "it is intelligible to its subject" as offering "awareness of a feature of objective reality," that is, "a seeming glimpse of the world," as emotions do. See *Mind and World*, 54. My emphasis.

their content seriously. But what is at issue in our affective life is nothing less than our sense of reality—in other words, our emotions have to do with how we are faring and how things are going, as far as we are concerned. We sell ourselves short, and ignore a uniquely beneficial mode of awareness, if we dismiss their cognitive content as negligible just because they are not reflective judgments, not impersonal, not subject to voluntary control, or not necessarily based on linguistically formulated thoughts.[51] Of course, there are many ways in which our felt apprehensions differ from our relatively dispassionate judgments. Yet we should not make the mistake of overlooking their rational structure and their intentional content simply because they are embodied feelings.[52] At the same time, we also ought to avoid disregarding their felt quality merely because not all emotions involve trembling, violent palpitations, dramatic facial expressions, sweltering feverishness, or any other obvious bodily disturbance. Somatic changes in emotion can be precise feelings with complex intentional content even if they incorporate only subtly felt agitation.[53] A slight feeling of relief, for instance, can be no more phenomenally conspicuous to us than the barely felt sense

51. Cf. Mikko Salmela, "True Emotions," 388. See also Nussbaum, *Upheavals of Thought*, 200. On how emotion has an integrity of its own, distinct from other states, see Steinbock, *Moral Emotions*, 3–7; Raja Bahlul, "Emotion as Patheception."

52. O. H. Green makes this point in *The Emotions*, 130–131. On the way that affective arousal need not involve any dramatic "feeling of bodily changes," see Michael Stocker, "Intellectual and Other Nonstandard Emotions," 406–409. An unapologetic advocate of the extreme view that emotions *lack* object-directedness is Demian Whiting: see, e.g., "The Feeling Theory of Emotion and Object-Directed Emotions," 281–283.

53. As I noted earlier, the somatic feelings involved in certain emotions are better defined in terms of subjective experience than in terms of measurable physiological arousal. For a good account of "intuitive, nonpropositional," and "meaning-apprehending feelings," see Mark R. Wynn, *Emotional Experience and Religious Understanding*, 111. On the body as "obscurely [or conspicuously] felt," see Colombetti, *The Feeling Body*, 122–128: while acknowledging the possibility of feelings that are not conspicuously bodily, she claims that the "feeling body" is typically "the medium through which one . . . makes sense of the world." Cf. Ronald de Sousa, *The Rationality of Emotion*, 153.

of having just remembered something one had intended to do this morning but had forgotten until this instant:[54] yet it registers in our felt awareness just as our former nagging frustration about what we forgot had been present in the background. The intelligence of emotions consists in their ability to provide us with an apprehension of significant truths that we could not have glimpsed apathetically. Emotions provide us with a distinctive kind of understanding— and, as I shall proceed to argue, they are also involved in the configuration of our own identity, the shape taken by our lives over time, and our personal conception of what is real and meaningful. It is for all of these reasons that we ought to view affective cognition as an indispensable mode of experience, which provides us with a crucial means of being in touch with the world.

54. Here I borrow an example from Eugene Gendlin, *Experiencing and the Creation of Meaning*, 92. See also Gendlin, *Focusing*, 37–38 & 56–57.

PART III

THE REASONS
OF THE HEART

Chapter 5

On the Emotional *A Priori*

So far, I have explained why it is that emotions ought to be understood as an epistemically indispensable mode of experience for human beings, because they involve our living bodies in the recognition of what is meaningful within our world of concern, thereby making us aware of the reality and significance of whatever is affecting us. In other words, to be emotionally moved is to have some aspect of the world be revealed to us in a specific manner: in fear, as a threatening danger; in grief, as a serious loss; and so on. And it is because what we come to know through our emotions could not be adequately grasped by any other means that the emotions embody a distinctive mode of cognition. What is disclosed to us in the experience of wholehearted emotional knowing would be otherwise inaccessible—either to "mere" reason *or* to "mere" feeling, that is. Our affective responses allow us to perceive significant truths, or so I have argued, and their felt quality is intrinsically related to the awareness that they provide. The present chapter will investigate the question of how it is that we have a "world of concern" in the first place, in which things (including situations, persons, events, possibilities,[1] etc.) *matter* to us; in short, what are the enabling conditions

1. On "the possible" as a property of existing beings or realities, in relation to a human perspective, see, e.g., Sartre, *Being and Nothingness*, 149–150. See also Ratcliffe, *Experiences of*

that make us capable of having emotions? Also, how do these conditions *ground* affective experience as a capacity that is potentially capable of revealing something true?

AFFECTIVE DISPOSITIONS AS GROUNDING CONDITIONS OF PARTICULAR EMOTIONS

To begin, let me reintroduce a distinction between long-standing "attitudes of love and concern," on the one hand,[2] and the emotional responses that we are experiencing at any particular instant or interval of time, on the other. This might be conceptualized as the difference between *dispositions toward* and *episodes of* emotion, or in terms of *background* versus *situational* emotions, as Richard Wollheim and Martha Nussbaum respectively do.[3] The dispositional affective states are those that serve as background to, or precondition for, the episodic emotions that arise in particular situations, because they *dispose* us *toward* emotional responses. Once you care about something, you are liable to have a variety of discrete emotions about it, in response to happenings in the world that pertain to what you care about. For instance, if you love a child, this renders you liable to experience relief (and perhaps gratitude) when he or she arrives home safely despite the icy roads. Your concern for this child is a long-standing disposition with a specific focus: before the safe arrival of the child whom you love, you feared for his or her

---

Depression, 41–53, on the phenomenology of sensing what is (and is not) possible in the world we inhabit.

2. These attitudes, as I have previously noted, "establish in us a readiness for being affected," and in this chapter I will expand upon and further develop this claim: see Furtak, *Wisdom in Love*, 10.

3. See Wollheim, *On the Emotions*, 9–11; see also Nussbaum, *Upheavals of Thought*, 69–70.

safety in a way that you did *not* fear for just any and every child who might be similarly at risk. If we change the example so that it is not today's road conditions that give you reason to fear for this child's safety, but a heart condition that renders the child more vulnerable throughout his or her life, then it is still your underlying care for him or her that allows you to be worried about his or her health. Here, the care is the affective disposition, and the worry—no matter how long it might persist—is derived from the care. Your care *disposes* you to become worried. An episode of emotion may last a long time, as anyone who has lived through profound grief knows quite well.[4] Yet we grieve only the loss of what we love or care about, and in this sense even prolonged grief is an emotional response that depends upon a more fundamental affective disposition—and *not* a disposition in its own right.[5] The same can be said for any other type of emotion, from resentment and pride through shame and indignation, that can arise in an episode of longer or shorter duration based upon what concerns us.

The affective dispositions of love, care, or concern (which could also be described as modes of interest or attachment) constitute the felt background to our experience of the world. These dispositional passions play a foundational role in establishing the realm of what matters to a person, what Merleau-Ponty calls the "things which

---

4. Studies have shown that our ordinary-language concept of emotion (as revealed when people are asked to report, or write about, their emotions) embraces many episodes of longer duration, even if we limit ourselves to episodic emotions that are not moods or other affective dispositions. See, e.g., Frijda et al., "The Duration of Affective Phenomena." Cf. Oatley and Duncan, "Incidents of Emotion in Daily Life." See also Frijda, *The Laws of Emotion*, 180–182: "The fashion to consider emotions as fast emergency responses, made by measure by evolution to grab prey . . . or vanish from predators, is wrong. It is a romantic stereotype. Such emotions may occur and do occur, but they do not form the rule."

5. This is one reason why moods cannot be sufficiently distinguished as such by their persistence over time, as is noted by Giovanna Colombetti in *The Feeling Body*, 77–78.

count and exist for me."[6] In this way, my loves, cares, and concerns determine what I am liable to have other emotions about—what has reality and value, from my vantage point, because it is not indifferent to me (as I am not indifferent to it). This is why, once I know that you care about a particular blueberry shrub, I can understand why you would be frightened by a looming hailstorm. Now, rather than saying that you "care about" this shrub, I might equally well have said that you are "attached to" it, or that you have "taken an interest in" it, or even that you are "enthusiastic about" the plant, and I would in each case be pointing out a grounding emotional disposition which inclines you to experience fear and other emotions in response to whatever impacts your blueberries for worse or for better.[7] The same is true if you love a certain child, or if you are concerned about the state of the environment: what a person is dispositionally *passionate about*, he or she is disposed to feel episodic passions or emotions toward. This is why "concerns, cares, loves, interests, attachments, and enthusiasms are dispositions to emotions":[8] because we must already care about something in order to become afraid when that thing is threatened by danger, delighted when it is thriving, angry when it is harmed by someone else, sorry and regretful when we ourselves have done it harm—and so on, through the entire variety of particular emotional responses that are predicated upon our underlying care and can arise from it.

6. Maurice Merleau-Ponty, *Phenomenology of Perception*, 333. What has "practical reality" for us "must appear both *interesting* and *important*," as James notes in "The Psychology of Belief," 331.

7. See Robert C. Roberts, "Existence, Emotion, and Virtue," 185–186: he notes that "any concern (passion, interest, enthusiasm, attachment, involvement) can give rise to any or all of the whole range of emotions." Nussbaum makes a similar claim, that "love or attachment to some thing or person" forms the basis of a background or dispositional emotion: *Upheavals of Thought*, 71–74.

8. Roberts, *Emotions*, 79–80. Cf. Nussbaum, *Upheavals of Thought*, 87–88.

LOVE, CARE, AND RELATED ASPECTS OF
THE EMOTIONAL *A PRIORI*

In contemporary emotion research, although virtually "everyone agrees that love is an emotion,"[9] there is not so much agreement about (or recognition of) the way that love, care, and concern, along with other dispositional emotions, ought to be understood as categorically different from anger, jealousy, fear, and the like. The latter—episodic emotions, those that have been my primary theme in the earlier chapters of this book—are not members of the same category into which love would most accurately be placed, although that is *not* because love is unrelated to fear or grief. On the contrary, love (or care, concern, or interest) is a condition of possibility for the very existence of emotions which arise in particular situations or circumstances. Now, it has frequently been argued that love is not exactly *based* upon reasons, in the same way that grief, anger, or worry typically are: we can explain that we're angry at someone for a specific reason (*because* he or she did this or that), but explanations of love do not take the same form. As one philosopher has written, "love in general is not thought to require reasons"; indeed, "the citation of particular reasons" may "seem like the bringing in of ulterior motives," which casts doubt on whether one's affective state should be identified *as* "love" at all.[10] And, as Frankfurt has observed, even if "the beloved invariably *is* . . . valuable to the lover," nevertheless "perceiving that value is not at all an indispensable *formative* or *grounding* condition of the love."[11] However, this does not

---

9. James A. Russell and Ghyslaine Lemay, "Emotion Concepts," 493.

10. Jerome Neu, *A Tear Is an Intellectual Thing*, 90–91. See also, e.g., Jean-Luc Marion, *The Erotic Phenomenon*, 79–81. Cf. Michael D. Barber, *Guardian of Dialogue*, 118–120.

11. Harry G. Frankfurt, *The Reasons of Love*, 38.

entail that love is irrational, nor does it rule out the possibility that love may in some sense have *reasons of its own.*

Later I will explore in more detail the question of how love *in its own way* can be reasonable or truth-revealing, although not in quite the same way that grief or fear can be rational. At present, I am focusing on the phenomenon of love in order to clarify the concept of the emotional *a priori.* The notion of the emotional or affective *a priori,* as I am employing it, is meant to capture the set of background affective dispositions such as love, care, and concern that grounds our whole emotional life. It performs this basic function by opening us to what is of value, enabling what is meaningful or significant to be disclosed to us. Or, to suggest an analogy between the domain of what moves us emotionally and the realm of visible objects: our capacity to love or to care has less in common with anything that is illuminated by the sun, and more with the source of light that allows things to be seen. Even in the absence of "the empirical findings showing that all knowledge is driven by interest, attention, or love," Scheler maintains, reflection on our own experience would justify the conclusion that "love provides the foundation for every sort of knowing."[12] Our own perceptual awareness provides evidence for this view: namely, in the difference between what we see and what escapes our notice, even though the latter is

---

12. Max Scheler, *The Constitution of the Human Being,* 391–392. Cf. Scheler, "Ordo Amoris," 110: "*love* is always what awakens both knowledge and volition; indeed, it is the mother of spirit and reason itself." See also Jean-Luc Marion, *The Erotic Phenomenon,* 87–88. On the universality of personal love, see Jankowiak and Fischer, "A Cross-Cultural Perspective on Romantic Love," 154; and Aron et al., "Romantic Love," 595. Although some have argued that love is a "basic" emotion (see Shaver, Morgan, and Wu, "Is Love a 'Basic' Emotion?") in Paul Ekman's technical sense of the term (see Ekman, "An Argument for Basic Emotions"), my aim is not to take a stand on this issue. Rather, when I refer to "basic" affective dispositions, I mean that they have a foundational place in the emotional life of human beings.

"there to be seen," in an important sense.[13] What stands out to us as salient, and what recedes into the background or goes unnoticed, are conditioned by the primary affective dispositions that lay the ground for affective cognition, allowing us to perceive significance in the world. And we know that something has value only to the degree that we can emotionally feel a sense of its value.

How is it that our capacity to love enables us to know and appreciate significant features of the world, which would otherwise remain unknown to us? Following Scheler, I believe that this is because love, care, and concern dictate "the sense and meaning" of our lives, grounding our "many-sided interest in the things of this world,"[14] and thereby providing us with focus and orientation as moral agents. What we love and care about is disclosed to us as bearing inherent value, as something that is worthy of existence in its own right. Here, I am speaking about our love of persons, but also about our care for such abstract ideals as fairness or equality; our love of places, such as particular towns, valleys, or ecosystems; and our concern for concrete political causes, such as indigenous land rights or prison reform. It is the same class of affective dispositions that underlies our emotional attachment to other human beings, to traditions or institutions, and to the artistic or scientific pursuits to which we are devoted. Love, in this broad sense, is what makes us aware of anything as axiologically salient, and—against those who view it as therefore an irrational bias or a distorting influence—I will try to explain why it instead ought to be understood as potentially

---

13. Scheler is the phenomenologist best known for pursuing this idea that there might be an *a priori* logic of the heart, and my account here is indebted to him in ways that will become more apparent as the discussion proceeds. Cf. Scheler, *Formalism in Ethics and Non-formal Ethics of Values*, 63–64. Mikel Dufrenne defines the "corporeal" *a priori* as a capacity for "revealing . . . certain aspects of the world." See *The Notion of the A Priori*, 154–155.

14. Scheler, "Ordo Amoris," 98 & 119–120. The latter passage in Scheler's essay, which I cite first, is italicized in the original. Here, I have removed the emphasis.

truth-revealing. Yet this requires that I first clarify my statement above that love, care, and concern form the emotional *a priori*, providing the enabling conditions of possibility for particular types of affective recognition.

In making this claim about the emotional *a priori*, I am arguing that we cannot accurately understand the nature of the world known by human beings unless we take into account the structure of human subjectivity, *in this respect* specifically. Within the realm of human emotions, the relevant idea is that a meaningful world of experience is disclosed only to a loving or caring person. As Merleau-Ponty suggests, if we attempt to see how any significant reality comes to exist *for us* through love, then "we shall thereby come to understand better how things and beings can exist in general."[15] Love, in other words once again, plays a world-disclosing role because it enables us to perceive things as meaningful or significant. Things exist *for* us because they matter *to* us, and it may be that our best mode of access to their value is an unselfish love that "wants the object to be nothing other than what it is."[16] Rather than being just one element among others within the horizon of human experience, love shapes the way that a world comes to light for each of us. As Kierkegaard points out, "it is generally true that something manifests itself to the one who loves it"—and it is also true that we are made most emphatically cognizant of anything when we care about it for its

---

15. Merleau-Ponty, *Phenomenology of Perception*, 178. He prefaces this claim with the comment that, if we wish "to bring to light the birth of being for us, we must finally look at that area of our experience which clearly has significance and reality only for us, and that is our affective life."

16. Scheler, *On Feeling, Knowing, and Valuing*, 153. John Drummond defines phenomenology in general as the attempt to find conditions of possibility "for objects and a world to be experienced—to disclose themselves—as having the significance they have for us." This is from " 'Cognitive Impenetrability' and the Complex Intentionality of the Emotions," 111.

own sake.[17] Indeed, our awareness of what we love and care about orients our attention and defines what has reality and value in our eyes. Thus, the affective dispositions that constitute the emotional *a priori* organize our world of experience, enabling certain things to stand out—to be obvious and apparent to us.

This is the sense in which love, care, or concern is a condition of possibility for the disclosure of what is real and what matters. Without the affective dispositions by virtue of which we take an interest in the world, what sort of awareness or knowledge would we be lacking? Episodes of emotion, whether the mundane (becoming annoyed by a conversation I'm overhearing on the train) or the weighty (experiencing prolonged grief over the loss of a close friend), involve apprehensions of significance: in grieving or in being annoyed I am responding to something that seems more or less meaningful to me. It commands my attention and stands out prominently, while other things withdraw into the background. In *what* we see, and in *how* it appears to us, features of the world are discovered through our emotions.[18] Every time we walk down the street, look at the news headlines, or enter the grocery store, our consciousness is drawn toward whatever seems to be significantly dangerous, calming, or wonderful: the stray dog approaching us, or

---

17. Søren Kierkegaard, *Journals and Papers*, no. 2299 (entry from 1847, IX A 438). On loving or caring about something "for its own sake" see Frankfurt, *Necessity, Volition, and Love*, 135. Cf. Iris Murdoch, *Existentialists and Mystics*, 215–216: "Love is the perception of individuals," the recognition "that something other than oneself is real," and in this sense it is "the discovery of reality." Love, in other words, is "the apprehension of something else, something particular, as existing outside us."

18. Empirical research in psychology confirms this observation that our emotions influence both *what* we see and *how* it appears to us: see, e.g., Klaus Fiedler, "Affective Influences on Social Information Processing"; also, Joseph P. Forgas and Patrick T. Vargas, "The Effects of Mood on Social Judgment and Reasoning," 351–354. For a striking phenomenological description of how the world is *given* to us through our emotions, see Alphonso Lingis, *The Imperative*, 119–122.

a report of a political tension that has eased, or sunlight from behind a cloud that suddenly illuminates the contours of the canyon in which we are hiking. In spite of what certain prevalent biases might encourage us to assume, we do not experientially inhabit a world of inert objects devoid of axiological salience; rather, the world as we know it is filled with things that allure and repel us, gladden or worry us, disappoint and fascinate us. To be clear: my point is *not* that our emotions *give* meaning to life, or that our lives are meaningful *because* we have emotions. More precisely, it is *through* our emotions that we human beings encounter meaning or significance *within* our lives, in all the numerous ways that we can apprehend by means of these responses. And what I am highlighting right now is the affective background that must be *always already* in place, in order for us to experience particular episodes of emotion.

In the first chapter of this book, I stated that only a being able to perceive itself as threatened can be afraid. What I am now adding is the claim that only if we already care about the life and well-being of a person—whether oneself or another—are we disposed to react with fear when that person is threatened. And it is only *if* I have some degree of concern for a particular situation *that* I am liable to become upset, in one way or another, upon learning some significant information about it. When a person loves or cares about something, "he makes himself vulnerable" to becoming emotionally affected insofar as what he or she cares about "is diminished or enhanced."[19] Heidegger makes the same point when he observes

---

19. Frankfurt, *The Importance of What We Care About*, 83. Regarding what follows, see Scheler's comments on the "a priori" in relation to how "the person is always the *correlate* of a 'world'," and on how there is a "*world* corresponding to every individual person." The "essential interconnection between person and world," he adds, explains the "personal" nature of the "truth about the world" as revealed through feeling. See *Formalism in Ethics and Non-formal Ethics of Values*, 393–395.

that it is by way of our positive and negative passions that we encounter the beneficial and the harmful—the features of the world that we find uplifting or dismaying, in light of our concerns and how we are disposed.[20] Aspects of our surroundings are susceptible to being experienced as distressing or uplifting by virtue of the fact that we *do* care, and *are* concerned. In this way, underlying affective dispositions function as the lenses through which we view the world: without them, we could not discern the meaning or value of anything whatsoever. And everything about which we *can* experience emotions has already been revealed as significant through the dispositional affective background that I am characterizing as the "emotional *a priori*." It serves as the condition of possibility for the experience of passions that arise within particular situations, and it does this by rendering us capable of recognizing the world we inhabit as a realm of significance in which things matter.

Most of the time, in designating aspects of the emotional *a priori*, I will speak of *love, care, concern,* and *interest*. For our purposes, "care" and "concern" are the most nearly synonymous terms, as well as the broadest in scope. When we say that we *love* someone or something, we tend to mean that we care about whatever or whomever we love with an especially intense concern, to an exceptional degree—what we love, then, is a subset of what we care about.[21] While I will have

---

20. See Martin Heidegger, *Basic Concepts of Aristotelian Philosophy*, 34–35 & 83. See also Charles Guignon, "Moods in Heidegger's *Being and Time*," 238: "What we initially encounter in the world [are] things that are useful, harmful, fascinating, dull, messy, appealing, or disgusting." As James Gibson agrees, the "perceiving of an affordance is not a process of perceiving a value-free physical object to which meaning is somehow added"—it is, rather, "a process of perceiving a value-rich ecological object."—Gibson, *The Ecological Approach to Visual Perception*, 140. On the relational properties thereby perceived, see Hufendiek, *Embodied Emotions*, 17–18 & 120–124.

21. As Socrates claims in the *Republic*, one cares most about what one loves: Plato, *Republic* 412d, using a variant of the verb μέλω, which also has a nominal relative in Greek. Frankfurt describes love as "an especially notable variant of caring," in which we care about something as an end in itself, and which enables us "to engage wholeheartedly in activity that

more to say later about different forms of love, and about what distinguishes love from other modes of care, right now I leave aside any such distinctions, in order to understand love in a wide, inclusive sense. This "wider" sense of the term comprises many varied ways of loving and various types of beloved, but in each case what is loved is cared about intensely, as something whose very existence matters emphatically to us. It matters *for its own sake* or *as an end in itself*, we might add, though not in such a way as to factor the loving subject out of the equation. Now, if we understand love as an unequivocal, other-centered mode of care or concern, then we can locate *interest* at the least vehement end of the spectrum: it is an affective disposition in which one is "not entirely indifferent," or "barely more than nonchalant,"[22] about something.

Interest may be described as the faintest passion—the affective state of caring, or being concerned, to a minimal extent but perhaps no more than this. Since interest amounts to nothing more than a slight regard in certain cases, some would claim that it should not qualify as a passionate state at all.[23] And it is true that a person whose

is meaningful."—see *The Reasons of Love*, 10–11 & 90. The foundational affective states or dispositions of "care, concern, and interest" are highlighted by Michael Stocker: see *Valuing Emotions*, 53–54. Others who have defended a broad conception of love include Sigmund Freud, in *Group Psychology and the Analysis of the Ego*, 29–30. See also Frankfurt, "Duty and Love," 4; Marion, *The Erotic Phenomenon*, 221.

22. Annette Baier searches for a name to characterize the feeling which is opposed to nonchalance, suggesting "chalance" or "souciance," in "Feelings That Matter," 203. Also, Giovanna Colombetti speaks of affectivity as a living being's "capacity to be sensitive to what matters," based in "a *lack of indifference*" about its existence—*The Feeling Body*, 1–2.

23. See, e.g., Patrick Stokes, *Kierkegaard's Mirrors*, 48–50: he argues that we should not "conflate" passion and interest, since that would suggest that there is something passionate about even the state of "watching an excruciatingly boring game of chess." However, to insist that interest must be distinguished from passion runs the risk of missing the point that even such minimal attention is continuous (and linked, by degrees) with states of intense passionate concern. On how interest "constitutes the nonneutrality of the conscious subject," see Stokes, *Kierkegaard's Mirrors*, 51.

cares and concerns amounted to nothing more than weak, barely perceptible interest would be in a deplorable condition. Yet this should not prevent us from recognizing that even the state of being minimally interested can be located on a continuum with states of greater concern. To adapt an Aristotelian example to the matter at hand, we could say that it is because we have an interest in knowing that we enjoy looking around, with no purpose other than to see.[24] In the simple case of noticing what surrounds us, we are employing to a slight degree the same affective ability that is engaged much more wholeheartedly in the abiding care that motivates a person's dedication to a lifelong project: this is true as soon as we have begun to take an interest in our surroundings, as opposed to being utterly indifferent or oblivious. And this explains why some emotional researchers argue that *interest* is an affective state or disposition that orients and inspires human beings in all of their "day-to-day functioning," by focusing attention and guiding perception.[25] The point they are making is similar to that made by Scheler when he says that love plays a world-disclosing role, guiding our thought and action and governing the meaning of our lives. Of course, love and deep concern allow a life to become more robustly meaningful than mere interest ever could. Nonetheless, someone who takes an interest in anything (however negligible) is already beginning to care about it (albeit slightly). The ways of being affectively disposed—ranging from bare interest, through care or concern, to love in its various forms—can be located along a spectrum of incremental shades, not

---

24. Cf. Aristotle, *Metaphysics* 980a.

25. Carroll Izard, *Human Emotions*, 209–213. He refers to interest as one of "the most frequently experienced" emotions. On the emotion of interest in relation to knowledge, see also Paul Silvia, *Exploring the Psychology of Interest*. Hubert Dreyfus speaks of the "interested attitude" and of our "interested dealings with the world," e.g., in *Being-in-the-World*, 60 & 137. Yet he does not link this notion as explicitly as he might with the Heideggerian concepts of care and concern.

one of categorical differences. And this accounts for why interest can, at least to a slight extent, perform the same kind of function that is more obviously accomplished by other dispositional affective states.

Because the affective disposition of interest allows us to perceive the significance of the world (or, more precisely, those aspects of it in which we have *taken* an interest), it moves us from a state of indifferent neutrality to one of personal involvement. It is in our emotional capacity to become interested or concerned that we should find the key to understanding what William James refers to as "the mystery of . . . selective attention"[26]—that is, how we notice certain things that become conspicuously manifest to us, while others are overlooked. What we care about does not remain in the background of our awareness, but comes forward and impresses itself upon us as meaningful. And if I am right to explain love as a particular way of caring, then our ability to care (even in an understated way, as manifested in merely taking an interest) is an expression of what in its strongest form is love. Although "care" and "concern" are more inclusive terms, it is essential in thinking about the emotional *a priori* to bear in mind that our emotional life is fundamentally grounded in the same dispositional affective capacity that shows itself most powerfully in love, and most faintly in mere interest.

Heidegger speaks more frequently of care, rather than love, yet he makes it clear that his notion of care is *not* intended to *exclude* love—for instance, when he rejects a proposal that his account "needs to be supplemented with 'love,'" to remedy an alleged omission. His reason for rejecting this emendation is that, "correctly

---

26. James, "Are We Automata?," 8. Elsewhere, he characterizes our emotional interests as "the real *a priori* element in cognition."—*Essays in Philosophy*, 11n. On how we might fail to detect things whose value is unfelt, see Scheler, *Formalism in Ethics and Non-formal Ethics of Values*, 266–267.

understood," he claims, "care is never distinguishable from 'love.'"[27] Thus, when Heidegger says that human existence "is characterized by *caring*," which is "a fundamental mode of being" for us,[28] or that the world is encountered as being of concern to us only *because* it is dependent upon care, we could revise Heidegger's language (based on the identity he affirms in the passage cited above) as implying that our life in the world is experienced as meaningful *because* we are fundamentally loving beings. Indeed, the claim that each particular human existence is defined by *care* could also be rephrased in these terms:[29] that love forms the heart of every human being, shaping the way the world appears to him or her as real and significant. Now, some ways of describing the emotional *a priori* are preferable to others, for instance by virtue of capturing a wider range of affective phenomena, or specifically characterizing one distinctive expression of the emotional *a priori*. Yet what is most important, I think, is that we recognize the phenomenon which is being named in each of these various ways, and that we appreciate its basic place in our affective life.

For this reason, even some of the less felicitous terms often used in referring to aspects of the affective *a priori* are worthy of mention. To care about something is not necessarily to *desire* it, for example,

---

27. Heidegger, *Zollikon Seminars*, 190–191. The proposal comes from Ludwig Binswanger: see his *Being-in-the-World*, e.g., 173 & 219.

28. Heidegger, *Ontology*, 66. Regarding what follows, see *Being and Time*, §§ 41 & 43(c). Cf. Jonathan Lear, *Happiness, Death, and the Remainder of Life*, 32–33: "we are ontologically constituted by care," or by love, in such a primary sense that by ceasing to care, if this were even feasible, we would no longer inhabit a recognizably human world.

29. On how love "forms the heart" and grounds all elements of our world as personally meaningful, see Søren Kierkegaard, *Works of Love*, 12 & 215–216. That love can be viewed as "a concretion" of "concern" (*Sorg*) is indicated by Kierkegaard in *Papers and Journals: A Selection*, 128 (entry of 5 July 1840, III A 4). Cf. Sharon Krishek, "Kierkegaard on Impartiality and Love," on how care or concern ought to be understood as "encompassing" different forms of love. See also Frijda, *The Emotions*, 335–344.

although some forms of caring may lead to wishing or wanting:[30] as when we want to preserve a wild area *because* we care about it, or wish good fortune for a child whom we love. These desires and wishes are not primary, but predicated on the fact that we already love or care about someone or something. In the same way, our aims and goals are based upon what already matters to us, what we are concerned about. By virtue of caring in the ways that we do, we find a goal to be worth striving toward or pursuing. This is why, for similar reasons, I view it as inexact to claim that either desires or goals are grounding conditions of our emotional responses.[31] What we find personally significant includes but cannot be reduced to either what we desire or what is relevant to our pursuit of goals. It is more accurately identified as what we are *not* uninterested in, what we are *not* unconcerned about. To formulate the point without a double negative, then: the realm of what we find significant (and thus of what we are disposed to have particular emotions about) is coextensive or *identical* with the realm of what we regard with interest, care, or concern. Yet theorists of emotion who argue that goals or desires are essential features of emotional response do seem to be designating or pointing toward the same affective background which is constituted on my account by various forms of love or care. I hope to acknowledge the common ground on which we converge, even though I favor different explanatory language.

---

30. Cf. Frankfurt, *Necessity, Volition, and Love*, 155. As he points out, the notion of desire tends to be deployed "rather carelessly, in a variety of different roles," yet frequently what moves us to act "is not that we merely *want* one thing or another," but "that there is something of which it is both more precise and more pertinent to say that we *care about it* or that we *regard it as important.*" See also Frankfurt, *The Reasons of Love*, 10–12.

31. So I disagree on the one hand (regarding whether desiring or wanting is necessary for emotion) with, e.g., Graham Oddie and Michelle Maiese; and, on the other hand (regarding whether goals must ground emotional responses), with Richard Lazarus. See Oddie, *Value, Reality, and Desire*, 75–76; Maiese, *Embodiment, Emotion, and Cognition*, 64; and Lazarus, "Appraisal," 210.

Is there a felt valence that accompanies the background affective disposedness to which I refer? Not always, and thus perhaps not necessarily. The emotional *a priori* is always with us, yet not in such a manner as to be phenomenally obvious at each and every moment. However, we should refrain from concluding that there is nothing it is like—that is, nothing that it *feels* like—to have ongoing cares or concerns. Embodied affect, subtle enough to be hardly noticed at all, may accompany us in ordinary life so constantly that it does not command notice, while being crucial for our ability to orient ourselves and understand our circumstances. Evidence that this is indeed the case can be found in conditions involving a deficiency of background affective valence, in which the world (including the world of other human beings) seems radically flat, unfamiliar, and somehow *not real*. A number of severely incapacitating psychiatric conditions that involve a general diminishment of emotional feeling show that the affective *a priori*, if lacking, is experienced as glaringly apparent in its absence. Sufferers report that when their accustomed emotional awareness is missing, their surroundings seem "artificial," "strange," or "unreal," as if even the faces of loved ones are unrecognizable, "inhuman" or "fake," like "wax models."[32] When nothing exerts an "affective pull" on a person, his or her world as a whole seems profoundly foreign and alienating, and things within the world are deprived not only of meaning but also of substance

---

32. Quoting first-person accounts from Sechehaye, *Autobiography of a Schizophrenic Girl*, 31–38; Simeon and Abugel, *Feeling Unreal*, 73–79; Ratcliffe, *Experiences of Depression*, 202–208; Stone and Young, "Delusions and Brain Injury," 327–337; Radovic and Radovic, "Feelings of Unreality," 274–275; Ratcliffe, "The Phenomenological Role of Affect in the Capgras Delusion," 211; Ellis and Young, "Accounting for Delusional Misidentifications," 241; Ratcliffe, *Feelings of Being*, 147–159; and Medford et al., "Understanding and Treating Depersonalisation Disorder," 93–95. See also de Sousa, *Emotional Truth*, 166–167; Pacherie, "Perception, Emotions, and Delusions," 117–119; and Merleau-Ponty, *Phenomenology of Perception*, 390.

or solidity, in some cases making him or her feel convinced that these things do not actually exist.[33] Needless to say, for such a person the ability to know and recognize anyone or anything is gravely impaired. What this suggests is that, when we are not so unfortunate as to be afflicted with a deficit of background affective feeling, we are probably relying upon an emotional sense that pervades our felt experience so completely that we often take it for granted. Because it is conspicuous when absent, the emotional *a priori* must normally be present as the unobtrusive horizon of human existence, framing our affective involvements and allowing us to be open and receptive to whatever significance our lives might contain. We should therefore not assume that we could easily be conscious of the world around us without love, care, or interest.

TOWARD AN ACCOUNT OF LOVE, SUBJECTIVITY, AND TRUTH

What we know as the surrounding world is permeated by the affective disposition of the subject. As one Nietzsche scholar remarks, "the concept of 'objective reality' can only be elucidated with the help of such notions as interest, concern," and the like.[34] To that observation, I think we should add this: the fact that our cognition involves a mode of subjectivity, such as an affective disposition, need not imply that this cognition is thus *merely* subjective.

---

33. Once again, the phrase "affective pull" is from Husserl, *Analyses Concerning Passive and Active Synthesis*, 98. On how the world "manifests itself as real," and we experience a "sense of [its] reality," in "contexts of meaningfulness," see also Heidegger, *Basic Problems of Phenomenology*, 85–86.

34. Peter Poellner, *Nietzsche and Metaphysics*, 89–102. That this is not just a Nietzschean theme, but a Kierkegaardian one as well, will become more apparent in the next chapter.

More needs to be said about this, but we are already in a position to appreciate how the emotional *a priori* is a condition of possibility for the objective world to come to light in its reality and significance. Furthermore, it should by now be clear that we have reason to take seriously the notion that our capacity to be affected allows things to be objectively moving. In order to explain how a personal affective orientation can be justified in any case as potentially truth-revealing, I must account for the nature of the significant truths that appear to be disclosed to us in emotional experience. For each person, what follows from the human capacity to have things matter is a particular way of having things matter to him or her: another topic that needs further explanation, therefore, is how a person's emotional point of view could be more or less reliably truth-disclosing. What follows in the remaining chapters of this book is, initially, an account of why love or care is capable of revealing significant truths; and, later on, an examination of how an individual human being's affective vantage point could be justifiably described as truthful.

Chapter 6

Love's Knowledge; or, The Significance of What We Care About

We have begun to see how the emotional *a priori* is a condition of possibility for the world around us to appear real and significant. In this chapter, I will explain further why love and care (and concern, and interest) *can* be reliable capacities, able to reveal meaningful truths. In the process of doing so, I will rely on the work of numerous other thinkers who have been inspired by Pascal's remark that the heart has its reasons—from Søren Kierkegaard and Max Scheler to Harry Frankfurt and Jean-Luc Marion[1]—and will also return to the work of philosophers who have already been cited frequently in earlier chapters, such as William James and Martha Nussbaum. Early in his treatise *Works of Love*, Kierkegaard presents a series of images having to do with the obscure "origin" at the ground of human existence from which love flows, "along many paths," to illuminate our world in all of its rich and intricate significance.[2] He

---

1. Again, see Blaise Pascal, *Pensées*, 216. This passage is quoted or alluded to approvingly by both Scheler and Marion. See *Formalism in Ethics and Non-formal Ethics of Values*, 255 and *The Erotic Phenomenon*, 217.
2. Søren Kierkegaard, *Works of Love*, 8–13.

portrays love both as an unseen source of light and as an unfathomable wellspring from which water flows. The common theme that unifies his imagery is that our capacity to love is like the hidden ground of a visible reality, and what is tacitly implied by this series of metaphors is something akin to a transcendental argument. By virtue of our experience of "love in its manifestations," he claims, we can justifiably conclude that love must be the "ground of all things" in a more profound sense: that is, even if we cannot empirically verify that love is the basis of life as we know it, we still have good reason to make this inference.[3] That is because love must be posited as a pervasive influence in order for what *is* apparent to us to be the way it appears. Without love, or care, as a basic affective disposition, we would not have access to those features of the world that attract our attention and that move us to respond emotionally. As Scheler claims, on a related note, love enables the "showing of something" to us, making significant knowledge possible,[4] and allowing us to grasp what is other than ourselves. If we find the world to be charged with value, this is because we are "always already" loving or caring beings.

RECOGNITION OF VALUE AND CONDITIONS OF POSSIBLE EXPERIENCE

Whether I am getting angry at someone who has just slighted a friend of mine, or feeling constant anxiety throughout a period of poor health, every episode of emotion that I experience involves an

---

3. Kierkegaard, *Works of Love*, 9 & 225. Cf. *Works of Love*, 215: here, Kierkegaard identifies love as the source of all things and as the deepest ground of meaningful experience.
4. Scheler, *The Constitution of the Human Being*, 391.

awareness of someone or something that I value.[5] These valued persons, places, and things (including abstract entities, such as ideals) define my world of concern: they stand out prominently, while everything else withdraws into the background. In general, when we view the world with the intense attention and concern that a loving disposition brings, we find it charged with meaning or importance. As Helm points out, following Frankfurt, "love is a form of caring," and part of what it means to love or care about anything is that it seems "worthy of your attention."[6] Because love is an affective state in which we pay heightened attention to a person (when it is a person whom we love) and feel acutely concerned for his or her well-being, it is—as Nietzsche remarks—a bad sign if someone must *compel* himself to pay attention to us when we are speaking.[7] A loving or caring outlook disposes us toward noticing, and appreciating the significance of, things whose reality and value might otherwise have been invisible to us. Our emotions focus on whatever in our environment matters to us, so an indifferent person to whom nothing matters will not notice very much of what is competing for his or her attention. And is this not consistent with our experience when we are in a state of profound boredom? When we have no appreciable interest in our surroundings, we generally find that "our responsiveness to ordinary stimuli flattens," as "differences are not noticed and distinctions are not made."[8] Boredom, as Marion

---

5. On how a concern for what is what is threatened enters into the sense of fear, see (for instance) Roberts, *Emotions*, 100–101; Düringer, *Evaluating Emotions*, 6–7.

6. Bennett Helm, "Love, Identification, and the Emotions," 42–43. Cf. Harry Frankfurt, *Necessity, Volition, and Love*, 165: here, Frankfurt states that love "is a mode of caring." See also Frankfurt, *The Reasons of Love*, 11.

7. See Friedrich Nietzsche, *Human, All Too Human*, 274: "Assorted Opinions and Maxims," § 247. He concludes, perhaps a shade too cynically, that this constitutes "a valid proof that he does not love us," or "loves us no longer."

8. Frankfurt, *The Reasons of Love*, 54.

observes, "renders indifferent every difference"—for, as he adds, "that which is, if it does not receive love, is as if it were not."[9] Now, consider what this implies: if indeed we cannot distinguish anything that does not seem even minimally valuable or significant, then a person who was completely devoid of love or care would suffer a comprehensive loss of the world. That we are loving or caring beings structures how the world seems to us—what seems real and significant, what appears to be possible, as well as what arouses our attention and moves us to respond. This is why we "cannot dispense with love," as Kierkegaard claims, even for the sake of our epistemological interests:[10] this affective disposition gives us an enhanced mode of awareness, while one who loves or cares only minimally apprehends considerably less and inhabits a diminished world.

Most of the time, fortunately, we do not find ourselves in such an emotionally desolate place. Yet insofar as we *are* moved to recognize anything, it must be that we *do* feel some sense of its value, or (in other words) that we are not indifferent about it. To say that we do not feel indifferent about something is logically equivalent to saying that we care about it, whether more or less. As we have seen, to care about anyone or anything is to regard what we care about as meaningful or significant. And for someone or something to be *loved* is for him, her, or it to be cared about in an especially intense and emphatic manner. When we love, our affective regard "flows in a warm affirmation of the beloved," as Ortega writes. "Think of what it is to love art or your country . . . it is like recognizing and confirming at every moment that they are worthy of existence."[11] If we understand love as an intensified

9. Jean-Luc Marion, *God without Being*, 123 & 134. On boredom as the state of mind in which nothing appears to "interest us at all," in which "we do not ascertain anything, nor do we grasp anything," as the world loses intelligibility, see also Heidegger, *Fundamental Concepts of Metaphysics*, 97–99.

10. Kierkegaard, *Works of Love*, 5–7.

11. José Ortega y Gasset, *On Love*, 16–17.

mode of care, then as I have noted we can locate both love and care along a continuum that extends from the most slight interest, or non-indifference, all the way to love in its most powerful forms—including love for another person for his or her own sake. This warmly felt appreciation of someone's existence in its own right, as a life that matters passionately to us as an end in itself, can be directed toward anything that has (strictly or metaphorically speaking) a life of its own—one we can affirm, and wish to be going well. It is in this way that love "makes visible" what is loved, so that its existence becomes strikingly evident to us;[12] and this is why nothing would appear to have "definitive and inherent worth," as far as we could perceive, if not for its being loved. As viewed from the perspective of someone without loves or cares, the world would be deprived of its usual axiological salience. Each of us *is* aware of the meaning and value of things because of these foundational affective dispositions.

In order to appreciate what it is that we can apprehend emotionally, we need to acknowledge that the nature of the objective world—insofar as it is knowable by human beings—cannot be established without taking into account the structure of the subject by whom it is known. (And those who are unsure about this widely accepted, but still controversial, thesis must be willing to give it serious consideration.) If our capacity to love and care performs a world-disclosing role, it is because it enables us to experience things as meaningful: opening us up to an awareness of what is meaningful, love shapes the way each person views the world. It determines what comes to light as significant, out of the entirety of everything that is in principle available for our attention (much of which escapes our notice altogether). Love and care specify the "axiological nuance[s]" of reality for each of us, in Scheler's terms, defining what

12. Jean-Luc Marion, *The Erotic Phenomenon*, 87–88. Regarding what follows, see Frankfurt, *The Reasons of Love*, 55.

falls within "the value realm accessible to a being."[13] These affective capacities dispose us to *feel*, emotionally, the reality of what otherwise remains hidden. This is why Merleau-Ponty rightly asserts that by understanding how anything significant comes to exist *for us* (to become real in our eyes, and in our felt experience) by virtue of love, we should also understand better how things and beings can exist for us in general.[14] We become fascinated by what is other than us when we open ourselves up to "selflessly" caring about what we love, as Frankfurt says, "for its own sake."[15] Love has a unique authority due to its formative role in human life: it so comprehensively organizes our world of experience that what we are able to *know* depends on our affective disposition or attunement, our way of caring.

As I began to explain in the previous chapter, the fact that love makes us aware of the significance of things does not necessarily entail that this significance is *projected* onto the world by our own minds. Our capacity for love, care, concern, or interest could function more like the aperture in a camera, opening the eye of the beholder so that he or she has access to what is truly "out there" beyond us. For instance, when a friend is waving her hand in greeting, this bodily movement is a meaningful gesture whether or not I perceive it as such. The same is true when a student in class is raising his hand to ask a question. These significant gestures are also measurable physical movements of objects in space, yet neither is adequately described as *only* this material fact. We do, experientially, inhabit a context of significance or meaningfulness: from a human point of view, the world is axiologically charged or valenced rather than flat or value-neutral.[16]

---

13. See, e.g., Max Scheler, *Formalism in Ethics and Non-formal Ethics of Values*, 17–18 & 261. See also Peter H. Spader, *Scheler's Ethical Personalism*, 260.

14. Again, see Merleau-Ponty, *Phenomenology of Perception*, 178.

15. Frankfurt, *The Reasons of Love*, 59; see also *Necessity, Volition, and Love*, 135.

16. Cf. Martin Heidegger, *Basic Problems of Phenomenology*, 83–84: "When I see the acquaintance greeting me and in factical seeing warmly return his greeting, I saw [*sic*] him greeting. I did

Kierkegaard's notion that our phenomenally experienced world is "an objectivity which takes shape in a corresponding subjectivity"[17] reminds us that we need not abide by the terms of a gratuitous dichotomy. We need not, that is, assume that value must either be "merely" subjective or else have totally mind-independent objectivity, as "the Good" has been supposed by some philosophers to provide an absolute standard against which we can measure our all-too-human emotional responses. Rather, love and care enable us to perceive features of the world that are not of our own fabrication, but that are not manifestly evident apart from our affective receptivity either. What registers upon us, in our felt recognitions of significance, could be characterized as "the anthropocentric-cum-subjective real but non-natural properties that are there to discover ('in the world' as one says)."[18] The perception of value can thus depend upon love, although love does not involve the *bestowal* of value. This is a topic to which we shall return.

ON LOVING AND CARING ABOUT ONE'S NEIGHBOR

If love is understood as a disinterested concern for the well-being of whomever or whatever is loved, then what it means to love my neighbor—who could be, literally, the person who lives next

---

not at all see [only] the movement of a material body in objective space." See also Stephen Mulhall, *On Being in the World*, 197–202: the reductive presumptions that might lead us to ask *if* meaning *could* possibly be expressed by another human being's gestures exemplify a conception of human existence which is "not only confused, but demeaning and offensive."

17. Søren Kierkegaard, *Journals and Papers*, no. 6360 (entry from 1849, X 1 A 146).
18. David Wiggins, *Needs, Values, Truth*, 346. Wiggins embraces the sort of "cognitivism" which holds that we can *know* something true through our perceptions (he would say "judgments") of value—moral, aesthetic, etc. See *Needs, Values, Truth*, 140–141.

door—is to take an interest in her life and to value her well-being as an end in itself. It means caring selflessly about how she is doing, and being "personally affected" by her good or bad fortune as a result.[19] Because my neighbor's life is defined by *her* interests, my concern for her must extend to whatever *she* cares about. My (modest, yet sincere) love for my neighbor entails caring about her wish to arrive at work on time. This matters to me—for no other reason except that it matters to her. Let's also say that I see her and say hello as I head out for a morning run, and notice that she seems to be flustered: she has just discovered that her car won't start, and now she is almost late for work. I am affected by her plight, enough to offer her a ride in my car—even if this means that I won't have time to go running now, and even though I value my morning run more than anything I myself might gain by driving my neighbor to work. In all of this, I have hardly achieved a saint-like extreme of unselfish, other-focused concern; yet I have transcended my own interests, and gone out of my way, for the sake of my neighbor's well-being. I care about her, *not* "as an instance of a type" or as "an indifferent thoroughfare for . . . impersonal rational activity,"[20] but as an individual person with her own specific set of interests and concerns, and it is in terms of these that the situation makes a claim on me, to which I respond. This is how, by virtue of love, one person allows another to become a significant reality for herself or himself: a reality that registers in her or his own emotional world. Through this process, our life is both augmented and made more complicated, as we are liable to

---

19. Frankfurt, *The Reasons of Love*, 61. On love as a disinterested concern for the flourishing of the beloved, see also *The Reasons of Love*, 42–43. As Kierkegaard says, a "truly loving" person "loves every human being according to his distinctiveness; but 'his distinctiveness' is what for him is *his own*; that is, the loving one . . . loves what is the other's own."—*Works of Love*, 269.

20. I cite, respectively, Frankfurt, *The Reasons of Love*, 80; then, Scheler, *Formalism in Ethics and Non-formal Ethics of Values*, 372–373.

become emotionally affected by anything that impinges upon a person whom we care about.

Thus, by loving or caring, we develop a "many-sided interest in the things of this world."[21] Our basic affective capacity to care grounds a meaningful world of concern for each human being who is emotionally engaged. When I take an interest in the interests of another person, I succeed to some degree at caring about whatever *she* cares about (loving what she loves). This is what it means to love the neighbor "as thyself": to be affectively disposed toward what is *hers*, just as we are toward what is *our* own to love and care about. Since what it means to love oneself, on many accounts, is to love these "other things" that we care about wholeheartedly—to love them well—it makes sense that to love one's neighbor in a similar manner is to care about what she loves.[22] Again, because caring about others means "loving each one individually," affirming the distinct existence of *this* person, the wish for another person's life to be going well must involve reference to what that person loves and cares about. If I love you, I will be motivated to water your garden while you're away—initially, not because I am independently convinced of its value or importance, but because I know how much the garden matters to you, how much you care about it. Knowing this moves me emotionally to cherish it for your sake; and that, once again, is what it means to take an interest in the interests of another. Through you and because of your love of gardening, I may end up becoming more appreciative of the plants you cultivate—more concerned that they be alive and thriving, in their own right. For this reason, loving what you love

21. Scheler, "Ordo Amoris," 98–99. On pages 110–111 of the same essay, Scheler describes how a person's loves define his or her range of "contact with the universe."

22. See Frankfurt, *The Reasons of Love*, 77 & 85–86. In the following sentence I cite Kierkegaard, *Works of Love*, 66–67.

expands the scope of my affective awareness, broadening my contact with axiological reality.

Some loves and concerns transform our existence so profoundly that we can no longer imagine what our lives might be like without them. Yet our capacity to love is not operative only in such extreme, overwhelming cases. My discussion here also pertains to the ordinary experience of acting in accordance with what we love and are concerned about, whether or not these affective dispositions are brought overtly to our attention.[23] From our most powerful loves and enthusiasms, to what we care about to a moderate degree, to that which interests us only slightly, there is a spectrum which differs from one end to the other not in *whether* something is important to us but in *how* significant it is. What I am now suggesting is that, in the absence of love, nothing would hold *any* significance for us, and there would be no such thing as affective intentionality. This, I presume, is what Frankfurt must have in mind when he asserts that loving or caring "is essential to our being creatures of the kind that human beings are."[24] If we did not love or care about anything even minimally, nothing and no one would stand out saliently to us and solicit our attention. Insofar as we *do* care, when something or someone *does* stand out in this way, we are also subject (for the sake of truthfulness) to this demand: to love the *actual* beloved. The wish to "project non-existent perfections" onto another person, supplanting his concrete actuality with imaginary fantasies of what we want him to be, threatens to put us affectively out of touch with the world.[25] We must, rather, endeavor to be "sensitive to the

---

23. Cf. Theo Van Willigenburg, "Reason and Love," 58.
24. *The Reasons of Love*, 17. Cf. Michael Stocker, "Some Considerations about Intellectual Desire and Emotions," 139: "without care, concern, and interest, nothing would be salient, indeed the world would have no categories."
25. José Ortega y Gasset, *On Love*, 21–23.

individuality and uniqueness of the other," capable of "discerning his or her value, and appreciating it."[26] We long to be seen—that is, to be emotionally perceived in each case as *this particular* being, apprehended in our utterly singular distinctiveness. That is why we are dismayed when someone seems to love us based on a false notion of who we are, or without any recognition of what distinguishes us as this specific person.

The character Beatrice, as depicted in Dante's *Purgatorio* and *Paradiso*, can be regarded as a model of truthful love, in which a person is loved according to his unique individuality. With regard to Dante, she views him with an honest vision that overlooks nothing, loving "what is the other's own," and what identifies him as the person he is.[27] Because any characteristic of Dante can contribute, in a minor or a major way, to his own "personal distinctness," her love does not neglect or disregard any of his particular traits. She knows and cares about his literary aspiration—indeed, what would it mean to love Dante without being aware of this guiding passion? Yet she is also conscious of (and concerned about) his deviation from the goals that ought to be governing him, the ways in which he has not lived up to his own standards. Late in the *Purgatorio*, Beatrice admonishes Dante in a way that reminds him of his own orientation toward what is good—how *could* you have lost your way, she asks, appealing to his conscience. Yet she speaks gently, with a smile, aiding his own vision. All the idiosyncrasies of his biography so far, including the way that she herself has inspired him, are part of what she loves in him. Realizing that Dante is more than his history, she does not confine her love for him to what has been already

---

26. Sharon Krishek, *Kierkegaard on Faith and Love*, 156.
27. Cf. Kierkegaard, *Works of Love*, 269–272. See also M. Jamie Ferreira, *Love's Grateful Striving*, 115–116: "Genuine love, in this account, amounts to an honest . . . vision of concrete individuals, focusing on them 'as they are' rather than trimmed to our measure."

manifested in his life, but she loves him also as a subject with rich possibilities who is still in the process of becoming. Furthermore, as Nussbaum points out, Dante's "very body is, for her, a part of his identity: she calls him by name, recognizes him," and "looks at him with love."[28] Beatrice acknowledges his most worthy pursuits as well as his faults, and toward the latter she seeks a "mitigating explanation," viewing him in a way that is clear-sighted and fair, yet also forgiving. Viewing him with a friendly eye, making a charitable interpretation, she apprehends much about Dante that would be missed by another observer: one who was guarded or distrustful, or who focused mainly or merely on his faults. We ought to be reminded, in considering this example, of Iris Murdoch's phrase: "a just and loving gaze directed upon an individual reality," which when directed toward a person sees her "as she really is,"[29] and in the best light available. This illustrates why it is that we cannot dispense with love or care without losing access to truthful insights.

Love for one's neighbor means caring for that specific person, therefore, with a love that does not remain "proudly independent of its object," but embraces that human being himself or herself. It means "to will to exist" for that person, as Kierkegaard says, affirming his or her life and well-being.[30] Similar formulations can be found in Scheler, who writes that our most truthful mode of access to others (when we can manage this) is an unselfish love that "wants the [being] to be," and "to be nothing other than what it is," flourishing in its distinct existence.[31] This, as I noted above, means

---

28. Martha C. Nussbaum, *Upheavals of Thought*, 571–573. See Dante, *Purgatorio* XXXI: 28–30 and XXXIII: 94–96. Regarding what follows, see Søren Kierkegaard, *Works of Love*, 289–292.

29. Iris Murdoch, *Existentialists and Mystics*, 327–329.

30. Kierkegaard, *Works of Love*, 83–84.

31. Scheler, *On Feeling, Knowing, and Valuing*, 153.

loving what is *their* own just as we love what is *our* own, or at least in a similar way—that is, to care about this person's life, to want her to be doing well. If a human being were nothing else but the vehicle of impersonal reason, then to love Socrates would simply mean to love the rational principle that happens to be embodied in him—but not in him *only*, so it would be irrational to mourn his death. Then again, if Socrates is defined by what he loves, then the pursuit to which he was wholeheartedly devoted *does* specify his identity—although not in the same way. If this is the case, then we cannot authentically love Socrates without appreciating his dedication to philosophy; however, we appreciate *his* particular manner of practicing the love of wisdom. That includes the way in which he raises questions, how he loves to talk, his tone of voice, and his characteristic gestures and expressions, including the peculiar way in which he sometimes gets lost in thought and falls into a trance. We recognize that Socrates leads the examined life in a way that is utterly his own, and we love how he shares this life with those who are drawn to him, displaying a playful kindness toward his friends, along with an ironic sense of humor which cannot be separated from his tendency to pester us relentlessly with questions. We believe in the reality and meaning of his existence, we rejoice in his distinct being, and we will miss him irreparably after he is gone. As in each of the other examples I have mentioned, to love Socrates is to care about him as a certain individual with his own conception of the good and a unique set of concerns. It is, in other words, to love him as a valuing subject with a distinct and irreplaceable perspective on the world.

There is "a significance in things" which is not simply of my making, yet which can be revealed only through my subjectivity.[32] I am

32. See Merleau-Ponty, *Phenomenology of Perception*, 507–510.

not at liberty to give the world whatever meaning I choose, but to a dispassionate observer its meaning would not be disclosed. My heightened awareness of those whom I love and care about allows me to appreciate things that I would not otherwise have been able to perceive.[33] To mention one more brief example, a child who has difficulty with language and who struggles in school might have creative gifts that only a loving and perceptive mother could detect, affirm, and encourage. Now, love does not have a magic power to create value that simply isn't there (no amount of motherly love could bring into being an inclination or aptitude that doesn't exist). Yet the gaze of a loving person who views what *is* there in the most favorable light *can* uncover possibilities that are not apparent to anyone else.[34] Through my affective disposition, I become able to appreciate what I would not have observed in any other way. In loving you, my neighbor, I am attentive both to your actual existence and to "a truth that has yet to manifest itself—yours and that of the world revealed through and by you."[35]

ON VALUING, AND ON THE PARTICULAR SIGNIFICANCE OF WHAT IS LOVED

In speaking of "the significance of things," we are dealing with an aspect of our environment that depends on our subjective outlook

---

33. Cf. Furtak, "Love as a Relation to Truth," where I elaborate further on some of the examples that have been mentioned here.
34. As Marion says, the other person "appears only if I gratuitously give him the space in which to appear." See "What Love Knows," 166. Cf. William Luijpen, *Existential Phenomenology*, 228–230.
35. Luce Irigaray, *I Love to You*, 116–117. This attention is my "support for your becoming," she adds.

in a way that other features of the world arguably do not.[36] The lovable properties of a friend, a hometown, or a favorite song are not like the volume and mass of a solid object, which can be confirmed by any and every observer. Instead, they are phenomena that *can* be well founded, since we are capable of describing them and pointing them out to others—to some degree, and to some others—but which are *not* evident from all perspectives. When we succeed at explaining to another person some qualities that we find moving in the song, we prompt him to notice and hear these also, and if he hears them in anything like the way that we do, then he should find the song moving in *something* like the way that we do. We have better conceptual resources to account for the relation between what moves us and how we feel moved by it than to conceive of these as an inscrutable outward cause of a private, unintelligent inner condition.[37] Rather, here as in other cases a more adequate account of our affective experience will capture the intimate link between intentionality and phenomenal feeling.[38] And yet: with regard to that favorite song of mine, whenever somebody else responds to the song in anything like the way that I do, hearing it and being

---

36. Cf. Robert C. Solomon, *True to Our Feelings*, 55: he makes a similar point about the nature of axiological qualities. As Roger Fitterer points out, we must in some way distinguish "between the kind of objectivity proper to the hard sciences and that [which is] proper to ethics": see *Love and Objectivity in Virtue Ethics*, 4. I'll return to this suggestion in the next chapter.

37. The sort of conceptual resources that I've already rejected as inadequate and to which we need not revert would include, for instance, Hume's notion of the passions as having no representative or intentional content whatsoever: on this, see chapter 1 above. I also have in mind John Locke's equally mystified account of the relation between what pains us and our pain: see, e.g., *An Essay Concerning Human Understanding*, Book II, chapter 8. On "what or who we love" as not "merely the cause . . . of a state arising in us," see Heidegger, *Fundamental Concepts of Metaphysics*, 89.

38. Cf. York Gunther, "The Phenomenology and Intentionality of Emotion," 45–49. See also Robert C. Roberts, who makes an analogous claim in *Emotions*, 80: emotional construal is not a matter of "interpretation laid over a neutrally perceived object," but a way of seeing, and feeling toward, the object of our emotion.

emotionally moved (being thrilled or delighted by it, even *loving* it), there remain vastly more human beings who will register the song as audible sound but not be moved by it in a remotely similar way. In appreciating music versus hearing mere noises,[39] we differ more greatly in our capacities—in the former case, something more personal and maybe peculiar to our disposition is involved, something which (as I have been arguing) nonetheless both reveals aspects of the world and lies at the heart of who we are, who each of us is.[40] I have argued that by making us capable of discovering the significance of other persons and things, love brings to light the axiological dimension of reality, the value in our surroundings; that love, care, and concern are what make it possible for us to have experiences in which things delight and threaten us, alarm and calm us: in sum, that our affective dispositions allow us to experience our world as intricately meaningful and as warranting all variety of emotions. Through this mode of experience, we discern things that dispassionate reason is blind to, "as ears and hearing are blind to colors."[41] This doesn't mean that what is disclosed to us in such experiences somehow flies in the face of rationality or logic, only that we are relying upon a different faculty when value is perceived. Our emotional

---

39. Nietzsche suggests that a "mechanistic" interpretation of music, which reduced it to nothing but quantified sound waves, would be among the *"stupidest"* possible views, disregarding the *"value"* of the music and insisting that music, and by extension the world, is "lacking in significance" and "essentially *meaningless*."—*The Gay Science*, § 373. Cf. Roberts, *Emotions*, 52–55.

40. On the way that, according to Scheler, love discloses real features of the world to us and at the same time engages what is rightfully called the "heart" of the human being, the capacity to "love and to feel the order of values," see again *Formalism in Ethics and Non-formal Ethics of Values*, 261–262 and see also Manfred Frings, *LifeTime*, 66.

41. Max Scheler, *Formalism in Ethics and Non-formal Ethics of Values*, 254–255. See also Scheler, "Ordo Amoris," 117–118. On why it is that our partial and charitable interpretations, how we are moved by what and whom we love, can vary from one of us to another without being out of touch with reality, see Troy Jollimore—who claims that, if you saw (or heard) what I love *as I do*, then you would also love it the way I do—in *Love's Vision*, 68–70.

responses embody a mode of vision, but what they enable us to see would be invisible to anyone without the necessary sort of affective attunement. When a person views the world with the heightened attention and concern that a loving disposition brings, he or she finds that it is not neutrally valenced but permeated with tangible meaning. Still, more needs to be said about this.

Prevailing and deep-seated (if nihilistic) habits of thought can lead us to wonder, in certain moods, whether the apparent significance of what we love and care about is merely illusory—perceived by us as meaningful, but actually meaningless. On the one hand, we do not experience ourselves as actively endowing the objects of our love with the very attributes we point to when we are describing what we love about them.[42] It would be phenomenologically inaccurate to claim that what I find so moving about the austere beauty of a desert valley, or a friend's gentle way of rebuking me, is emanating from me onto the landscape or the person. When I love someone, it is likely that I am especially aware of her good qualities, because these are amplified in the light of my radiant and charitable gaze. This is not tantamount to admiring a falsified image of the person, which obstructs my view of her as she really is. If it were, then it would make no sense to speak about cases in which we "fail to see the individual because we are completely enclosed in a fantasy world" of our own creation.[43] Yet we do, rightly, make a distinction between delusional images projected by our own soul and

---

42. Cf. Rolf Johnson, *Three Faces of Love*, 103–104. A similar point is made by Iain Thomson: see "Ontotheology," 118–120.

43. Iris Murdoch, *Existentialists and Mystics*, 215–216. Love, she explains further, is the "difficult" realization "that something other than oneself is real. . . . It is the apprehension of something else, something particular, as existing outside us." Of what love reveals, Marion contends: "I did not foresee it, cannot expect it, and will never comprehend it."—*The Erotic Phenomenon*, 103.

the captivating features of those whom we love that impact us and arrest our attention, which strike us unexpectedly. One good reason for making this distinction, and for believing that love *can* put us in touch with truths not fabricated by us, is that we could not possibly have anticipated much of what we have, in fact, been affected by. In order to account for what I love and care about, I must acknowledge that it all depends upon my encounter with actual persons, places, and things whose existence is independent of mine. And the contingency of these encounters, like other occasions for perception—had you not been there, you would not have seen—shows that the truth we perceived and our perception of it were circumstantial facts, not rationally necessary.[44] Yet rationally necessary truths are not the only ones available to us, or the only ones that ought to qualify as such.[45]

On the other hand, however, even if the perceived beauty and value of what we love is not simply bestowed onto it by the beholder, recognizing this beauty does involve a kind of affective receptivity on our own part. When I describe what I love and care about, I am revealing something about how *I* view the world, or how it seems to me: and

---

44. If "knowledge" in the strictest sense is about universal and necessary truths, what is always the case and must be the case, then as Aristotle notes we cannot gain knowledge through perception. See *Posterior Analytics* 87b–88a. Yet he soon qualifies this claim (see my very next note).

45. Not every philosopher would agree with this statement, since there are forms of rationalism that would claim that nothing other than rationally necessary truth—what cannot be otherwise—*can* be known. Aristotle's way of moderating his strict definition of knowledge as ἐπιστήμη is to argue that "there are some things which are true and are the case, but which can also be otherwise." I cite *Posterior Analytics* 88b. In *Nicomachean Ethics* 1139b, he counts this as one of *five* ways in which we grasp the truth—one of five modes of knowing, one might say. Those rationalists who would count only knowledge of necessary truth as knowledge properly speaking are likely to reject the idea that human emotions could even potentially reveal something truthful. Yet most readers who are unsure about the truthfulness of emotion are not committed to philosophical rationalism, but unsure because of other considerations—and they ought to concede my point that rationally necessary truths are not the only truths available to us.

this is not equivalent to an impersonal description of how the world is. William James asks us to contemplate what *that* might be like:

> Conceive yourself, if possible, suddenly stripped of all the emotion with which your world now inspires you, and try to imagine it *as it exists*, purely by itself, without your favorable or unfavorable, hopeful or apprehensive comment. It will be almost impossible for you to realize such a condition of negativity and deadness. No one portion of the universe would then have importance beyond another; and the whole collection of things and series of its events would be without significance.[46]

At one point, this thought experiment almost veers into absurdity, as James invites us to contemplate a world that exists purely in itself. Since this is arguably what we cannot have any conception of, it is a rather unfair basis of comparison. Yet his main thesis is well worth taking seriously: insofar as we *could* envision the world as it might appear to an observer totally devoid of emotion, it would seem to be entirely lacking in value or significance. From this insight, however, he draws the wrong conclusion. Immediately after the passage cited above, he asserts that the meaning and value that animate "our respective worlds" are "thus pure gifts of the spectator's mind," and he identifies the "passion of love" as "the most familiar and extreme example of this fact."[47] That does not obviously follow. Without the right kind of affective outlook, we cannot experience the significance of things. But this does not entail that the significance of

---

46. James, *The Varieties of Religious Experience*, 140–141.
47. James, *The Varieties of Religious Experience*, 141. Nietzsche, who ought to know better, sometimes makes similar claims: see, e.g., *The Antichrist*, 29, § 23: "Love is the state in which man sees things most widely different from what they are. The force of illusion reaches its zenith here."

things is a distortion imposed on them by our own perspective:[48] one could equally well argue that an apple *truly* has no color if we try to view it in a dark room. Keeping in mind that we have access to the world only through its effect on sentient beings such as ourselves,[49] we should not conclude that love gives us a false view of things just because it enables us to see *more* than the cold eye of dispassionate reason could discern. Recognizing a tone of resentment in the voice of someone we love, which a neutral observer would fail to notice, may lead us to worry about the relationship. And this worry could be founded on actual evidence, providing us with insight into objective reality of the epistemically desirable kind. If we didn't love this person, then we could easily remain cool-headed, impartial, unworried, and thus oblivious to a fact that might be transparently evident to anyone who cared enough to perceive it.

Even if there *is* no standpoint from which our impressions of the world could be compared with the world as it "absolutely" is, we still have reason to hold onto the goal of truthfulness, of being in touch with the world. If we give up on this, as Williams has written,

48. Where Frankfurt stands on this matter is a contested question. I have argued elsewhere that *letting things become significant* may be a better way to characterize what he has in mind, rather than *projecting value onto things*. The former is more compatible with many of his statements, such as that it is liberating to be "captivated by our beloved" (*The Reasons of Love*, 65–66), or to be "seized by" the beloved (*The Importance of What We Care About*, 89). Its meaning attracts us because it is there *to be met with*, although not *absolutely* there, since a loving subjectivity is an essential condition of apprehending this particular truth. If I am wrong, and if Frankfurt does wish to defend the view that all value is falsely projected onto the beloved by the one who loves, then some of his claims are true for the wrong reasons. On such a reading, he would be right to argue that love is a condition of finding value in the world, but incorrect in holding that this value is just an illusory projection. See Furtak, "Love as the Ultimate Ground of Practical Reason," 233–234.

49. John McDowell makes this point, for instance, in *Mind, Value, and Reality*, 114. Regarding the "eye of reason" and the perspective of love, see also Max Scheler, *The Nature of Sympathy*, 150. Hilary Putnam writes that, since the time of Berkeley, it has been well known that "the arguments against the idea that things are colored in the way they seem to be" also undermine the idea "that they are *shaped* in the way they seem to be, *solid* in the way they seem to be, etc." I quote from *The Threefold Cord*, 39.

"we shall certainly lose something, and may very well lose everything."[50] Yet, at this point, we should understand why it would not be obvious that anything *deserves* to be loved, to a detached or indifferent observer. This is a consequence of the fact that a certain affective disposition is needed in order for us to perceive the significance of anything. In other words, what we see depends in part on our way of seeing. Taking notice of another person's suffering, for example, requires more than just pointing one's eyes at him while he is located in a well-lit place:[51] it also requires that we view him with the attention and concern that highlight whatever we love and care about. Drawing an analogy between emotional perception and color vision, Kierkegaard points out that it is only "if you yourself have loved" that you know what it is like to experience the world in this light, in the same way that "the blind person cannot know color differences."[52] The person with normal eyesight, of course, does not generate a world of visible and colorful objects out of his own mind. Rather, he must be constituted in a certain way in order to perceive what is visible: namely, real features of the world that can be detected only by those who are capable of taking them in. We are creatures for whom the world presents itself as meaningful in ways that elicit our emotional responses; however, its meaning is revealed to us only if it is approached under favorable conditions and in the appropriate way. Once we have rejected the incoherent notion of an absolutely subject-independent objectivity viewed "from nowhere," we lack any basis for the assumption that there is a value-neutral world "out there" that our emotional responses project value *onto*.[53]

50. Williams, *Truth and Truthfulness*, 7–17.
51. Cf. Anthony Rudd, *Expressing the World*, 121.
52. Kierkegaard, *Christian Discourses*, 237.
53. As Bernard Williams asks of projectivist accounts: "What is the screen?"—*Ethics and the Limits of Philosophy*, 129.

This is especially true with respect to the kind of knowledge we gain in becoming acquainted with other persons, as they are and as they might possibly become. Rather than simply altering our view of someone who is already quite well known to us, love is what allows the person to show up and be noticed in the first place. This is why Scheler claims that love is knowledge: *because* we come to know an "individual personality" only through "the act of loving," which discloses the person in his or her particularity.[54] Love or care performs a revelatory function in the realm of value experience, enhancing our awareness and expanding our "range of contact with the universe."[55] Frankfurt notes the "ineluctably particular" significance to the lover of what he or she loves, adding that it is precisely the "specific particularity" of the beloved that one loves about her or him.[56] This is how a significant world takes shape around the vantage point of each individual person, as love or care allows us to encounter meaningful aspects of the vast, complex, and multifaceted universe that surrounds us. Out of all that is worthy of love, we each have access to a limited part: this places an outer boundary on what we are emotionally capable of knowing. We *cannot* love everyone or everything, so we finite human beings are condemned to an inevitable partiality with respect to what we love and care about.

Each case in which we care about someone's existence for its own sake, wishing for this person's life to be going well—which, as I pointed out earlier, we can wish on behalf of anything that has (strictly or metaphorically speaking) a life of its own—lets value

---

54. Scheler, *The Nature of Sympathy*, 166–167. As Marion says, "only love opens up knowledge of the other as such." See "What Love Knows," 160.

55. "Ordo Amoris," 110–112.

56. Frankfurt, *Necessity, Volition, and Love*, 166–170. His claim is echoed by Eric Santner: "When one truly loves another person, one loves precisely what is *not* generic about them, what cannot be substituted for by someone else, in a word, what is irreplaceable." See *On the Psychotheology of Everyday Life*, 73.

and disvalue show up in relation to that existence, and thus renders us vulnerable to being emotionally affected. If we want someone to be doing well, we regard an animal whose venom or saliva (a rattlesnake, a rabid dog) is poisonous to that someone as a source of potential danger, in relation to this life.[57] Granted, these substances are dangerous only because of how they interact with human physiology, and only in relation to the life and thriving of a particular being: yet, given a concern for this life, they are truly harmful.

Lest we forget that our emotional responses are answerable to a world outside of our own mind, I should reassert that this emphasis on subjectivity is entirely consistent with our legitimate concern for being in touch with reality, and not being deluded. Our interest in knowing the world truthfully, however, would be poorly served by the effort to abide by some criteria of what is objectively lovable or worth caring about. In love, there is always something gratuitous or unjustified, an excess that we cannot explain—and were this not the case, it could not play the role that it does in human life. "If God is love," as Frankfurt observes, "the universe has no point except simply to be."[58] This is because the inherent value of being is disclosed to us only when we love or care; we are thereby moved to affirm the existence of what we love. From this, it follows that we regard its objects as valuable in their own right *and* that we view them as significant in a way that pertains to us. Rather than seeing the qualities of the beloved as "pure gifts," projected by the one who loves,[59] I think we should link the idea that love enables us to see with a modest realism about what it brings into view. It is, after all, a realist who can most readily

57. Cf. Stephen Mulhall, *Inheritance and Originality*, 251–252. On "relational properties," which are real whether or not perceived, see also Rebekka Hufendiek, *Embodied Emotions*, 120–122.

58. Frankfurt, *The Reasons of Love*, 63.

59. As James does: see again *The Varieties of Religious Experience*, 141.

acknowledge that any object of our emotional awareness "exists even while we think of it in ways that we do not know."[60] There is always more to what we love, and to the world more generally, than what has been already revealed to us at any given point in time. This is another reason for thinking that we will always fall short in attempting to validate our loves and cares in terms of objective merit. Love helps us recognize "less obvious aspects of what is really there," and also to make a charitable interpretation of what is not self-evidently deserving.[61] I am not in a position to know all that is worthy of love in someone or something when I stand at a critical distance and judge whether or not he, she, or it is worthy. The antecedent demand for justification, in terms of objectively lovable qualities, can preclude the discovery of precisely what one is supposedly looking for. This, I think, is why Marion says that "the project of knowing" another person adequately, "even before loving her," has "no meaning" whatsoever.[62] What we love does not come entirely into view, or into the most appreciative light, until we love it. It is there *to be met with*, although not simply "objective," because a loving subjectivity is a necessary condition of our apprehending this particular truth.

PERSONAL LOVE

Building on Frankfurt's account, I have been endorsing the view that love is "a particular mode of caring" which includes affirmation and "concern for the existence and the good of what is loved," whether what is loved or cared about is "a life, a quality of experience, a person, a group," an ideal, "a tradition," or "whatever" the

---

60. Stephen R. L. Clark, *God's World and the Great Awakening*, 69.
61. John Armstrong, *Conditions of Love*, 94–96. See also C. D. C. Reeve, *Love's Confusions*, 21: "love can discover value where nothing else can."
62. Jean-Luc Marion, *The Erotic Phenomenon*, 79.

case may be:[63] in each case, what is loved or cared about is a "concrete individual," so it would make sense that the beloved could also be a "country or an institution," a "personal project," or an abstract yet specific goal such as "social justice," or "scientific understanding," or "beauty in music or in other arts."[64] On the same page, he continues:

> The lover's concern is rigidly focused in that there can be no equivalent substitute for its object, which he loves in its sheer particularity and not as an exemplar of some general type. His concern is nonutilitarian in that he cares about his beloved for its own sake, rather than only as a means to some other goal.[65]

The particularized focus which is emphasized here has also been stressed, for instance, by Heidegger, who claims: "Love is never blind: it is perspicuous."[66] Perspicuous, that is, because lucid and perceptive regarding what lies within its focus; and blind, we might add, only by virtue of what it excludes from its scope due to the special attention paid to what is loved or cared about. Love and care specify what interests and concerns us: out of the great "sea of being," to use Scheler's image, the realm of what emotionally moves us rises up "like an island"[67]—while all else that remains susceptible of being loved, yet outside the purview of our concern, is submerged and hidden from us: invisible, because beyond our notice. Some of what we *do* love and care about is valued instrumentally; if, for instance, a person "care[s] about social justice only because

63. Frankfurt, *Taking Ourselves Seriously and Getting It Right*, 40–41.
64. I cite *The Importance of What We Care About*, 81; *Necessity, Volition, and Love*, 165–166; and "Duty and Love," 4–5.
65. Frankfurt, *Taking Ourselves Seriously and Getting It Right*, 40.
66. Martin Heidegger, *Nietzsche*, 48–49. Regarding what follows, see also Troy Jollimore, *Love's Vision*, 29–30.
67. Max Scheler, "Ordo Amoris," 111–112. On how much is "susceptible of being loved," see Albert Camus, "Losing a Loved One," 206.

it reduces the likelihood of rioting,"[68] justice is for this person *not* of intrinsic value. However, in such a case we can trace the merely instrumental significance of justice to something else that *is* cared about for its own sake, in this case presumably the safety of "me and mine," threatened in one's opinion by rioting. For the conceivable person imagined here, social justice may fall off the island, so to speak, if it ceases to be in his eyes a means toward the end of reducing the likelihood of riots. For someone else, of course, justice or fairness might be cared about in its own right. Scheler's imagery captures what I think is an all-important distinction, between all that affects us and matters to us—defining "the framework of standards and aims in terms of which we endeavor to conduct our lives"—and, on the other hand, everything to which we are indifferent.[69] The latter, as far as we are aware and concerned, may as well not exist.

By contrast with the indefinitely vast set of things in which we take no discernible interest, our intense concern for the well-being of what we love, indeed even for its very existence, is striking. This is what we *affirm*, when by virtue of loving we wish for the loved one to be, and also to be doing well. The affirmation of the beloved's being is at once an acknowledgment of his validity, of the fact that his existence matters, and an attempt to uphold and support him in his life and striving (to "make strong," just as the etymology of "affirm" would suggest).[70] Granting that the

---

68. Frankfurt, *The Reasons of Love*, 42. The phrase "me and mine," used in the following sentence, is employed by Lazarus to characterize *that in relation to which* what moves us emotionally must have some connection—for example, "me and mine" is what an offensive remark must be *about*, in order to make us angry. See, e.g., *Emotion and Adaptation*, 122–123 & 222.

69. Frankfurt, *The Reasons of Love*, 22–23.

70. Above, I cited Frankfurt's reference to love as a concern for the existence *and* the good of what is loved; see also *The Reasons of Love*, 41–42. That the beloved's very being is important to us is underscored by Ralph D. Ellis in *Love and the Abyss*, 97. On affirmation, see Kierkegaard, *Works of Love*, 209–224.

for-its-own-sake-ness highlighted by Frankfurt among many is one characteristic feature of love, versus less other-centered ways of caring or being concerned, we ought to identify the sense in which someone (colloquially speaking) cares about the health of the environment, not for any ulterior motive but for its own sake, as a form of love. And we ought not to be surprised that an account of the emotional *a priori*—of care, concern, and interest, that is—will often center on love especially.[71] Love is what allows us to find significance in the world, through the persons, aspirations, pursuits, and vocations that abidingly guide us, clarifying the meaning of our existence by enabling us to discover and feel convinced of the reality and value of what is not ourselves. In our love for another person, we are oriented toward the *truth* of the world as disclosed to her, the unique personal vantage point she embodies, as it continues taking shape through her experience, including the striving and suffering she undergoes in relation to all that she cares about.[72] Accordingly, truthfulness is at issue in our own life as loving, caring human beings in such a manner that we ourselves are challenged to recognize honestly what, whom, and how we love, at the risk of otherwise becoming radically confused about what our life means.

"What is love," Nietzsche asks, "but understanding and rejoicing at the fact that another lives, feels and acts in a way different from . . . ours?" Then he adds: "If love is to bridge these antitheses

---

71. In a discussion of Heidegger on care and concern, Iris Murdoch states that "Heidegger's *Sorge* may be thought of as a humbler but not less energetic force than Plato's Eros."—"*Sein und Zeit*: Pursuit of Being," 106–109.

72. See Peter Hadreas, *A Phenomenology of Love and Hate*, 29. See also Ellis, *Love and the Abyss*, 22–23 & 133. Cf. M. Guy Thompson, *The Truth about Freud's Technique*, 130. Again, see Irigaray on your truth, and the truth of the world manifested through you: *I Love to You*, 117.

through joy it may not deny or seek to abolish them."[73] That second sentence, following immediately after the first, admits that the otherness we are here encouraged to embrace and affirm joyfully is difficult for us to accept. Not only is this difficult because of individual differences we have trouble understanding, and due to the demands those differences make upon us (including a demand that we become and remain open to another perspective, and even to being transformed by it). It also has to do with the "profoundly vulnerable position" in which we find ourselves when we love a finite, separate person, by virtue of that very finitude and separateness—and of the precarious and painful lack of control we thereby accept.[74] For one who loves a specific other person, so much of one's well-being and life's meaning depends upon another, as this literary character learns: "Since she was no longer a reliable person for him, there was no stable point in the valueless chaos that is the world. . . . He felt a strange melancholy apathy overtake him. Not apathy about her but apathy about everything."[75] And the loves, on which our ability to find ourselves *in* a world of coherent significance depends, are not only our romantic attachments: close friendship, familial love, as well as other relationships of emotional intimacy can have similar importance. "My friends," Nehamas writes, "are people from whom . . . I don't yet know exactly what I want to get, because I trust them enough to let them influence what I believe," to "give them a part in determining *what* my sake actually is, what sort of person I shall turn out to be as a result of

---

73. Friedrich Nietzsche, *Human, All Too Human*, 229–230: "Assorted Opinions and Maxims," § 75.

74. Cf. Sharon Krishek, *Kierkegaard on Faith and Love*, 10–12 & 170. See Nussbaum, *Upheavals of Thought*, 458–462; and see also William A. Luijpen, *Existential Phenomenology*, 318.

75. Milan Kundera, *Identity*, 104–105. Because of this dependency, as Roger Scruton notes, "Love that is unrequited is therefore desperate, and love that is cut short by death is tragic."—*Sexual Desire*, 241–242.

our friendship."[76] To love another particular existing human being, as she or he unfolds over time, is to be in an uncertain and insecure predicament: what he does and what he *is* affects us; and so does everything that impacts him emotionally, as we suffer through his own sufferings.

If love indeed has a logic of its own, then the exclusiveness and singularity of its vision must give us unique or unequalled access to a kind of truth which it reveals. And it is the love of concrete individuals, especially persons, that most obviously shows this mode of knowing. Failures to see someone whom we love (about which, more later), for instance when we view her so pervasively through the lens of something we *want* from her that we can perceive little else but what pertains to this focus, must be contingent failings of an affective capacity that aims toward being truthful—toward revealing what is the case, or disclosing the person as he or she truly is.[77] Kierkegaard speaks of "true love" as being attentive "to the person's distinctiveness," viewing and caring about him or her "according to" this distinct individuality.[78] Someone "for whom a world exists," a

---

76. Alexander Nehamas, *Only a Promise of Happiness*, 58–59. That, as he adds, we tend to find our friends beautiful, and that the romantically beloved is one kind of friend, justifies further the near resemblance I find between or among different ways of loving persons. Marion, who also favors a unified concept of love that cuts across these divisions (see *The Erotic Phenomenon*, 5), says that "love lacks neither reason nor logic; quite simply, it does not admit reason or logic other than its own."—*The Erotic Phenomenon*, 217. Cf. Scheler, *Formalism in Ethics and Non-formal Ethics of Values*, 254.

77. See Paul Voice, "The Authority of Love as Sentimental Contract," 95–97, on accounts of love as at least *potentially* discerning versus as *essentially* irrational. That Proust's narrator is plagued by an inability to love without the sort of distorting "lens" I have just described is noticed by him, and by Joshua Landy in *Philosophy as Fiction*, 88–89. Articulating a Schelerian view, Michael Barber writes that "authentic love" opens one's eyes to potentially "higher values in the loved person." "Become what you are" is what the lover wishes for the beloved, not "be this way or that way." See *Guardian of Dialogue*, 118–119.

78. Kierkegaard, *Works of Love*, 270–272. I owe the phrase "for whom a world exists," meant to capture what distinguishes the kind of thing a person is, to Troy Jollimore: see *Love's Vision*, e.g., 90–91 & 125.

mortal embodied creature with his or her own literally inimitable perspective and way of being, a subject of experience who loves and cares like no one else and therefore senses and feels things as nobody else does, is not easy to know. Intricately complex beyond description at each moment, a person in the midst of her or his existence is never at *any* time a determinately specifiable entity but rather an unfinished being in process: she or he is enacting a continuous history of indefinite but finite duration, and must be loved as such. Although all our loves and cares are incorporated into our own ongoing biography, love for other persons must above all be "open-ended" due the nature of what is loved.[79] This is why to love a person is an infinite task. As limited human beings, we do not have inexhaustible resources of emotional cognition, and in fact our best attempts to love well are at most partially successful: which is to say, partial failures.

Whatever good may exist in a person, or in the world more generally, becomes apparent to us only if we adopt a charitable vantage point. To demand "loveworthiness" in advance, prior to loving, is to assume a detached stance that prevents us from finding what we are ostensibly searching for. We simply do not appreciate all that is susceptible of being appreciated if we insist that love for a person must be strictly in proportion to his or her value or worthiness, as it would appear to an impartial observer. To stand at a critical distance, and to adopt an impartial standpoint, is to enact a disabling prejudice. As Troy Jollimore remarks, love offers "a way of seeing the world that makes possible insights and understandings that cannot

---

79. Here I am relying, not just for this term, on Robert Brown's *Analyzing Love*, 106–107. On how what we love and care about is related to our ongoing concern with the story of our own lives, see Frankfurt, *The Importance of What We Care About*, 83–84. Regarding "the complexity of what a person cares about," see Giovanni Stanghellini and René Rosfort, *Emotions and Personhood*, 312.

be achieved" by "more dispassionate modes of engagement." What is needed to be appreciative "is precisely *not* a state of detachment but a state of engagement."[80] Jollimore offers the example of how we might attend to the poetry written by a friend: what comes easily to us is to be dismissive of its value, whereas the effort of paying more charitable attention (through loving eyes) is more likely to let us appreciate what our friend has written. "The sort of interested, involved, predisposed-to-find-something-of-value stance" that a friend takes toward another "is precisely the sort of stance" that we must take "in order to give *any* work a reasonable hearing."[81] His overtly atheistic standpoint shows that one need not have embraced any form of theistic personalism in order to recognize the compelling reality that a person is. Humbert Humbert is moved, despite his initial interest in using Dolores Haze as a means to gratify himself, to acknowledge that she is a person (a unique someone, for whom a world exists) whom he has irreparably harmed. He recognizes this by virtue of having noticed how she feels, for example when "a chance combination of mirror aslant and door ajar" lets him glimpse an unspeakably helpless and despondent look on her face. It then begins to trouble him that he "did not know a thing about my darling's mind," since it had been his habit "to ignore Lolita's states of mind while comforting my base self"—although, he adds,

---

80. Jollimore, *Love's Vision*, 53–56. Cf. *Love's Vision*, 88–90. See also pages 62–64: "If the lover is blind to certain . . . interpretations," namely those which "tend to see the beloved in unflattering or negative terms," it is also true that the "detached observer is blind" toward "more sympathetic" interpretations; and, he adds, that the detached observer's blindness may be the worse epistemic impediment. Kierkegaard would agree: see *Works of Love*, 5–6. It is not as though we could fall into error *only* by regarding what we love in too charitable a light. On the importance of vision in our moral and emotional response to others, see also Stokes, *Kierkegaard's Mirrors*, 136. Scruton claims that love gives us "a full understanding of what it is for persons to be 'ends in themselves.'" See *Sexual Desire*, 250–251.
81. Troy Jollimore, *Love's Vision*, 57.

addressing himself to her, "there were times when I knew how you felt, and it was hell to know it, my little one."[82]

The same is true of our love and care for other concrete individuals, whether they be places or traditions, ideals or pets, artists or authors, and so on. The way of seeing that love provides is utterly unlike the impartial vantage point of universal, impersonal reason: it is through love that we learn, and feel, what it means for each human life to have intrinsic value, or to be an end in itself. That this involves feeling is crucial: while love is sometimes phenomenally present in the background only as an inconspicuous affective disposition, we can at certain moments feel struck (or even overwhelmed) by the distinctive meaning and significance of another person or thing that exists, of its unmistakable reality. It is in such felt experiences that we recognize most compellingly how much another life means—in itself, and also to us.[83] To express the point even more emphatically, it is "by feeling concretely the radical finitude confronting a person's attempt to be who she is" that we can emotionally apprehend "the

82. Vladimir Nabokov, *Lolita*, 282–285 & 287. Quite possibly, he says, "behind the awful juvenile clichés, there was in her a garden and a twilight and a palace gate—dim and adorable regions which happened to be lucidly and absolutely forbidden to me." This all follows the overwhelming realization that washes over our narrator on pages 277–279, which makes him aware of how much he loves her (apart from all his desire to use her and to possess her), that she is a subject in her own right, and that he has damaged her and deprived her of her youth.

83. Cf. Jesse Prinz, "The Emotional Basis of Moral Judgments," 38: I can, as Prinz points out, have an "emotional disposition" such as love without always having a conspicuously felt experience. If, however, over time I *never* experience more intense emotional feelings of love, then I'm insincere in claiming to love someone or something. As I noted in chapter 5, some nonordinary conditions that involve a general diminishment of emotional feeling show that the affective *a priori*, if lacking, is experienced as strikingly apparent in its absence. For those who suffer from what is known as the Capgras delusion, the faces of loved ones seem unrecognizable, "inhuman," or "fake," like "wax models." And this suggests that a low-level affective "feeling of familiarity" is a critical aspect of our ordinary experience of those whom we love. See Ronald de Sousa, *Emotional Truth*, 166–167; see also Prinz, *Gut Reactions*, 182.

extreme value of that existentially embattled being."[84] Once again, we see how emotional upheavals enable significant realizations to "hit home" with us.

I have promised to examine how an individual human being's emotional vantage point could be legitimately described as truthful, and this account of personal love shows some of the difficulties that inhere in such an explanatory task. When Aristotle, talking about love for friends, claims that we can love only a limited number of people ("great friendship can only be felt towards a few people"), he notes that one reason why we *could* not have noninstrumental love toward many friends is that it would overtax our passionate capacities "to rejoice and to grieve in an intimate way with many people."[85] And the partiality of attention and concern that we direct toward a beloved other whom we truly wish to understand (even when it is as free as it realistically can be from selfish distortions, misconstrual, or projection), shapes and governs our sense of what matters, what is real, and what is possible. As I have argued, each person's world of concern is grounded fundamentally in what this person loves and cares about, and this dispositional affective grounding anchors us in a coherent world of meaning and significance, rather than the "valueless chaos" in which the literary character cited above found himself at a time when he was experiencing radical doubt about what

---

84. Ellis, *Love and the Abyss*, 9–16.
85. Aristotle, *Nicomachean Ethics* 1171a. I cite the Revised Oxford Translation. Aristotle also says that attempting to befriend too many might place us at odds with ourselves, as when we needed at once to be pleased with one friend's good fortune while we also mourn with another. Cf. Troy Jollimore, *Love's Vision*, 112: Values "are, in a sense, incoherent, or at any rate pluralistic; not all value bearers, and indeed not all values, can be fully recognized or incorporated into a single life." Nehamas echoes the point that what makes it extremely difficult to have many close friends, since love is always addressed toward "particular individuals," is that this would become "psychologically costly and confusing."—*On Friendship*, 50–51.

he loved. We differ so much in our emotional sense of reality, and of what is important, that each person's idiosyncratic conception of the world (based as it is upon what she loves and cares about) will fail, unquestionably, to meet standards of universal rationality.

> For it is the very essence of reason to be universally applicable: a reason for you is a reason for anyone. Anyone in the same circumstances, that is. The qualifier is essential . . . for circumstances are never the same.[86]

De Sousa expands on this claim as follows: "if you respond differently from me, each of us owes an account of some relevant difference between our cases." All the same, he adds that "there is no serious prospect of getting another to see your beloved as you do," by virtue of the complexities, many of which are contingent, that define each person's distinct emotional perspective.

In the final chapter of this book, I will venture an explanation of how a person's attunement to the world, his or her affective point of view, could reveal something true and therefore embody and make possible a kind of knowing—if not what we ordinarily think of as knowing. This will require that I say more about the multifaceted and always debatable nature of the truth that is revealed to us emotionally, as well as how our own subjectivity can, as I have said, be epistemically enabling rather than an impediment to truthful apprehension. Our felt sense of the world, biographically and idiosyncratically formed though it is, can (as I will argue) allow us to know and understand what would otherwise be unavailable to us.

---

86. Ronald de Sousa, *Love*, 56–57 & 74. The following quotations are also from these pages. See also, in this regard, Stanley Cavell, *The Claim of Reason*, 241: the "truth of skepticism," he writes, is that what binds a human being to the world is "not what we think of as knowing," according to the standards of what he calls "traditional epistemology."

Furthermore, the ways in which our temperament and personality underlie our entire emotional standpoint must also be taken into account. This is what remains to be further explained, in order to complete this investigation into affective experience as capable of disclosing significant truths about self and world.

Chapter 7

Attunement and Perspectival Truth

As I have argued, emotions involve our living bodies in the recognition of value or meaning, by making us aware of significant matters of concern. Whenever we become emotionally agitated, we are having some aspect of the world impact us as axiologically salient—decidedly *not* as indifferent or meaningless. What registers in our awareness through our affective experience could not be adequately grasped by any other means, and our emotions therefore constitute an indispensable mode of embodied cognition. Furthermore, our affective dispositions—our loves, cares, and concerns—define our sense of what has reality and value. I have also provided an account of why love may provide distinct insights of its own, and have *begun* to offer a defense of the idea that we have good reason to reject categorical skepticism about the potential legitimacy of our emotional apprehensions. Yet even if you grant that these claims are plausible, you might nonetheless have doubts about whether the most personal aspects of our affective life could be truth-disclosing. How could our pervasive moods, our temperaments, and our idiosyncratic passionate outlooks find a place within an account of emotions as felt recognitions of significance which are capable of being more or less truthful? This is the question to which I now turn.

REASONS FOR SKEPTICISM ABOUT MOOD
AND ATTUNEMENT

Without revisiting terrain that was covered earlier, we can now briefly remind ourselves of certain arguments (some better, some worse) purporting to show that emotions in general are irrational: that, for instance, affective experience has no role whatsoever in the disclosure of truth. If episodes of emotion such as fear and grief are not accurately tracking anything in the world, then the loves and cares on which these types of emotion are based must also be subject to doubt as to their reasonableness, or lack thereof. And we do find philosophical analyses of care and love putting forward all the same arguments against the intelligence of emotions that have been dealt with in earlier chapters.[1] All the more so, one might think, for moods and overall attunements to our surroundings: might these not be simply painting the world in our own colors, as a popular cliché suggests?[2] Even philosophers who neither assume nor argue

1. For example, Düringer asserts that "care-based emotions" are comprehensively unreliable, and that whether a situation really is dangerous or a person deserves admiration (for instance) is much "better assessed" if we remain "calm and collected" rather than becoming afraid or feeling admiration. See *Evaluating Emotions*, 121. And Brogaard, writing about love specifically, reverts to the dubious claim examined in chapter 2 above (and, to some degree, in chapters 3 and 4 as well) that emotional processing is segregated between two pathways in the brain, one so fast that it conveys what she calls "unconscious" information "long before" (i.e., a split second before) the slower pathway has informed us of anything: see *On Romantic Love*, 152–153. The conflation of allegedly subcortical passions with unconscious affectivity adds one more layer of confusion to this account: Dehaene identifies this notion as one of several "simplistic dichotomies" which have been proposed, and refuted, about brain function above and below (or to the left and right of) a dividing line. See *Consciousness and the Brain*, 52–55. Regarding grief's dependency on love, see Robert Solomon, *True to Our Feelings*, 74–78; see also Martha Nussbaum, *Upheavals of Thought*, 39–85.
2. As, e.g., Roberts suggests they are, lending a "coloration" to the world: see *Emotions*, 112–115. My characterization of this bias against the very idea of affective cognition is indebted to Stephen Mulhall, "Can There Be an Epistemology of Moods?," 191—he describes, but does not endorse it.

that our affectively charged experiences ought to be distrusted compared to our relatively cool or apathetic reasonings often speak (whether or not on purpose) of our patterns of caring as "creating" significance, or "making" life meaningful—as if to hint that, in fact, this apparent meaning or significance is merely a fabrication.[3]

More well-founded skeptical doubts about whether moods might be capable of revealing something true begin with the observation that our affective state of mind is likely to dispose us toward feeling certain emotions—those that are consonant with whatever mood we happen to be in. "Life is a train of moods," Emerson writes, "and each shows only what lies in its focus"; thus, "I am always insincere, as always knowing there are other moods."[4] Contemporary research shows that people who are in irascible moods tend (unsurprisingly) to get angry at a slight provocation, while a person in an "elated" mood might be inclined toward evaluating things as wonderful.[5] Moods have therefore been identified as *propensities* toward appraising or responding to aspects of the world in particular ways.[6] The happy person *finds* many reasons for happiness in his or her situation, dwelling in a world that appears to be this way. And there is evidence that a state of joy, or sadness, will likewise dispose us

3. Helm, *Emotional Reason*, 60–67; Solomon, *True to Our Feelings*, 2. Even as Helm disavows any intent to make it sound as though value is merely "projected onto the world," he continues to talk of "import" as a "constitution" imposed by the subject, as a consequence of "her caring."—*Love, Friendship, and the Self*, 57–66. Cf. Solomon, *True to Our Feelings*, 55–56: although love is not a "distort[ion]," he says, it is a "bestow[al]" of value that lies only in the "eye of the beholder," not in the beloved: what we perceive is not "objective[ly]" there. Solomon also speaks of *creating* meaning in life, which is "provide[d]" by our passions and emotions and is itself their "product."—*The Passions*, xiv & 7.
4. Quoting respectively from the essays "Experience" and "Nominalist and Realist," in Ralph Waldo Emerson, *Essays and Lectures*, 473 & 587.
5. See, e.g., Matthias Siemer, "Mood Experience," 258–259; Siemer, "Mood-Congruent Cognitions Constitute Mood Experience"; Eric Lormand, "Toward a Theory of Moods," 400. See also Forgas and Vargas, "The Effects of Mood on Social Judgment and Reasoning."
6. See, e.g., Brian Parkinson et al., *Changing Moods*, 216–217.

toward discerning what further justifies our positive or negative affective state. "When bad things happen to someone whose general mood is euphoric," they typically "fail to produce the expected distress."[7] This has been called "the influence of incidental mood [on] cognition"; and (in keeping with our prevailing biases) the "influence of affective feelings on judgment" has been stigmatized as a kind of *contamination*, which is liable to give rise to false or distorted emotional cognitions:[8]

> Mood-based feelings are easily misattributed to whatever stimulus is being processed at the time. Hence, general moods (and moodlike conditions such as depression) are much more likely than are specific emotions to result in contamination of judgments.

The apparent problem here, which leads these authors to suggest that our moods taint or impair affective cognition, is that the power of our emotional disposition to focus our attention in specific ways can also blind us to whatever lies beyond its focus. This can be confirmed in our everyday experience, when (due to our general background mood) we pay selective attention to reality, perceiving only what reinforces our affective state.[9] Feeling discouraged, we find additional reasons for discouragement; whereas, when we are happy, we are less likely to recognize anything that is discordant

---

7. Richard Lazarus, *Emotion and Adaptation*, 265–266.
8. I first cite Griskevicius et al., "Influence of Different Positive Emotions on Persuasion Processing," 190; then, in what follows, Clore and Ortony, "Cognition in Emotion," 45–46. Reasons to consider moods as having only a diffuse relation to objects are weighed by Rolls in *Neuroculture*, 131–132.
9. See Michael Stocker, *Valuing Emotions*, 120–121 & 188; Richard Sorabji, *Emotion and Peace of Mind*, 192. Regarding what follows, see Samuel Todes, *Body and World*, 69: "Local dissatisfaction gives us a sense of dissatisfaction with our world."

with our happiness, taking notice mainly of whatever might warrant a jovial state of mind.

What seems to us a response to how the world *is* can, therefore, be—if not a *projection*, exactly—a subjectively *filtered* perception of things in general. We distrust the phenomenon of "rose-colored glasses," in which all is viewed through a tinted lens and the world seems more rosy than it is (or else, we see *only* what is rosy). And we feel that "something has been lost" which was formerly there when we are depressed and find, "not just that things no longer make one feel happy," but that "a sense of their even having the potential to do so is gone." Ratcliffe continues, commenting on a first-person account of depression:

> The sufferer . . . knows that something is gone and is able to speak of what has been lost, [yet] there remains something she cannot fully conceive of, an appreciation of things that none of her thoughts or words are able to evoke. It is the possibility of actually experiencing things as mattering in the ways that they once did which she cannot entertain. . . . Depression thus involves a transformation of deep mood, a shift in the kinds of concern that structure experience of people, things, and also, of course, oneself. . . . The sadness of severe depression is not adequately characterized as an intensification or generalization of some intentional state. The world is experienced through the sadness. It is how one finds oneself in the world rather than an emotion that one has within the world.[10]

The futility of being told, when depressed, to "cheer up"—or, less vacuously, of having someone try to point out aspects of the world

---

10. Matthew Ratcliffe, "The Phenomenology of Mood and the Meaning of Life," 360–361. He refers to Sally Brampton, *Shoot the Damn Dog*, 29 & 171. See also Ratcliffe, *Experiences of Depression*, 276, which also pertains to what follows.

that are *not* so bleak—is because of this pervasive, all-encompassing darkness or gloom, through which everything is felt. One cannot step outside of this emotional state and see how the world appears without it. A loss of the sense that one inhabits a meaningful space, in which things are worth hoping for and pursuing, can leave a person questioning whether that previously apparent value was just a falsification of the world that is now felt to be so empty and bare.

Earlier, I claimed that our background affective dispositions are the conditions of possibility for particular episodes of emotional recognition: it is because we care about a friend that we grieve her loss or departure; and our concern for what is threatened is the basis for fear. (The same is true for other types of emotion.) In some cases, this interest or care is simply lacking. When Scheler notes that our "attitudes of interest and love" establish in us "a readiness for being affected," he adds that our feeling of what matters, of what is significant, is "peculiar to each" of us.[11] This peculiarity is often thought (although not by Scheler) to cast doubt upon the potential truthfulness of our affective experience, the validity of what it reveals. My world of concern is not the same as your world, just as the world of a happy person differs from that of someone who is unhappy,[12] or even of the same person in a different mood. In order to explain why our aspirations to purify ourselves of "mere subjectivity" and attain a dispassionate vantage point are misguided, we must appreciate why they *can* seem so compelling. How is it reasonable to be affectively disposed toward perceiving meaning, value, or significance in the world? If we believe that someone who is suffering from depression, for whom the possibility of feeling that anything is significant seems

---

11. Max Scheler, "Ordo Amoris," 101–107. Cf. Robert Solomon, *True to Our Feelings*, 240. On the idiosyncratic "framework" that allows for "personal knowing," see also Michael Polanyi, *Personal Knowledge*, 30–31.

12. Cf. Ludwig Wittgenstein, *Tractatus Logico-Philosophicus*, 106 (§ 6.43).

to be absent, has an impaired capacity to care due to the depression, then we are assuming that caring *is* reasonable and that it can reveal the world accurately. Yet this assumption is susceptible to being questioned. As Frankfurt notes, "one version of skepticism with regard to these matters is the view that there is really nothing worth caring about."[13] Since no rational criteria dictate what ought to be axiologically salient to us, what should command our attention, the selective focus of our emotions and affective dispositions (which is particular to us in each case) could be banished to the realm of the irrational. The emotional atmosphere that is determined by a person's mood can seem to *create* the world we inhabit—as if meaning lies merely in the eye of the beholder, and as though our moods *do* paint the world in false colors.

Before asking, what color is it *really?* we should first consider other varieties of confusion to which our moods are vulnerable. A particular experience of disappointment or discouragement can expand into a generalized mood of despondency that permeates the world. A physical illness can have the same effect upon us. Going through grief over a long period of time can leave us in a "funk," to such a degree that we may begin to wonder if we are suffering from endogenous depression, or a similar affective state, which is no longer *about* anything.[14] Or is it about *everything*? This could mean that our wide-ranging emotion *does* have intentionality but is about something as broad as the state of the world, or "how my life is going." Alternatively, our affective state could be "about everything"

---

13. Frankfurt, *The Importance of What We Care About*, 91. De Sousa contends, relatedly, that "no logic determines *salience*: what to attend to," etc.—"The Rationality of Emotions," 136. See also, on selective attention, Michael S. Brady, *Emotional Insight*, 20; and, on how moods constitute our world, Jonathan Flatley, *Affective Mapping*, 19–20.

14. See, e.g., George Graham, "Melancholic Epistemology." On disappointment, discouragement, and despondency, see Furtak, *Wisdom in Love*, 4–5.

in the sense that our mood acquires a "*covert intentionality*," and functions as a "background tonality or atmosphere that contaminates my whole field of awareness," influencing how everything appears.[15] Zahavi attests that it is "doubtful whether it is possible to be dizzy, anxious, [or] nauseous without at the same time perceiving some objects," such that even our internal, nonintentional bodily states can indeed be "forms of disclosure," because what we apprehend emotionally gets filtered through them. As he proceeds to say about our "bodily sensibility,"

> Although one must distinguish between intentional feelings, such as . . . admiration for a particular person, and more general and pervasive moods, such as the feeling of elation, sadness, boredom, nostalgia, or anxiety, etc., the latter are *not* without a reference to the world. . . . They all lack an intentional object [yet] they do not enclose us within ourselves, but are lived through as pervasive atmospheres that lend their coloration to our intentional objects and deeply influence the way we meet the world.[16]

The deeply somatic nature of depressive states has been remarked upon by many,[17] and (due to the palpably embodied aspect of moods) we should expect that conditions such as dizziness, nausea, headache, jitteriness, anemia, trembling, fatigue, or even jet

---

15. René Rosfort and Giovanni Stanghellini, "The Person in between Moods and Affects," 258–260. "How my life is going" is a fair paraphrase of what moods "make manifest," according to Heidegger. See *Being and Time*, § 29. On moods as "about everything," see also Robert Solomon, *True to Our Feelings*, 42.

16. Dan Zahavi, *Self-Awareness and Alterity*, 125–126. See also Strasser, *Phenomenology of Feeling*, 46–47. Cf. Colombetti, *The Feeling Body*, 80–81: she portrays moods as being intentionally " 'open' to the world," even when not otherwise possessing intentionality.

17. See, e.g., Matthew Ratcliffe, *Experiences of Depression*, 75–78. See also Fredrik Svenaeus, "Depression and the Self," 9–12; Giovanni Stanghellini and René Rosfort, *Emotions and*

lag can affect our felt sense of reality—*acquiring* a kind of intentionality, a reference to the world. Once again, we see how the sense of one's living body is also simultaneously a sensibility *through* which we perceive what is around us, which is experienced through or "by means of" the lived body.[18] Although, when Heidegger explains what is disclosed by a person's mood and attunement, contending that moods (generally speaking) *are* indeed revelatory, he acknowledges that in what he calls "bad moods," the human being "becomes blind to itself" and "the surrounding world" is "veiled."[19] In another discussion of "bad mood," he specifically remarks that conditions of physical illness and other bodily states are never merely internal but lived through. Because affective feeling, he writes,

> as feeling oneself to be, always just as essentially has a feeling for beings as a whole, every bodily state involves some way in which the things around us and the people with us lay a claim on us or do not do so. When our stomachs are "out of sorts" they can cast a pall over all things. What would otherwise seem indifferent to us suddenly becomes irritating and disturbing; what we usually take in stride now impedes us.[20]

Personhood, 254. On the perceptibly embodied quality of moods, see Ronald de Sousa, *The Rationality of Emotion*, 47; and Matthew Ratcliffe, *Feelings of Being*, 184–185.

18. See Edmund Husserl, *Phenomenology and the Foundations of the Sciences*, 9–10.

19. "Something like an affect would never come about under the strongest pressure and resistance . . . if attuned being-in-the-world were not already related to having things in the world matter to it in a way prefigured by moods."—Heidegger, *Being and Time*, § 29. The passages about "bad moods" are from this section too. Cf. Quentin Smith, "On Heidegger's Theory of Moods," 220–221.

20. Martin Heidegger, *Nietzsche*, 99. On bodily illness, and how the psyche "pervades the whole organism," see also Heidegger, *Zollikon Seminars*, 77–79. Cf. Cataldi, *Emotion, Depth, and Flesh*, 93–94.

Heidegger concedes that certain moods *can* hinder our understanding—closing us off from the surrounding world, rather than making us receptive to it. So even a philosopher who places great emphasis on what our attunements can make known to us, by showing us how we are doing as well as how things are going in the world, concedes that *some* moods are not trustworthy.

WHY MOODS CAN REVEAL ASPECTS OF THE TRUTH

All of these worries about our moods lending a subjective coloration to the world in a contaminating manner, either distorting everything we perceive or filtering out any features of the world that are discordant with our own state of mind, may deter us from accepting that truthfulness is at stake in our current or characteristic attunement. But, to begin by pushing back against the last of these worries (which I mentioned at the end of the prior section): what is it like when we find ourselves in a depressive, languid, or apathetic condition, which includes a morbid sense of our own body as heavy and sluggish, as if it were "getting in our way" and obstructing us from action? Is this not also, simultaneously, a feeling that the world withdraws out of reach because it affords us no clear opportunities to become meaningfully engaged—that enticing possibilities (as far as we can discern) are less available to us? It is similar to the case in which I am bored, and I feel that the world is "dull and uninviting,"[21] even if this is because of a bodily condition such as chronic fatigue, anemia, or overexertion. As Merleau-Ponty points out, it is not possible "to set limits to physiological explanation" *or* "to set limits to

---

21. John Russon, *Human Experience*, 44–45.

consciousness," to say where a merely "internal" corporeal affliction ends and where the embodied mind's openness toward the world begins.[22] For this reason, I think the burden of proof ought to lie on those who argue that a mood is just an inner somatic and affective state that stretches out into the world, tainting our sense of things and persons.[23] That a mood is "about nothing" should not be our default assumption. Such an assumption leads us to imagine that a preference for pleasant rather than painful moods is as light a matter as a preference for sweet flavors over bitter ones. And this would be yet another way to trivialize our affective experience, by telling ourselves not to take it seriously. Especially when thinking about our overall emotional outlook, we should refrain from making this mistake. Fortunately, there has been increased appreciation (and a growing body of evidence to confirm) that indiscriminately maximizing "good moods" impairs cognition:[24] and that even depressive states may be "truthful" or "reasonable" in that they "capture important truths" and accurately depict actual "states of affairs in the world," and are thus misunderstood if regarded as nothing other than unwelcome ailments.[25] For any mood, we ought to assume that there could be a "peculiar truth or manifestness that lies in this attunement as in every attunement in general."[26]

---

22. Maurice Merleau-Ponty, *Phenomenology of Perception*, 142. Cf. Giovanna Colombetti, *The Feeling Body*, 13–14 & 79–80. She provides the example of how *the way the world appears* and *how I feel* are unified in experience just as the warmth of the bathwater and the warmth of my skin when I'm immersed in that water are not distinguished.

23. Alluding to Heidegger, *Being and Time*, § 29. On the sense in which every mood contains its implicit (not theoretical or thematized) understanding, see also *Being and Time*, § 68. Regarding what follows, see Valérie de Prycker, "Critical Remarks on Shortcuts to Happiness."

24. See, e.g., Joseph P. Forgas, "On the Downside of Feeling Good," 303–313 (with references).

25. Jennifer Hansen, "Affectivity," 37–38; George Graham, "Melancholic Epistemology," 407–419.

26. Martin Heidegger, *Fundamental Concepts of Metaphysics*, 138–139.

That every mood shows only what lies in its focus, in Emerson's terms, could be nothing worse than a sign of how completely our attention is oriented by moods: and we are "selectively attentive *whenever* we adopt a point of view," whether it be affective or "moral, prudential, or scientific."[27] Even the outlook appropriate to theoretical cognition is not the absence of mood, the entire obliteration of perspective, but one way of being attuned to the world. Think of the manner in which we must view the area at the airport where arriving passengers enter the main terminal, if we are gathering data about how many have arrived each hour: our care for getting an accurate count is what ought to orient our awareness, and any other concern that might change our state of mind (even something as innocuous as being moved to wonder whether the fish market will still be open when it's time to go home, and hoping that it will be) is irrelevant right now, and would interfere with the kind of affective attention we need to be paying. On the other hand, if we are awaiting a particular arriving passenger, then it would be a distraction to keep count of how many people are entering the terminal, or to start feeling curious about how many of them are wearing a new cut of jeans, rather than being disposed to take notice of the friendly face of the person whom we are there to greet. That we *have* a vantage point, and are selectively attentive through our emotional attunement, does not prove that mood in general is a *contaminant*—particularly if it is true that a mood-free perspective is not available to us, and that we get out of one mood only by getting into another. Although the metaphor of discoloration lends itself to us so easily, we should

27. Cheshire Calhoun, "Subjectivity and Emotion," 109. My emphasis. Cf. Alison Jaggar, "Love and Knowledge," 160–161: observation involves "selection and interpretation," and "what is selected and how it is interpreted are influenced by emotional attitudes." See also Alexander Nehamas, *Nietzsche*, 48–50. On this selectivity of attention, including how it moves us to retrieve mood-congruent memories, see Joseph LeDoux, *Synaptic Self*, 222.

ask ourselves if this is because we are envisioning the most reliable point of view as "pure" and clear of any determinate characteristics, as no human standpoint ever *can* be. To see is always to see from somewhere, *and* in some way.

In an unhappy mood, we notice saddening features of the world and find sad memories coming to mind: as long as these aspects of our world and our past are not our own delusional projections, however, this way of being "tuned in" need not involve any falsehood or distortion. Likewise, if a war veteran while in a nostalgic mood recalls at the moment only the joyful camaraderie shared with fellow soldiers, what would make this a flawed epistemic outlook would be if these memories of joyful camaraderie were the *only* truths about the experience of war that the soldier *ever* felt aware of—just as a sad person would be in a deplorable condition if her affective disposition prevented her from *ever* perceiving anything besides what further reinforced her prevailing sadness. It is via our moods that we apprehend in our environment everything which in its existence or nonbeing, in how it is doing, matters to me, can register with me, and be recognized as significant.[28] What makes it a shame to be trapped too predominantly or exclusively in a depressive mood (or a mood of nostalgic sentimentality, or of being surrounded by vague threats against which I must be on guard) is that the way the world seems to us when we are depressed, or in another affective state, is not the *only* way it is.

Speaking of what he calls the epistemology of moods, and bringing forward an Emersonian and Thoreauvian idea, Stanley Cavell invites us to take seriously the claim "that moods must be taken

---

28. Alluding here to Merleau-Ponty, who himself is paraphrasing and citing Scheler's *Formalism*: see *Phenomenology of Perception*, 274. Again, see Heidegger, *Being and Time*, §§ 29–30.

as having at least as sound a role in advising us of reality as sense-experience has; that, for example," finding in the world "the qualities 'mean' or 'magnanimous' . . . may be no less objective or subjective than . . . attributing to [an apple] the colors red or green."[29] Thoreau, for instance, claims that many attunements can lead us "to a perception of the truth," and that we thus ought to respond to things "in various moods" and "from many points of view," in order to know the world in its varied aspects.[30] That meanness or magnanimity, just like inconsiderate remarks and kind gestures, *could* be part of the fabric of reality, is more than many philosophers will be prepared to acknowledge. Yet we are all too readily taken in by axiological nihilism. In observing that the qualities we perceive are dependent on the meeting between self and world, we are easily led to conflate several ways in which our subjectivity is involved. The features of the world that cannot be revealed except through our faculties are not *for that reason* unreal, nor are they mistaken attributions to our surroundings of what in fact dwells *entirely* within us. Few, if any, perceived qualities depend completely on the perceiver and not at all on the object. Perhaps the nature of axiological reality and our emotional perspective on it need to be understood as interdependent, in ways that we have yet to appreciate well philosophically. The world revealed through our affective feelings, and through our entire temperament and affective outlook, is one in which a plurality of (always contentious) values exist. It therefore

29. Cavell, *The Senses of Walden*, 124–127. McDowell points out that the contrast between world-experience that is *less* conspicuously dependent on the subject and that which is *more* so "is not a contrast between veridical and illusory experience." See *Mind, Value, and Reality*, 136. See also *Mind, Value, and Reality*, 145: here, McDowell adds that both values and evaluative outlooks are essentially "contentious."

30. Henry David Thoreau, journal entries of 4 November 1851 and 24 March 1857, cited in Furtak, "The Value of Being," 124–125.

makes sense, both to believe that one's experience of a situation *may* be legitimate or accurate, *and* to bear in mind also that even a truthful emotional apprehension is likely to capture only one "side" of the truth. Nietzsche notes that a "diversity of perspectives and affective interpretations" are "useful to knowledge," due to the multifaceted and pluralistic world of value that we inhabit.[31] I have already commented on the sense in which what we are able to know depends upon our attunement or our way of caring. Yet what shows up for us at any particular moment is not exclusively delimited by what mood we happen to be in. An episode of emotion can erupt into our awareness at any moment, making us aware of another side of the truth.

Here is a defense lawyer's firsthand account of being in the courtroom when a man who had been long imprisoned unjustly was—following an arduous battle against racism and fabricated evidence—finally exonerated, as his family members and other supporters rejoiced:

> All of a sudden, I felt strangely agitated. I'd expected to be exuberant. Everyone was in such a good mood. The judge and the prosecutor were suddenly generous and accommodating. It was as if everyone wanted to be sure there were no hard feelings or grudges. Walter [the defendant] was rightfully ecstatic, but I was confused by my suddenly simmering anger. We were about to leave court for the last time, and I started thinking about how much pain and suffering had been inflicted on Walter and his family, [and] the entire community. . . . I thought about how certain it was that hundreds, maybe thousands of other

---

31. Nietzsche, *On the Genealogy of Morals*, Third Essay, § 12 (a section to which we shall return), in Taylor Carman's translation: see *On Truth and Untruth*, 102–103.

people were just as innocent as Walter but would never get the help they need.[32]

What follows is his description of how, in that jubilant and triumphant moment, he felt impelled to make a few remarks about "how easy it was to convict this wrongly accused man for murder," putting him in prison and then on death row, and how difficult it was "to win his freedom after proving his innocence," exemplifying what serious institutional problems and biases remain widely in place despite this victory. Being open to noticing emotionally that something important was at risk of being concealed in a moment of joyful celebration, he was moved to break away from the prevailing mood and to point out that, as I said above, how the world seems to us in a particular affective orientation is not the *only* way it is. In this case, a pervasive mood of joy is capturing *part* of the truth, but not the whole truth—so, by becoming momentarily angry, the speaker allows other features of the situation to register in his awareness.

That brief narrative demonstrates a few things: first, that although an overall mood disposes us toward specific emotions that are in accordance with our mood, it is possible for an episode of emotion *discordant* with the mood to arise. When it does, as when the lawyer in this story begins to feel "simmering anger," this can echo through one's broader mood—and alter it. The anger in the midst of joy is a felt recognition of significant aspects of the truth to which he had not been attuned a moment before. If this lawyer still feels that it's appropriate to be joyful, *now* his mood is transformed into one of greater affective complexity, which gives him a more

32. Bryan Stevenson, *Just Mercy*, 224–225. The systemic violences that are a large part of US history are also relevant to this lawyer's emotion: see, e.g., Ta-Nehisi Coates, *Between the World and Me*, 6–11.

intricate sense of the world: it is one in which a bleak situation has just been redeemed (such things *do* happen), but in which obstacles to fair treatment continue to be distressingly present. We see what would be—not necessarily false, but simplistic—about *mere* cheerful rejoicing.[33] And this makes us realize that someone who actually *did* simplify the wrongfully imprisoned man's story enough to perceive *nothing* but its joyful outcome might be falsifying it so much that his sense of what has taken place *would* be largely untrue. At the same time, we ought to recognize the superficiality of any account of emotion that cannot make sense of affective experiences such as the lawyer's anger-revised mood: that is, experiences in which one feels an admixture of (for example) ecstatic jubilation and burning outrage.[34] Such an account also assumes a shallow view of the circumstances that we human beings live within. When we feel that the world is not simply good nor simply bad, but that matters are more complex, we are probably right. An attunement shows what lies in its focus, and we can see in this case how a transformation in the lawyer's mood brought more significant truth into view.

Justice (and, by contrast, injustice), bigotry and perjury, as well as the worth of a human being's life, are axiological realities with reference to which we understand the story of a man framed for a murder with which he had nothing to do: if his story affects us, it is because we see it as something other than a series of value-neutral

---

33. See Mark Jefferson, "What Is Wrong with Sentimentality?," 526–527; David Pugmire, *Sound Sentiments*, 129. See also Mikko Salmela, *True Emotions*, 121–122. Giovanna Colombetti draws an analogy between "the relationship between moods and emotional episodes," on the one hand, and "that between climate zones and weather," on the other: *The Feeling Body*, 78–79. I find this image helpful, but more applicable to the relation between temperament and particular moods.

34. I spoke in chapter 4 of theorists, such as Robinson and Greenspan, who cite the fact that one can feel that a situation is good in some respects and bad in others as proof of the irrationality of emotional experience in general. See, e.g., Robinson, *Deeper Than Reason*, 19–20.

facts. If we are unsure what to feel when he is finally released, it is due to the elaborate composite of variegated significance that we apprehend in his case and its wider context—what is realistically facing us is *not* a world upon which our affective attunement is a subjective imposition onto meaningless data. And yet we still hear people, even philosophers who are writing about love and emotion, showing incredulity about (for instance) the notion that a person's life has intrinsic worth. Of another philosophical author who defends this notion, Singer asks: "How does he know this to be the case? His belief is not open to empirical verification."[35] Consulting our own experience, though, we are reminded that the felt significance of what we perceive is, as Scheler and Husserl would agree, the more *initially* given fact—from which we must abstract to construct an artificial, but allegedly more "empirical," reality that is devoid of meaning.[36] What we continue to learn about oxytocin, dopamine, and phenylethylamine in relation to mood states may become useful in ways that are yet unforeseen: this kind of information, however,[37] is misconstrued if interpreted as negating the world-oriented, meaning-responsive nature of emotions

35. Irving Singer, *The Nature of Love*, 3: 402.
36. See, e.g., Max Scheler, *Ressentiment*, 117; Edmund Husserl, *The Crisis of European Sciences and Transcendental Phenomenology*, 53–55 & 99–100. How Johnston and Malabou can dismiss Husserl's critique of scientism as "obsolete" is not clear, since the dismissal is made quickly and without explanation: they are either misconstruing Husserl or misunderstanding the intellectual situation in which we find ourselves. See *Self and Emotional Life*, xi.
37. About which see, e.g., Zdeněk Fišar et al., "Neurotransmission in Mood Disorders"; Vaishnav Krishnan and Eric J. Nestler, "The Molecular Neurobiology of Depression"; Larry J. Young, "Love: Neuroscience Reveals All"; and Arthur Aron et al., "Reward, Motivation, and Emotion Systems Associated with Early-Stage Intense Romantic Love." Although the naturalistically minded Paul Griffiths observes that a long-standing affective disposition "is hardly going to be analyzed as a rapid response which had survival value for our phylogenetic predecessors," Singer and others prefer a more reductive view. See *What Emotions Really Are*, 99. Cf. Ronald de Sousa, *Emotional Truth*, 43–44. Here is Paul Redding's coda: "Reason must navigate on a sea of biological and other natural forces . . . without which it could go nowhere. Affect is our most immediate awareness of [this] fact."—*The Logic of Affect*, 158.

and moods. It should not lead us to mistakenly adopt (as some-how more empirically valid) the impersonal vantage point "from which all is seen but nothing is cared for."[38] Scientific investigation, as Ratcliffe argues, itself requires certain moods, and would hardly be intelligible to a person who was entirely free of attunement:

> In a world devoid of all significance, an objective account of the structure and origin of the universe could be of no more worth than a comprehensive account of the precise configuration of all the grains of sand in a bucket. There would be no motivation for formulating a scientific theory, no sense of it being of any poten-tial interest or consequence. It is doubtful that scientific theo-ries would even be intelligible to someone in such a mood. . . . One would be presented with a series of hollow claims that one might indifferently assent to or deny but which one could not fully *grasp*.[39]

In other words, an observer who is not attuned in *any* way—if, just for the sake of argument, we go along with the idea that such a human being could exist—would not notice or record anything. Rather than being an ideally neutral observer, such a subject would lack the focus and orientation required in order to be capable of investigating and understanding the world. He or she would sim-ply not *feel* aware of *why* that might be worth doing.[40] The imagined

---

38. Margaret Olivia Little, "Seeing and Caring: The Role of Affect in Feminist Epistemology," 125–126.
39. Matthew Ratcliffe, "The Phenomenology of Mood and the Meaning of Life," 362. He adds that anyone who "actually lived" in accordance with the reductively mechanistic views to which many people nominally assent would experience "a derealization so crippling as to prohibit them from assenting to any doctrine" whatsoever. See *Feelings of Being*, 289–292.
40. On the affective orientation of the scientific observer, and the emotions involved in research and discovery (such as what Richard Feynman describes as the *enjoyment of finding things*

attunement-free standpoint, and the model of knowledge which is correlated with it, must be rejected once and for all.

THE VIEW FROM HERE

The manner in which we are attuned to our surroundings at any given time, the mood that we embody, opens us toward what we encounter and conditions how we take it in. Through these dimensions of our affective experience, we have a felt awareness of "the way we find ourselves to be with ourselves," and thereby at the same time how it is "with beings that we ourselves are not." Thus, Heidegger concludes: "Every feeling is an embodiment attuned in this or that way, a mood that embodies in this or that way,"[41] a determinate sense of how (hence, "in this or that way") we are faring, how things stand in our world of concern. Our attunement governs what we perceive and apprehend yet also *how* it seems: far from being objectless or lacking intentional world-directedness, moods *can* be revelatory. Moreover, what they reveal to us are features of the objective world (such as the injustices which led to the false imprisonment of the lawyer's client) *as well as* the contours of our own perspective (such as the lawyer's concern for exactly this kind of social injustice, and his care for the particular man whom he defended). An emotional attunement brings some of our surroundings to light, while also showing what concerns us and our specific *way* of being concerned. It is both outwardly and inwardly revealing. While one person may

---

out), see Paul Thagard, *Hot Thought*, 171–187. Regarding what follows, see also Friedrich Nietzsche, *The Will to Power*, § 560: to speculate about what things are like *entirely* apart from "interpretation and subjectivity," is to entertain a "quite idle hypothesis."

41. Martin Heidegger, *Nietzsche*, 98–100.

perceive and respond to a challenge with a mood of confidence, another is more likely to experience this challenge with nervous anxiety or through the "inferiority complex" that shapes his affective attunement—and that could be deeply ingrained in his cognitive and bodily comportment, but also intensified right now due to an event as slight as just having been looked at by a total stranger in what he perceived as a demeaning way.[42] Thus, on the macroscopic and microscopic levels of focus, one's entire "sedimented" life history *and* a brief recent episode of emotion can be relevant to one's current attunement toward the world.

Whatever may be the present state of our affective point of view, however we are emotionally disposed, our "take" on things is an illustration of what Nietzsche designates as "the perspectival character of existence."[43] That to which we are attuned is only *part* of a larger reality, viewed through a perspective which itself is *partial*. There are more significant truths than could ever be apprehended from one standpoint. Furthermore, the axiologically salient features of the world with which any person has felt acquainted, even if indeed "there to be seen" for one who is suitably attuned, also show how much a person's sense of reality and value is defined by peculiar features of who he or she is.[44] The world as revealed through a

42. Cf. Merleau-Ponty, *Phenomenology of Perception*, 513, on what he calls the "sedimentation of our life" by virtue of which an "attitude towards the world" is established, one which in this case (of the inferiority complex) is clearly an affective orientation. See also David Michael Levin, *The Body's Recollection of Being*, 49–51; Glen Mazis, *Emotion and Embodiment*, 208–209. Speaking about the "differences in our biographies" by virtue of which "we find significance . . . in different places," see Cheshire Calhoun, "Subjectivity and Emotion," 113.

43. Friedrich Nietzsche, *The Gay Science*, § 374. See also § 57, on the human contribution to how things appear.

44. See, e.g., Ronald de Sousa and Adam Morton, "Emotional Truth," 260: the "values" we perceive emotionally "depend in part on who we are." These values "are no less objective for that," but if so, then "what reflects my own individual nature" is "relevant to the objective world of value," i.e., the axiological contours of the world. On personal acquaintance with what affects us emotionally, see Roberts, *Emotions in the Moral Life*, 39–40.

distinct affective outlook must be understood as *real* in its own right yet also emphatically "*for us*," to adopt a phrase used with similar import by both Merleau-Ponty and Hilary Putnam.[45] Because what we are speaking about is the realm of what is emotionally recognized by any one specific person, what is at issue isn't just the world as it can be known by human beings universally, or as it appears to those within a particular society (for whom it will have culturally generic features)—instead, we must be able to appreciate that the world as it is known by *each* of us, emotionally known by each person in a distinct way, is still recognizably *the* world.[46] It is that upon which we *have* a point of view, that which is disclosed in our experience. Borrowing once more from Merleau-Ponty, we could say that in the "encounter between 'us' and 'what is,'" we "are interrogating our experience precisely in order to know how it opens us to what is not ourselves."[47] We must appreciate how a person's affective perspective can be biographically inflected and idiosyncratic, yet (not despite, but rather *due to* what distinguishes it in its utmost particularity) able to provide an angle of access to what is the case, disclosing important truths about one's surroundings. If we could validate

45. Putnam suggests that the best we can do in our "conceptions of something real" is "*objectivity for us*": see *Reason, Truth, and History*, 55. Merleau-Ponty considers how it can be that "there is *for us* an *in-itself*," since perceived things do exist but are also "inseparable" from the perceiver. See *Phenomenology of Perception*, 82–83 & 373–376.

46. Scheler claims that significant truth and insight might in some cases be available to one person alone: see, e.g., *Formalism in Ethics and Non-formal Ethics of Morals*, 76–78 & 493. In Putnam's terms, *our* conceptions are nonetheless "conceptions of something real." See *Reason, Truth, and History*, 54–55. Yet I think this must also be true for *my* conceptions, for *yours*, for each of ours. Heidegger elaborates: "Something can very well have universal validity and be binding universally [or within a community collectively] and still not be true. Most prejudices and things taken as obvious have such universal validity and yet are characterized by the fact that they distort beings. Conversely, something can indeed be true which is not binding for everyone but only for a single individual." See *Plato's Sophist*, 16–17.

47. Merleau-Ponty, *The Visible and the Invisible*, 159. Cf. "Eye and Mind," 186: in seeing, "the eye accomplishes the prodigious work of opening the soul to what is not soul."

our emotional responses only by appealing to universal consensus, then it would follow that my grief upon the death of someone whom I knew and appreciated as no one else did would qualify as irrational, whereas it *would* be reasonable to grieve the loss of an author or a political leader loved by many. And the significance of a person's life cannot plausibly be understood as varying this much simply as a consequence of how many others happened to know and appreciate him or her.

To return to an example that I brought up earlier, there is a moment in Proust's novel when the main character is overwhelmed by the realization that his grandmother is dead. Although she had passed away a year ago, it is only now for the first time that he learns that she is gone, in that her death and its meaning had not registered in his awareness until this instant. As Beckett comments, it is now in this experience that he learns and knows "that she is dead," and "knows *who* is dead."[48] The narrator "had to recover her alive and tender," not depleted by illness as she had become, "before he could admit her dead." The woman whose kindness toward him seemed boundless, who had comforted him in moments of distress, who loved rereading her favorite book and could gaze in contented rapture for hours out the window at the sea, who reassured him of her presence by gently returning his knocks on the wall between their two rooms at Balbec, would now never respond to him again. All of this is included in what he knows, in knowing *who* has died. Earlier, my point was that to register the significance of such a loss

---

48. Samuel Beckett, *Proust*, 27–30. See chapter 3 above. Proust writes, "I dared not put out my hand to that wall, any more than to a piano on which my grandmother had been playing and which still vibrated from her touch. I knew that I might knock now, even louder, and that I should hear no response, that my grandmother would never come again."—*Cities of the Plain*, 790. On how painfully *isolating* such an experience of loss can be, as one is surrounded by others for whom the loss means nothing, see Stolorow, *World, Affectivity, Trauma*, 43–44; see also *Trauma and Human Existence*, 14–15.

is to be grieved; so until I begin to feel grief, my understanding of what has taken place is lacking *because* I am not passionately agitated in the appropriate manner. And if we do not feel convinced that a person has died, then in an important sense we do not know that she is dead. Now, however, what is most pertinent is that the person who grieves the loss of a loved one can *know* the significance of that person's life *in* feeling aware of what has been lost. Marcel's closeness to his grandmother, and all the features of the relationship they shared, give him a vantage point that makes him aware—as not just any other Parisian contemporary, much less any other human being, *could* be aware—of the distinctive reality that was Bathilde's life. His affective comportment discloses aspects of the truth about this person that no one else might have glimpsed. In this case and in general, it seems that what we love about people includes that "elusive something" which "may be called their total vision of life, as shown in their mode of speech or silence, their choice of words," as well as "their conception of their own lives, what they think attractive or praiseworthy, what they think funny," all of which contribute to making up what Iris Murdoch calls "the texture of a man's being or the nature of his personal vision."[49] And all of this is what can best, if never completely, be known by someone who loves him—not in spite of, but again *due to*, the accidents of circumstance that allow this someone to become attuned to whom or what is loved. For the same reason that it would be unreasonable for us to assume that those who fail to appreciate what *we* love have somehow gone *wrong*,[50] it

49. Murdoch, *Existentialists and Mystics*, 80–81. Cf. Maurice Merleau-Ponty, *Phenomenology of Perception*, 382, on the distinct "style" that we recognize, "in an individual or a writer" whom we love. On Proust's novel itself as a concrete individual that can be known and loved in this manner, see Alexander Nehamas, "Only in the Contemplation of Beauty Is Human Life Worth Living," 9.

50. Cf. Frankfurt, *The Importance of What We Care About*, 90–91.

would be a mistake to expect *everyone* else to confirm intersubjectively what we find in a person, place, social issue, or work of art that moves us—and which we might be uniquely able to perceive. In "the experience of truth," such as the significant truth about his dear grandmother's death that Marcel apprehends, if it were possible "to lay bare and unfold all the presuppositions" of his affective recognition, "we should always find experiences which have not been made explicit, large-scale contributions from past and present," in short "a whole 'sedimentary history.'"[51] What has made Marcel affectively disposed to feel aware of what it means that Bathilde has passed away, to recognize the meaning of *this* other person's life which now has ceased to be, is an intricate history of impressions and interactions that have formed his point of view *on* her separate existence. Diverse biographically subjective factors such as these are enabling conditions of his emotional apprehension.

In such an experience one learns or is reminded of significant truths about self and world, especially about the world of others. Particular other persons are integral to our existence and well-being, as Marcel's grandmother was to his, and this renders us profoundly vulnerable. Moreover, in his grief he discovers much about *his* orientation toward those whom he loves, his own *way* of loving and caring: that, for instance, he is in need of exactly the kind of reliability and reassurance that his grandmother gave him for as long as she was here. Yet no one is *always* here. In relation to less reliable beloved others, his insecurity will bring out a possessive jealousy, which he identifies as "an anxious need to be tyrannical

---

51. Merleau-Ponty, *Phenomenology of Perception*, 459–460. Here, he credits Husserl with the term "sedimentary history." See also Bernard Williams, *Ethics and the Limits of Philosophy*, 51–52, on why the effort to abstract oneself from one's own dispositions might prevent one from forming "an adequate picture of the value of anything."

applied to matters of love."[52] So Marcel's emotional upheaval also informs him about his own fragility in relation to what he loves and cares about, regardless of whether or not this is a truth that he ever accepts. Another person might respond to a similar loss with regret, resignation, anger, or self-blame.[53] Each of these ways of "taking in" a situation emotionally is likely to reveal something about his or her entire way of being and caring. We can, in this manner, learn about our affective standpoint more broadly through particular moments of emotion. Gendlin describes, for instance, how a powerful feeling of what first seems like jealousy, upon hearing a friend tell of a favorable development in his career, and is subsequently deciphered as (more specifically) a "feeling of being left behind," may demonstrate that one's own emotional comportment toward one's work is that it will not allow one to do what one really wishes to be doing.[54] Becoming quite disturbed and disheartened upon hearing news about a violent battle in an international conflict, likewise, shows

52. Marcel Proust, *The Captive*, 112–113. Cf. Peter Goldie, *The Emotions*, 132–140; see also Martha Nussbaum, *Upheavals of Thought*, 462–479. On our fragility in relation to what we love and care about, due to the ungovernable otherness this places at the heart of our identity, see Stanghellini and Rosfort, *Emotions and Personhood*, 147–148.

53. Cf. Cheshire Calhoun, "Subjectivity and Emotion," 118–119. About a character in the narrative that she has spelled out, Calhoun remarks: "Jealousy, anger, self-recrimination, and regret may all be appropriate for *people in general* to feel in situations like Emilio's, but they may not all be appropriate for Emilio." My emphasis. That "biographically subjective" factors can nevertheless be epistemically enabling rather than disabling is an insight I trace to Calhoun's essay. Also, the "individual differences" noted by psychological studies such as Scherer and Ceschi, "Lost Luggage," are on a continuum with the sort of differences that Calhoun has in mind.

54. Eugene T. Gendlin, *Focusing*, 46–49; see also *Experiencing and the Creation of Meaning*, 35–36. See also Michael Stocker, *Valuing Emotions*, 56–57, including in relation to what follows. Michael Brady comments on how such emotional responses "can therefore promote understanding of our evaluative landscape *and* of the values that we ourselves hold."—*Emotional Insight*, 150–151. In this particular case, the jealous reaction is excessive in context but leads to another, well-founded, emotion. See also Freud, *On Dreams*, 14–25, on finding the basis for apparently irrational affects; he makes a similar point about phobias in *A General Introduction to Psychoanalysis*, 344–355.

me that I view the conflict not as merely another frustrating geopo-
litical affair (as I might have assumed I did, thinking that I was only
cynical about the whole matter) but as a *terrible* situation—one
whose extreme disvalue is *not* outside the range of my concerns. In
experiences such as these we see how aspects of the world, and of
the person, are revealed at once.

Although we "cannot look around our corner" and experience
from within what other "intellects and perspectives there *might* be,"
Nietzsche suggests that we ought at least to avoid "the ridiculous
immodesty of decreeing from our angle that perspectives are *permitted* only from this angle."[55] While trusting in our own way of experiencing the world emotionally, we must also remember that it isn't
uniquely or absolutely valid: ours is not the only view of the truth.
There are indefinitely many affective standpoints and interpretations, as Nietzsche points out in another passage: "There is *only* perspectival seeing, *only* perspectival 'knowing'; and *the more* affects we
bring to expression about any one thing, *the more* eyes—different
eyes—we know how to bring to bear on the same thing, the more
complete will be our 'concept' of that thing, our 'objectivity.'"[56] It
may be, however, that this ideal makes more sense for human beings
to aspire toward collectively than for any one of us to aim for. Each
of us can know only so much of what is emotionally knowable, so a
plurality of different affective subjects is required in order to apprehend more facets of the axiologically multifaceted world. If it is only
through an attunement of one kind or another that we can attend
selectively to *any* of the valenced features of reality—so that the fic-
titious ideal of pure observation from nowhere would, if possible,

---

55. Friedrich Nietzsche, *The Gay Science*, § 374. Cf. Nietzsche, *The Will to Power*, § 481: The
   world "is knowable; but it is *interpretable* otherwise" because it has "countless meanings."
56. Nietzsche, *On the Genealogy of Morals*, Third Essay, § 12, in *On Truth and Untruth*, 103–104.

discover nothing—we should not conclude that a person's affective vision is flawed simply because of its partiality of focus. As Nietzsche ought to have known, it is a dubious goal for a finite being to try to view things from all sides, and feel all plausible emotions about them.[57] My shame and outrage about the institution of slavery in my own country blocks me from genuinely feeling sympathy for those who advocated that individual states ought to have the right to preserve the institution; and, because I feel strongly that the massacre at Wounded Knee was a deeply regrettable tragedy, I cannot extend my sympathies toward the cavalry soldiers who died at Custer's last stand, sad though their loss may have been when viewed from other perspectives (such as those of their family members). Trying to spread ourselves so thin as to see "from everywhere" is dangerously similar to the false aim of attaining a "view from nowhere."

One kind of opportunity to widen our emotional outlook is offered to us when we love a friend who (in some respect, or in many respects) views the world differently, and feels differently about it, than we do. To understand better this person's affective *take* on the world, we must endeavor to appreciate how things *seem* through the lens of their subjectivity. Yet in order to imagine what another person, given her character, beliefs, and values is undergoing, instead of what we ourselves would feel in her situation, we need to develop "a sensitivity to the specific detail of the subjective stance of another."[58]

---

57. Here I am in agreement with Nehamas, *Nietzsche: Life as Literature*, 56. Lanier Anderson's *apologia* for Nietzsche's perspectivism, while textually well founded, derives from the Nietzschean insight that "different perspectives reveal different aspects of things" the implication that what we should seek is to discover "the limitations of our own perspective" and pursue "broader and less idiosyncratic" points of view, even if "we can never escape the limitation of perspective."—"Truth and Objectivity in Perspectivism," 18–21. This way of reading Nietzsche preserves an assumption that Nietzsche himself invites us to question: namely, that it is a kind of embarrassment, and also an epistemic handicap, to occupy a finite perspective.

58. McDowell, "Functionalism and Anomalous Monism," 396. Cf. Lawrence Blum, "Compassion," 510.

The difficulty of this task can hardly be overstated. "The grief and the anger of another have never quite the same significance for him as they have for me," and even if I am undertaking a shared project with my friend Paul, nonetheless "it does not appear in the selfsame light to both of us, we are not both equally enthusiastic about it, or at any rate not in quite the same way, simply because Paul is Paul and I am myself."[59] The unique vision or temperament of a person is described by Ronald de Sousa as "the mystery of personality," the "labyrinth of another's being"; as he adds, "the worlds of value," that is, "of emotional reality with which individual temperament and history endows us," are "just accessible enough . . . for us to know that they are irreducibly different."[60] When we do glimpse to some degree how the world appears to another person whose affective standpoint we trust, we realize that a "sharing of values and perspectives" and "a similar sense of what is important and what is worth doing" are not the only basis of our bond with each other: rather, "the specific difference" in our emotional outlooks is "absolutely important."[61] This is because our own view can be broadened when we appreciate

59. Merleau-Ponty, *Phenomenology of Perception*, 414–415. Proust's narrator remarks upon "that unknowable thing which . . . another person's life invariably is to us."— *The Captive*, 73–74. Not *entirely* knowable, he means (or ought to mean). See also Marion, *In Excess*, 126–127: "Only the one who has lived with the life and the death of another person knows to what extent he or she does not know the other." Cf. Nussbaum, *Political Emotions*, 173.

60. De Sousa, *The Rationality of Emotion*, 329–330. Cf. Joshua Landy, *Philosophy as Fiction*, 60–63. In spite of the "pluralism of values" which is entailed by de Sousa's axiological realism, he asserts that "we should not give up" on the notion that "our emotions connect us to the real world"—this world itself presumably being a multifaceted one, aspects of which are revealed by different emotions, as I pointed out above.

61. Richard J. White, *Love's Philosophy*, 27–28. He emphasizes how love and friendship involve the ways in which our evaluative standpoints are similar *and* the ways in which they differ. "Personal vision" is a phrase employed by William James in *A Pluralistic Universe*, 10–11: and these visions, he adds, "are usually not only our most interesting but our most respectable contributions to the world in which we play our part." See also William J. Wainwright, *Reason and the Heart*, 85–86.

(even if we do not come to share) aspects of the "otherness" *in* another's perspective—what, in her "personal vision" or way of being attuned, is unlike our own. Because what is at stake in our affective outlook is the apprehension of axiological reality, or the disclosure of being and value to the emotional knower, becoming sensitive to the attunement of another person enables us to know other sides of the truth and other significant truths.[62] At the same time, encountering different perspectives always poses a challenge and can even pose a threat to our own felt sense of how the world is. Truly acknowledging other affective standpoints is never easy to do, and is *feasible* only to a limited degree.

A pluralistic and perspectival conception of truth must concur with Merleau-Ponty that a thing is not accurately seen "from nowhere," but rather "from everywhere."[63] As I mentioned above, however, neither seeing things from all sides nor feeling all plausible emotions about them is an achievable ideal for a finite being. Hence arise "the many misunderstandings that so often separate persons of different temperament."[64] In the following narrative excerpt, what is proximally misunderstood by each of two characters is how the other feels about cemeteries, based upon what features of a cemetery each is familiar with by virtue of what they have experienced. As we see, each of their affective impressions is well grounded. For Sabina, "the only word that evoked in her

---

62. See Ronald de Sousa, *Emotional Truth*, 59–62; William A. Luijpen, *Existential Phenomenology*, 322. See also Cheshire Calhoun, "Subjectivity and Emotion," 120–121. She observes that to be critical of another person's emotional perspective, her "subjective style of thinking," is "to criticize the person, her memories, her way of life," as well as her evaluative framework.

63. *Phenomenology of Perception*, 79. Iris Murdoch writes that "to do philosophy is to explore one's own temperament, and yet at the same time to attempt to discover the truth." See Murdoch, *The Sovereignty of Good*, 46; *Existentialists and Mystics*, 337.

64. Kierkegaard, *Papers and Journals: A Selection*, 26 (entry of 29 July 1835, I A 68). Cf. Sharon Krishek, *Kierkegaard on Faith and Love*, 6–7.

a sweet, nostalgic memory of her homeland was the word 'cemetery.'" This is why:

> Cemeteries in Bohemia are like gardens. The graves are covered with grass and colorful flowers. When the sun goes down, the cemetery sparkles with tiny candles. . . . No matter how brutal life becomes, peace always reigns in the cemetery. . . . Against a backdrop of blue hills, they were as beautiful as a lullaby.

For Franz, on the other hand, "a cemetery was an ugly dump of stones and bones,"[65] and this is the only emotional connotation that cemeteries held for him. Later on in the novel, in another location, Sabina is feeling upset and, "according to her old habit, she decided to calm herself by taking a walk in a cemetery." This time, however, she is struck by the overdone grandeur of the gravestones:

> The cemetery was vanity transmogrified into stone. Instead of growing more sensible in death, the inhabitants of the cemetery were sillier than they had been in life. Their monuments were meant to display how important they were. . . . She thought about that stone all day. Why had it horrified her so? . . . Suddenly she missed Franz terribly. When she told him about her cemetery walks, he gave a shiver of disgust and called cemeteries bone and stone dumps. A gulf of misunderstanding had immediately opened between them. Not until [now] did she see what he meant. She was sorry to have been so impatient with him.

Seeing an aspect of the world in the way that Franz had seen it, feeling moved the way he had been moved by it, Sabina realizes that

---

65. Milan Kundera, *The Unbearable Lightness of Being*, 104.

with more time she and Franz might have grown to understand one another's affective vantage points: "But it was too late now."[66] The opportunity is lost for self- and other-understanding. Crucially, the "personal truth" apprehended by each of these characters is nevertheless a truth about the world, very much there to be seen and perceived, while being available only from certain emotional perspectives. Most important of all for my theoretical account is that Franz and Sabina are *not* out of touch with reality due to their selective affective attention: it would be a mistake to describe either of them as if they were in the epistemic position of someone who is hallucinating, dreaming, or seeing an afterimage.

AFFECTIVE TEMPERAMENT, AND TRUTHFULNESS AS AUTHENTICITY

In developmental psychology, the term "temperament" is often used to describe innate emotional tendencies such as shyness.[67] Sometimes this can also include factors in early childhood that influence our affective personality traits into adult life, as well as what is more likely to be genetically inherited and biologically ingrained. Whether we opt for a psychiatric or a phenomenological account of the "manic mode of being-in-the-world," for instance, such an affective tendency may well have a strong basis in our

---

66. Kundera, *The Unbearable Lightness of Being*, 123–124. Regarding what follows, namely the "essential interconnection between person and world," see also Max Scheler, *Formalism in Ethics and Non-formal Ethics of Values*, 393–395.

67. See, e.g., Jerome Kagan et al., "Initial Reactions to Unfamiliarity." See also Mary K. Rothbart, *Becoming Who We Are*, 10–15. See also Kagan, "Temperament"; Kagan and Snidman, *The Long Shadow of Temperament*.

inherited biology (which is not to say *only* in this).[68] Yet I will be using the term "temperament" in a sense that includes, but is not limited to, what is either innate or else acquired early in life through interactions with others and with our environment. Frijda, among others, has written about temperament in such a way as to allow this to include "emotional personality traits" that persist yet remain capable of undergoing shifts at any stage in human experience.[69] The notion of temperament can thus signify a person's entire affective standpoint: her concerns and way of caring, her characteristic attunements, and her manner of responding emotionally to particular situations. "Temperament" as a person's overall way of being affectively disposed, then, pertains to what William James depicts as one's "individual way of . . . seeing and feeling the total push and pressure of the cosmos."[70] In this final section I will consider how an emotional temperament can hang together—be true to itself—and also be accurately revelatory of the world.

Coherence as an ideal in affective life means more than just avoiding or resolving blatantly contradictory evaluations and concerns, or maintaining internal consistency in one's emotional outlook. It also means being genuinely responsive to the world, so that our temperamental attitudes and forms of attunement remain true to what has deeply moved us and who we have become. No one is, or should wish to be, invulnerable to a new discovery of value that might have a transformative impact on him, making him see and

68. See Ludwig Binswanger, *Being-in-the-World*, 143–145; see also Matthew Ratcliffe, *Experiences of Depression*, 181–183. On some of the biographical reasons for becoming "a student of moods," and of such conditions as mania, see Kay Redfield Jamison, *An Unquiet Mind*, 4–5.

69. Nico Frijda, "Varieties of Affect," 66. See also Peter Goldie, *On Personality*, 10–12.

70. William James, *Pragmatism*, 18. On "the range and kinds of value" accessible to each person, see also David Pugmire, *Sound Sentiments*, 112–113.

feel differently than he did before.[71] It is, as Salmela claims, essential to emotional authenticity "that one's coherent pattern of emotions, beliefs, and values" be "open to revision and change," making authenticity into a "regulative ideal,"[72] because any state of coherence among our affective dispositions is also a stage in an ongoing process of becoming that remains unfinished for as long as we continue to live. This can include, not only newly revealed significance, but later reappraisals of earlier passions. After deciding to reunite years later with a former teacher, lover, and friend, Hannah Arendt described this reunion as "the confirmation of an entire life," saying that her decision to visit Heidegger "mercifully saved me from committing the only really inexcusable act of infidelity and forfeiting my life."[73] Evidently what Arendt has in mind is the significance in her own life of what she and Heidegger had glimpsed in each other, including the potential he saw in her. The *fidelity* to which she refers has to do with being *true* to the self-defining affective experience, the event of having loved and been loved in return, which had a meaning that she appreciated only later, when she saw that betraying this love would constitute a betrayal of who she had become. This newly revealed emotional insight had to be incorporated into

71. As Jonathan Lear points out, "There is no such thing as an ego that is invulnerable to trauma," as "the psychological achievements of maturity do tend to be somewhat fragile. There is always and everywhere the possibility of being overwhelmed." See *Happiness, Death, and the Remainder of Life*, 110. See also Sue L. Cataldi, *Emotion, Depth, and Flesh*, 151–158: profound emotional experiences can bring about "changes in our identities" which make us realize that self and world no longer appear in the same light. Hence, for one who has been "deeply emotionally affected," the world may not seem the way it used to anymore.

72. Mikko Salmela, *True Emotions*, 98–99. Kym Maclaren remarks upon how some overwhelming affective experiences place us "into question," threatening our ability to make sense of what we are experiencing. See "Emotional Clichés and Authentic Passions," 59–60.

73. Hannah Arendt and Martin Heidegger, *Letters*, 59–60 (Letter no. 48). In what follows, I rely upon Iain Thomson's insightful interpretation. See his "Thinking Love."

a coherent, revised understanding of her life as a whole:[74] what she experienced was an affective recognition of deeply felt significance from an earlier time, a significance that was renewed and whole-heartedly endorsed.

What kind of truthfulness about oneself is at issue here? It shares something in common with what Nietzsche describes when speaking of how a human being can "get to know himself" by looking at what he has "truly loved" and through this finding "a law, the funda-mental law of your authentic self."[75] It involves an acknowledgment of what has mattered most to you, and how this has formed your affective standpoint, your set of concerns and way of being attuned, your distinct manner of emotionally apprehending meaning in the world. Because we are finite, we cannot appreciate everything of value, and consequently there is much that simply will not register in our awareness;[76] we can, however, strive to be true to what has deeply moved us, that for which we have felt an affinity. Profound affective upheavals bring to light our values and ideals, informing

74. Again, see Iain Thomson, "Thinking Love." Cf. David Pugmire, *Sound Sentiments*, 189–190. Also relevant is this comment by Annette C. Baier: "We can change our minds, or, if I am right, our hearts, about how much something mattered," but "changed values and priorities will usually show their genealogical links with earlier concerns."—"Feelings That Matter," 209–211.

75. Friedrich Nietzsche, "Schopenhauer as Educator," 174. See also Ronald de Sousa, "Truth, Authenticity, and Rationality," 328–329; Mikko Salmela, *True Emotions*, 83–87; and Quentin Smith, *The Felt Meanings of the World*, 292–294. On what Nietzsche famously por-trays as "the problem of nihilism," namely how to "find life to be significant . . . and worth affirming in light of the many reasons to be dissatisfied, perplexed, and skeptical about the value of the world," see James D. Reid, *Being Here Is Glorious*, 9–12. See also Furtak, *Wisdom in Love*, 108–136.

76. For good or evil, that is. As Nagel reflects, "the world comes to an end" for so many thou-sands of people each day, yet "we cannot regard all those deaths" with the interest they would deserve, for "sheer emotional overload prevents it, as anyone who has tried to sum-mon a feeling adequate to an enormous massacre knows."—*The View from Nowhere*, 230. On our finitude, and that for which we have an affinity, see Anthony Rudd, *Self, Value, and Narrative*, 133–137.

us of what someone or something means to us—how significant it *still* is, or is once again, or *that* it has become less so—thereby revising our understanding of self and world. I say "self and world" both, because learning more about how *my* world seems, by virtue of my emotional temperament, is also learning more about *the* world. When I am moved by a poem, I might clarify my sense of how much poetry means in *my* life while also appreciating an aspect of *this* poet's work that I had not previously recognized, but which is really there—and which I can now try to point out to others. Likewise, when an account of solitary confinement moves me to recognize for the first time what an inhumane form of punishment this is, a significant injustice in my society becomes apparent to me: one to which I had been blind before.

The way these things affect me emotionally also reveals my own temperamental perspective, what concerns me and how it does. If I am someone who cares about what is authentic and what is not in my affective experience, then I must engage in a healthy amount of self-questioning: my irascibility today must be taken into consideration when I ask myself how genuinely offensive *was* the remark to which I reacted, and so also must my characteristic way of being oversensitive to this sort of thing (if indeed I am). Similarly, when parents get inordinately upset at a child for some minor incident of misbehavior, there is likely an overall exasperation with the demands of parenting lurking underneath their excessive momentary emotion: this is yet another reason not to tell ourselves that our emotions disclose nothing true from which we could learn.[77] Simply

---

77. As Karen Horney says, we must not "be too easily satisfied with ready-at-hand explanations for a disturbance." Someone who has become extremely upset "about being cheated out of a dime" by a taxi driver "should not be content to tell himself that after all no one likes to be cheated," as a person "suffering from an acute depression must be skeptical about explaining his state on the basis of world conditions" alone. Thus "truthfulness" becomes

"pretending that a slight or disappointment isn't genuinely painful, or denying that we love someone whom we do, may culminate in a *complex* of denials strung together" until "we no longer know how we feel or what we believe."[78] By the same token, it is not harmless to indulge in moments of emotional dishonesty, sentimentally falsifying some aspect of the world or misrepresenting our care for it as serious when in fact it is temporary and superficial—*especially* if we never subject this response to critical examination. These kinds of self-deception can leave us in confusion about who we are and about what concerns us. The truth about my own emotional perspective is a sort of truth that cannot fail to interest me, and there exist facts about my affective outlook that I must *own* before I can even raise the question of whether or not I should reflectively endorse them.

The "real world includes the inner world,"[79] and our "inward" affective orientation is precisely what gives us access to outward reality. One's temperament, one's overall affective orientation or emotional way of seeing, never becomes an object that we can observe because it is that *through* which we look. It is disclosed in the ways that the world's significance shows up for us, and insofar as we know our own temperament, we can identify what about it we should try to adjust or alter (and, in the meantime, correct against), as well as the ways in which we can affirm it as revealing who we truly are and wish to be—and also what we care about (and wish to care about).

---

the relevant ideal in affective self-interpretation.—*Self-Analysis*, 153 & 256. Cf. Katherine Withy, "Owned Emotions," 25–26. See also Freud, *A General Introduction to Psychoanalysis*, 344–346, on the various "styles" of phobia that serve as masks for death anxiety.

78. M. Guy Thompson, *The Truth about Freud's Technique*, 130–132. He comments further upon the importance of "getting at the truth of experience and learning to accept the realities of a sometimes tragic existence," understood by Freud as "a form of ethic that is solely committed to *determining what is so*."

79. David Pugmire, *Sound Sentiments*, 53. On our perspective, or the framework through which we experience, see also Joshua Landy, *Philosophy as Fiction*, 113–116.

Of course, there is no infallibly secure ground upon which to make these evaluations and reappraisals, as Merleau-Ponty notes when he says that even in what I later come to regard as "illusory love,"

> I was willingly united to the loved one, she was for a time truly the vehicle of my relationships with the world. When I told her that I loved her, I was not "interpreting," for my life was in truth committed to a form which, like a melody, demanded to be carried on.

And he points out that

> Misguided love is revealed as such when I return to my own self. The difference is intrinsic. But as it concerns the place of feeling in my total being-in-the-world . . . and also as, in order to discern its mistaken nature I require a knowledge of myself which I can gain only through disillusionment, ambiguity remains.[80]

Ambiguity remains, that is, because affective self-understanding is by its nature always a work in progress, and the point of view from which we evaluate is *also* that which we are evaluating. A later outlook is not for that reason necessarily a more accurate one, as any emotionally honest person must acknowledge. The sad "misunderstandings that so often separate persons of different temperament,"[81] which I mentioned above, can even exist between younger and older versions of oneself. Someone who experienced during adolescence a spiritual crisis which he later interpreted as having been

---

80. Maurice Merleau-Ponty, *Phenomenology of Perception*, 439–444.
81. Again, see Søren Kierkegaard, *Papers and Journals: A Selection*, 26 (entry of 29 July 1835, I A 68).

nothing other than a psychotic episode may eventually decide that he got it right the first time, that his intervening years of complacent denial were just an attempt to talk himself out of taking seriously a religious experience. And the person whose passion for television was formed in the middle of life is right to keep in mind that during her young adulthood she would have regarded such a passion as corrupting her aesthetic standards, and to feel at least mildly bothered by this awareness.[82]

When we ask ourselves these questions, what is at stake is nothing less than the truth and meaning of one's own life. Yet a fallible capacity can still be one that enables us to know, and—as I have argued from the beginning—it is through our emotions that we perceive meaning in life, and by feeling emotions that we are able to recognize the value or significance of anything whatsoever. Furthermore, the kind of knowledge that our affective responses and dispositions are capable of providing to us is distinct from what other modes of knowing can bring. What our emotions reveal is our sense of reality and value—in other words, of "reality as we have felt it to be."[83] Whether or not this seems to us *well worth knowing about* must itself depend above all on what I have called our affective temperament. To take seriously what can be known through our emotions, I think, one must believe "in truth, in truthfulness, and in the meaning of an individual life."[84] This book has been an invitation to do so.

---

82. Adapting an example from Alexander Nehamas, "Only in the Contemplation of Beauty Is Human Life Worth Living," 13–14.

83. Marcel Proust, *Time Regained*, 277. This, the narrator says, is "our true life."

84. Bernard Williams, *Ethics and the Limits of Philosophy*, 198.

BIBLIOGRAPHY

E. M. Adams, *Ethical Naturalism and the Modern World-View* (Chapel Hill: University of North Carolina Press, 1960).

Charles Altieri, *The Particulars of Rapture: An Aesthetics of the Affects* (Ithaca, NY: Cornell University Press, 2003).

Adam K. Anderson et al., "Neural Correlates of the Automatic Processing of Threat Facial Signals," *Journal of Neuroscience* 23 (2003): 5627–5633.

R. Lanier Anderson, "Truth and Objectivity in Perspectivism," *Synthese* 115 (1998): 1–32.

Hannah Arendt and Martin Heidegger, *Letters: 1925–1975*, translated by Andrew Shields (Orlando, FL: Harcourt, 2004).

Jason M. Armfield, "Cognitive Vulnerability: A Model of the Etiology of Fear," *Clinical Psychology Review* 26 (2006): 746–768.

———. "Manipulating Perceptions of Spider Characteristics and Predicted Spider Fear: Evidence for the Cognitive Vulnerability Model of the Etiology of Fear," *Journal of Anxiety Disorders* 21 (2007): 691–703.

Jason M. Armfield and Julie K. Mattiske, "Vulnerability Representation: The Role of Perceived Dangerousness, Uncontrollability, Unpredictability and Disgustingness in Spider Fear," *Behaviour Research and Therapy* 34 (1996): 899–909.

Claire Armon-Jones, *Varieties of Affect* (Toronto: University of Toronto Press, 1991).

John Armstrong, *Conditions of Love* (New York: Norton, 2003).

Magda B. Arnold, *Emotion and Personality*, 2 vols. (New York: Columbia University Press, 1960).

———. "Historical Development of the Concept of Emotion," *Philosophical Studies* 22 (1974): 147–157.

Arthur Aron, Helen E. Fisher, Debra J. Mashek, Greg Strong, Haifang Li, and Lucy L. Brown, "Reward, Motivation, and Emotion Systems Associated with Early-Stage Intense Romantic Love," *Journal of Neurophysiology* 94 (2005): 327–337.

Arthur Aron, Helen E. Fisher, and Greg Strong, "Romantic Love," in *The Cambridge Handbook of Personal Relationships*, edited by Anita L. Vangelisti and Daniel Perlman (Cambridge: Cambridge University Press, 2006), 595–614.

Jorge V. Arregui, "On the Intentionality of Moods," *American Catholic Philosophical Quarterly* 70 (1996): 397–411.

James Averill, "Intellectual Emotions," in *The Emotions: Social, Cultural, and Biological Dimensions*, edited by Rom Harré and W. Gerrod Parrott (London: Sage, 1996), 24–38.

James Averill and Elma P. Nunley, *Voyages of the Heart* (New York: Free Press, 1992).

Albert F. Ax, "The Physiological Differentiation between Fear and Anger in Humans," *Psychosomatic Medicine* 15 (1953): 433–442.

Bernard J. Baars and Nicole M. Gage, *Cognition, Brain, and Consciousness: Introduction to Cognitive Neuroscience*, 2nd edition (Burlington, MA: Academic Press / Elsevier, 2010).

———, *Fundamentals of Cognitive Neuroscience* (Waltham, MA: Academic Press / Elsevier, 2013).

Raja Bahlul, "Emotion as Patheception," *Philosophical Explorations* 18 (2015): 104–122.

Annette C. Baier, "Feelings that Matter," in *Thinking about Feeling: Contemporary Philosophers on Emotions*, edited by Robert C. Solomon (Oxford: Oxford University Press, 2004), 200–213.

Michael D. Barber, *Guardian of Dialogue: Max Scheler's Phenomenology, Sociology of Knowledge, and Philosophy of Love* (Lewisburg, PA: Bucknell University Press, 1993).

Matthias T. S. Barker, "An Echo of Thought in Sight: Affective Perception in Emotional Intentionality" (Senior Thesis, Colorado College, 2009).

Luca Barlassina and Albert Newen, "The Role of Bodily Perception in Emotion," *Philosophy and Phenomenological Research* 89 (2014): 637–678.

Antoine Bechara, Hanna Damasio, and Antonio R. Damasio, "Emotion, Decision Making, and the Orbitofrontal Cortex," *Cerebral Cortex* 10 (2000): 295–307.

Samuel Beckett, *Proust* (New York: Grove Press, 1957).

Aaron Ben-Ze'ev. "Emotion as a Subtle Mental Mode," in *Thinking about Feeling*, edited by Robert C. Solomon (New York: Oxford University Press, 2004), 150–168.

———, *The Subtlety of Emotions* (Cambridge, MA: MIT Press, 2000).

Seth Bernstein, "A Time-Saving Technique for the Treatment of Simple Phobias," *American Journal of Psychotherapy* 53 (1999): 501–512.

Mukul Bhalla and Dennis R. Proffitt, "Visual-Motor Recalibration in Geographical Slant Perception," *Journal of Experimental Psychology: Human Perception and Performance* 25 (1999): 1076–1096.

Ludwig Binswanger, *Being-in-the-World: Selected Papers*, translated by Jacob Needleman (New York: Basic Books, 1963).

Simon Blackburn, *Ruling Passions* (New York: Oxford University Press, 2000).

Eric Blondel, "Nietzsche's Style of Affirmation," in *Nietzsche as Affirmative Thinker*, edited by Yirmiyahu Yovel (Dordrecht: Martinus Nijhoff, 1986), 132–146.

Lawrence Blum, "Compassion," in *Explaining Emotions*, edited by Amélie O. Rorty (Berkeley: University of California Press, 1980), 507–517.

Christopher Bollas, *The Shadow of the Object: Psychoanalysis of the Unthought Known* (New York: Columbia University Press, 1987).

Michael S. Brady, *Emotional Insight* (Oxford: Oxford University Press, 2013).

———, "The Irrationality of Recalcitrant Emotions," *Philosophical Studies* 145 (2009): 413–430.

Linda A. W. Brakel, "Knowledge and Belief: Psychoanalytic Evidence in Support of a Radical Epistemic View," *American Imago* 65 (2008): 427–471.

———, *Unconscious Knowing and Other Essays in Psycho-Philosophical Analysis* (Oxford: Oxford University Press, 2010).

Sally Brampton, *Shoot the Damn Dog: A Memoir of Depression* (New York: Norton, 2008).

Tad Brennan, *The Stoic Life: Emotions, Duties, and Fate* (New York: Oxford University Press, 2005).

Franz Brentano, *Psychology from an Empirical Standpoint*, translated by Antos C. Rancurello, D. B. Terrell, and Linda McAlister (London: Routledge, 1995).

C. D. Broad, "Emotion and Sentiment," *Journal of Aesthetics and Art Criticism* 13 (1954): 203–214.

Berit Brogaard, *On Romantic Love: Simple Truths about a Complex Emotion* (New York: Oxford University Press, 2015).

Leslie Brothers, *Mistaken Identity: The Mind-Brain Problem Reconsidered* (Albany: SUNY Press, 2001).

Robert Brown, *Analyzing Love* (Cambridge: Cambridge University Press, 1987).

Ross Buck, *The Communication of Emotion* (New York: Guilford Press, 1984).

Cheshire Calhoun, "Cognitive Emotions?," in *What Is an Emotion? Classic Readings in Philosophical Psychology*, edited by Robert C. Solomon and Cheshire Calhoun (New York: Oxford University Press, 1984), 327–342.

———, *Moral Aims: Essays on the Importance of Getting It Right and Practicing Morality with Others* (Oxford: Oxford University Press, 2016).

———, "Subjectivity and Emotion," in *Thinking about Feeling*, edited by Robert C. Solomon (New York: Oxford University Press, 2004), 107–121.

Serge Campeau and Michael Davis, "Involvement of the Central Nucleus and Basolateral Complex of the Amygdala in Fear Conditioning Measured with Fear-Potentiated Startle in Rats Trained Concurrently with Auditory and Visual Conditioned Stimuli," *Journal of Neuroscience* 15 (1995): 2301–2311.

Albert Camus, "Losing a Loved One," in *Youthful Writings*, translated by Ellen Conroy Kennedy (New York: Marlowe, 1976), 204–206.

Joshua M. Carlson et al., "Backward Masked Fearful Faces Enhance Contralateral Occipital Cortical Activity for Visual Targets within the Spotlight of Attention," *Social Cognitive and Affective Neuroscience* 6 (2011): 639–645.

Ulrika Carlsson, "Love as a Problem of Knowledge in Kierkegaard's *Either/Or* and Plato's *Symposium*," *Inquiry* 53 (2010): 41–67.

Quassim Cassam, *Self-Knowledge for Humans* (Oxford: Oxford University Press, 2014).

Sue L. Cataldi, *Emotion, Depth, and Flesh* (Albany: SUNY Press, 1993).

Stanley Cavell, *The Claim of Reason* (Oxford: Oxford University Press, 1979).

———, *The Senses of Walden: An Expanded Edition* (Chicago: University of Chicago Press, 1992).

Patricia S. Churchland, *Brain-Wise: Studies in Neurophilosophy* (Cambridge, MA: MIT Press, 2002).

Paul M. Churchland, *Matter and Consciousness* (Cambridge, MA: MIT Press, 1988).

Stephen R. L. Clark, *God's World and the Great Awakening* (Oxford: Oxford University Press, 1991).

Gerald L. Clore, "Why Emotions Require Cognition," in *The Nature of Emotion*, edited by Paul Ekman and Richard J. Davidson (New York: Oxford University Press, 1994), 181–191.

Gerald L. Clore and Andrew Ortony, "Cognition in Emotion: Always, Sometimes, or Never?," in *Cognitive Neuroscience of Emotion*, edited by Richard D. Lane and Lynn Nadel (New York: Oxford University Press, 2000), 24–61.

Ta-Nehisi Coates, *Between the World and Me* (New York: Spiegel and Grau, 2015).

Samuel Taylor Coleridge, *Poems*, edited by J. B. Beer (New York: Knopf, 1991).

Giovanna Colombetti, *The Feeling Body: Affective Science Meets the Enactive Mind* (Cambridge, MA: MIT Press, 2014).

David E. Cooper, *Existentialism*, 2nd edition (Oxford: Blackwell, 1999).

Amy Coplan, "Feeling without Thinking," *Metaphilosophy* 41 (2010): 132–151.

Randolph R. Cornelius, "Gregorio Marañon's Two-Factor Theory of Emotion," *Personality and Social Psychology Bulletin* 17 (1991): 65–69.

Arthur D. Craig, "How Do You Feel? Interoception: The Sense of the Physiological Condition of the Body," *Nature Reviews Neuroscience* 3 (2002): 655–666.

Antonio Damasio, *Descartes' Error: Emotion, Reason, and the Human Brain* (New York: G. P. Putnam, 1994).

———, *The Feeling of What Happens: Body and Emotion in the Making of Consciousness* (New York: Harcourt Brace, 1999).

———, *Looking for Spinoza: Joy, Sorrow, and the Feeling Brain* (Orlando, FL: Harcourt, 2003).

———, "Neuroscience and Ethics," *American Journal of Bioethics* 7 (2007): 3–7.

———, *Self Comes to Mind: Constructing the Conscious Brain* (New York: Pantheon Books, 2010).

Justin D'Arms and Daniel Jacobson, "The Significance of Recalcitrant Emotion (Or, Anti-quasijudgmentalism)," *Royal Institute of Philosophy Supplement* 52 (2003): 127–145.

Joyce Davidson, *Phobic Geographies: The Phenomenology and Spatiality of Identity* (Burlington, VT: Ashgate, 2003).

———, "Neural Substrates of Affective Style and Value," in *Neurobiology of Human Values*, edited by Jean-Pierre Changeaux, Antonio Damasio, Wolf Singer, and Yves Christen (New York: Springer, 2005), 67–90.

Richard J. Davidson, "Parsing Affective Space: Perspectives from Neuropsychology and Psychophysiology," *Neuropsychology* 7 (1993): 464–475.

———, "Seven Sins in the Study of Emotion: Correctives from Affective Neuroscience," *Brain and Cognition* 52 (2003): 129–132.

Richard J. Davidson and Carien van Reekum, "Emotion Is Not One Thing," *Psychological Inquiry* 16 (2005): 16–18.

Ivan E. de Araujo, Edmund T. Rolls, Maria Inés Velazco, Christian Margot, and Isabelle Cayeux, "Cognitive Modulation of Olfactory Processing," *Neuron* 46 (2005): 671–679.

Stanislas Dehaene, *Consciousness and the Brain* (New York: Viking Press, 2014).

John Deigh, "Concepts of Emotions in Modern Philosophy and Psychology," in *The Oxford Handbook of Philosophy of Emotion*, edited by Peter Goldie (Oxford: Oxford University Press, 2010), 17–40.

Craig DeLancey, *Passionate Engines: What Emotions Reveal about Mind and Artificial Intelligence* (New York: Oxford University Press, 2002).

Daniel C. Dennett, *Consciousness Explained* (Boston: Little, Brown, 1991).

Julien A. Deonna and Fabrice Teroni, *The Emotions: A Philosophical Introduction* (New York: Routledge, 2012).

Valérie de Prycker, "Critical Remarks on Shortcuts to Happiness," *Philosophica* 79 (2007): 57–70.

Ronald de Sousa, *Emotional Truth* (New York: Oxford University Press, 2011).

———, "Emotions," in *Thinking about Feeling*, edited by Robert C. Solomon (New York: Oxford University Press, 2004), 61–75.

———, *Love: A Very Short Introduction* (Oxford: Oxford University Press, 2015).

———, *The Rationality of Emotion* (Cambridge, MA: MIT Press, 1987).

———, "The Rationality of Emotions," in *Explaining Emotions*, edited by Amélie O. Rorty (Berkeley: University of California Press, 1980), 127–151.

———, "Truth, Authenticity, and Rationality," *Dialectica* 61 (2007): 323–345.

Ronald de Sousa and Adam Morton, "Emotional Truth," *Aristotelian Society Supplementary Volume* 76 (2002): 247–275.

John Dewey, "The Theory of Emotion," in *The Early Works*, vol. 4: *Early Essays and "The Study of Ethics: A Syllabus"*, edited by Jo Ann Boydston (Carbondale: Southern Illinois University Press, 1971), 152–188.

M. C. Dillon, *Beyond Romance* (Albany: SUNY Press, 2001).

———, *Merleau-Ponty's Ontology*, 2nd edition (Evanston, IL: Northwestern University Press, 1997).

Sabine A. Döring, "The Logic of Emotional Experience," *Emotion Review* 1 (2009): 240–247.

———, "Why Be Emotional?," in *The Oxford Handbook of Philosophy of Emotion*, edited by Peter Goldie (Oxford: Oxford University Press, 2010), 283–301.

———, "Why Recalcitrant Emotions Are Not Irrational," in *Emotion and Value*, edited by Sabine Roeser and Cain Todd (Oxford: Oxford University Press, 2014), 124–136.

George Downing, "Emotion Theory Reconsidered," in *Heidegger, Coping, and Cognitive Science*, edited by Mark A. Wrathall and Jeff Malpas (Cambridge, MA: MIT Press, 2000), 254–270.

Hubert L. Dreyfus, *Being-in-the-World: A Commentary on Heidegger's "Being and Time", Division One* (Cambridge, MA: MIT Press, 1990).

———, "Overcoming the Myth of the Mental," *Proceedings and Addresses of the American Philosophical Association* 79.2 (2005): 47–65.

John Drummond, "'Cognitive Impenetrability' and the Complex Intentionality of the Emotions," *Journal of Consciousness Studies* 11 (2004): 109–126.

Mikel Dufrenne, *The Notion of the A Priori*, translated by Edward S. Casey (Evanston, IL: Northwestern University Press, 1966).

Susan L. Dunston, "Philosophy and Personal Loss," *Journal of Speculative Philosophy* 24 (2010): 158–170.

John Dupré, *Human Nature and the Limits of Science* (New York: Oxford University Press, 2001).

Eva-Maria Düringer, *Evaluating Emotions* (New York: Palgrave Macmillan, 2014).

Donald G. Dutton and Arthur P. Aron, "Some Evidence for Heightened Sexual Attraction under Conditions of High Anxiety," *Journal of Personality and Social Psychology* 30 (1974): 510–517.

Paul Ekman, "An Argument for Basic Emotions," *Cognition and Emotion* 6 (1992): 169–200.

Paul Ekman, Wallace V. Friesen, and Ronald C. Simons, "Is the Startle Reaction an Emotion?," *Journal of Personality and Social Psychology* 49 (1985): 1416–1426.

Paul Ekman, Robert W. Levenson, and Wallace V. Friesen, "Autonomic Nervous System Activity Distinguishes among Emotions," *Science* 221 (1983): 1208–1210.

Hadyn D. Ellis and Andrew W. Young, "Accounting for Delusional Misidentifications," *British Journal of Psychiatry* 157 (1990): 239–248.

Ralph D. Ellis, *Love and the Abyss: An Essay on Finitude and Value* (Chicago: Open Court, 2004).

Phoebe C. Ellsworth, "Levels of Thought and Levels of Emotion," in *The Nature of Emotion*, edited by Paul Ekman and Richard J. Davidson (New York: Oxford University Press, 1994), 192–196.

Jon Elster, *Alchemies of the Mind: Rationality and the Emotions* (Cambridge: Cambridge University Press, 1999).

Ralph Waldo Emerson, *Essays and Lectures*, edited by Joel Porte (New York: Viking Press, 1983).

Dylan Evans, *Emotion: The Science of Sentiment* (Oxford: Oxford University Press, 2001).

Colin Falck, *Myth, Truth, and Literature*, 2nd edition (Cambridge: Cambridge University Press, 1994).

Luc Faucher and Christine Tappolet, "Fear and the Focus of Attention," *Consciousness and Emotion* 3 (2002): 105–144.

M. Jamie Ferreira, *Love's Grateful Striving* (New York: Oxford University Press, 2001).

Klaus Fiedler, "Affective Influences on Social Information Processing," in *Handbook of Affect and Social Cognition*, edited by Joseph P. Forgas (Mahwah, NJ: Lawrence Erlbaum Associates, 2001), 163–185.

Herbert Fingarette, *Self-Deception: With a New Chapter* (Berkeley: University of California Press, 2000).

Zdeněk Fišar, Jana Hroudová, and Jiří Raboch, "Neurotransmission in Mood Disorders," in *Clinical, Research and Treatment Approaches to Affective Disorders*, edited by Mario Juruena (Rijeca, Croatia: InTech, 2012), 191–234.

Helen E. Fisher, *Why We Love* (New York: Henry Holt, 2004).

Helen E. Fisher, Arthur Aron, and Lucy L. Brown, "Romantic Love," *Philosophical Transactions of the Royal Society of London B: Biological Sciences* 361 (2006): 2173–2186.

Philip Fisher, *The Vehement Passions* (Princeton, NJ: Princeton University Press, 2002).

Roger Fitterer, *Love and Objectivity in Virtue Ethics* (Toronto: University of Toronto Press, 2008).

Gemma Corradi Fiumara, *The Mind's Affective Life: A Psychoanalytic and Philosophical Inquiry* (Philadelphia: Taylor & Francis, 2001).

Owen J. Flanagan, *Consciousness Reconsidered* (Cambridge, MA: MIT Press, 1992).

———, "Neuro-Eudaimonics; or, Buddhists Lead Neuroscientists to the Seat of Happiness," in *The Oxford Handbook of Philosophy and Neuroscience*, edited by John Bickle (Oxford: Oxford University Press, 2009), 582–600.

Jonathan Flatley, *Affective Mapping* (Cambridge, MA: Harvard University Press, 2008).

Joseph P. Forgas, "On the Downside of Feeling Good," in *Positive Emotion*, edited by June Gruber and Judith Tedlie Moskowitz (New York: Oxford University Press, 2014), 301–322.

Joseph P. Forgas and Patrick T. Vargas, "The Effects of Mood on Social Judgment and Reasoning," in *Handbook of Emotions*, 2nd edition, edited by Michael Lewis and Jeannette M. Haviland-Jones (New York: Guilford Press, 2000), 350–368.

Harry G. Frankfurt, "Duty and Love," *Philosophical Explorations* 1 (1998): 4–9.

————, *The Importance of What We Care About: Philosophical Essays* (Cambridge: Cambridge University Press, 1988).

————, *Necessity, Volition, and Love* (Cambridge: Cambridge University Press, 1998).

————, *The Reasons of Love* (Princeton, NJ: Princeton University Press, 2004).

————, *Taking Ourselves Seriously and Getting It Right*, edited by Debra Satz (Stanford, CA: Stanford University Press, 2006).

Keith Frankish, *Mind and Supermind* (Cambridge: Cambridge University Press, 2004).

Sigmund Freud, "Consciousness and What Is Unconscious," in *The Ego and the Id*, translated by James Strachey (New York: Norton, 1960), 3–10.

————, *A General Introduction to Psychoanalysis*, translated by G. Stanley Hall (New York: Boni and Liveright, 1920).

————, *Group Psychology and the Analysis of the Ego*, translated by James Strachey (New York: Norton, 1990).

————, *On Dreams*, translated by James Strachey (New York: Norton, 1952).

Alan J. Fridlund, *Human Facial Expression* (San Diego, CA: Academic Press, 1994).

Nico H. Frijda, "Emotion Experience," *Cognition and Emotion* 19 (2005): 473–497.

————, *The Emotions* (Cambridge: Cambridge University Press, 1986).

————, *The Laws of Emotion* (Mahwah, NJ: Lawrence Erlbaum Associates, 2007).

————, "Varieties of Affect: Emotions and Episodes, Moods, and Sentiments," in *The Nature of Emotion*, edited by Paul Ekman and Richard J. Davidson (New York: Oxford University Press, 1994), 59–67.

Nico H. Frijda, Batja Mesquita, Joep Sonnemans, and Stephanie Van Goozen, "The Duration of Affective Phenomena or Emotions, Sentiments, and Passions," *International Review of Studies on Emotion* 1 (1991): 187–225.

Manfred S. Frings, *LifeTime: Max Scheler's Philosophy of Time* (Dordrecht: Kluwer Academic Publishers, 2003).

Rick Anthony Furtak, "Emotion, the Bodily, and the Cognitive," *Philosophical Explorations* 13 (2010): 51–64.

————, "Love as a Relation to Truth," *Kierkegaard Studies Yearbook* 18 (2013): 217–241.

————, "Love as the Ultimate Ground of Practical Reason: Kierkegaard, Frankfurt, and the Conditions of Affective Experience," in *Love, Reason, and Will*, edited by John Davenport and Anthony Rudd (New York: Bloomsbury Academic, 2015), 217–241.

————, "Martha C. Nussbaum's *Political Emotions*," *Phenomenology and the Cognitive Sciences* 13 (2014): 643–650.

————, "Poetics of Sentimentality," *Philosophy and Literature* 26 (2002): 207–215.

————, "The Value of Being," in *Thoreau's Importance for Philosophy*, edited by Rick Anthony Furtak, Jonathan Ellsworth, and James D. Reid (New York: Fordham University Press, 2012), 112–126.

———, *Wisdom in Love* (Notre Dame, IN: University of Notre Dame Press, 2005).

Hans-Georg Gadamer, *Truth and Method*, 2nd edition, translated by Garrett Barden and John Cumming, revised by Joel Weinsheimer and Donald G. Marshall (London: Continuum, 2004).

Sebastian Gardner, *Irrationality and the Philosophy of Psychoanalysis* (Cambridge: Cambridge University Press, 1993).

Tamar Szabó Gendler, "Alief and Belief," *Journal of Philosophy* 105 (2008): 634–663.

Eugene T. Gendlin, *Experiencing and the Creation of Meaning* (Evanston, IL: Northwestern University Press, 1997).

———, *Focusing*, 2nd edition (London: Rider Books, 2003).

———, "Thinking beyond Patterns," in *The Presence of Feeling in Thought*, edited by Bernard D. den Ouden and Marcia Moen (New York: Peter Lang, 1991), 25–151.

James J. Gibson, *The Ecological Approach to Visual Perception* (New York: Psychology Press, 1986).

Paul Gilbert and Kathleen Lennon, *The World, the Flesh, and the Subject: Continental Themes in Philosophy of Mind and Body* (Edinburgh: Edinburgh University Press, 2005).

Peter Goldie, *The Emotions: A Philosophical Exploration* (Oxford: Oxford University Press, 2000).

———, "Getting Feelings into Emotional Experience in the Right Way," *Emotion Review* 1 (2009): 232–239.

———, *The Mess Within: Narrative, Emotion, and the Mind* (Oxford: Oxford University Press, 2012).

———, "Misleading Emotions," in *Epistemology and Emotions*, edited by Georg Brun, Ulvi Doguoglu, and Dominique Quenzle (Burlington, VT: Ashgate, 2008), 149–165.

———, *On Personality* (New York: Routledge, 2004).

———, "Seeing What Is the Kind Thing to Do: Perception and Emotion in Morality," *Dialectica* 61 (2007): 347–361.

Daniel Goleman, *Emotional Intelligence* (New York: Bantam Books, 1995).

Robert M. Gordon, *The Structure of Emotions* (Cambridge: Cambridge University Press, 1987).

George Graham, "Melancholic Epistemology," *Synthese* 82 (1990): 399–422.

O. H. Green, *The Emotions: A Philosophical Theory* (Dordrecht: Kluwer Academic Publishers, 1992).

Patricia Greenspan, "A Case of Mixed Feelings," in *Explaining Emotions*, edited by Amélie O. Rorty (Berkeley: University of California Press, 1980), 223–250.

———, *Emotions and Reasons* (New York: Routledge, 1988).

———, "Learning Emotions and Ethics," in *The Oxford Handbook of Philosophy of Emotion*, edited by Peter Goldie (Oxford: Oxford University Press, 2010), 539–559.

Paul E. Griffiths, "Basic Emotions, Complex Emotions, Machiavellian Emotions," *Royal Institute of Philosophy Supplement* 52 (2003): 39–67.

———, *What Emotions Really Are* (Chicago: University of Chicago Press, 1997).

Paul E. Griffiths and Andrea Scarantino, "Emotions in the Wild," in *The Cambridge Handbook of Situated Cognition*, edited by Philip Robbins and Murat Aydede (Cambridge: Cambridge University Press, 2009), 437–453.

Vladas Griskevicius, Michelle N. Shiota, and Samantha L. Neufeld, "Influence of Different Positive Emotions on Persuasion Processing," *Emotion* 10 (2010): 190–206.

Elizabeth Grosz, "Philosophy," in *Feminist Knowledge: Critique and Construct*, edited by Sneja Marina Gunew (New York: Routledge, 1990), 147–174.

Charles Guignon, "Moods in Heidegger's *Being and Time*," in *What Is an Emotion? Classic Readings in Philosophical Psychology*, edited by Robert C. Solomon and Cheshire Calhoun (New York: Oxford University Press, 1984), 230–243.

York H. Gunther, "The Phenomenology and Intentionality of Emotion," *Philosophical Studies* 117 (2004): 43–55.

Peter Hadreas, *A Phenomenology of Love and Hate* (Burlington, VT: Ashgate, 2007).

Jonathan Haidt, *Moral Tribes: Emotion, Reason, and the Gap between Us and Them* (New York: Penguin, 2013).

———, *The Righteous Mind* (New York: Vintage Books, 2013).

Jennifer Hansen, "Affectivity: Depression and Mania," in *The Philosophy of Psychiatry: A Companion*, edited by Jennifer Radden (Oxford: Oxford University Press, 2004), 36–53.

R. M. Hare, "Nothing Matters," in *The Meaning of Life*, edited by E. D. Klemke (Oxford: Oxford University Press, 1981), 241–247.

Rom Harré, "Emotions as Cognitive-Affective-Somatic Hybrids," *Emotion Review* 1 (2009): 294–301.

Lawrence Hass, *Merleau-Ponty's Philosophy* (Bloomington: Indiana University Press, 2008).

Martin Heidegger, *Basic Concepts of Aristotelian Philosophy*, translated by Robert D. Metcalf and Mark B. Tanzer (Bloomington: Indiana University Press, 2009).

———, *Basic Problems of Phenomenology: Winter Semester 1919/1920*, translated by Scott M. Campbell (New York: Bloomsbury Academic, 2013).

———, *Being and Time*, translated by Joan Stambaugh (Albany: SUNY Press, 1996).

———, *Fundamental Concepts of Metaphysics: World, Finitude, Solitude*, translated by William McNeill and Nicholas Walker (Bloomington: Indiana University Press, 1995).

———, *Logic: The Question of Truth*, translated by Thomas Sheehan (Bloomington: Indiana University Press, 2010).

———, *Nietzsche*, vol. 1: *The Will to Power as Art*, translated by David Farrell Krell (San Francisco: Harper & Row, 1979).

————, *Ontology: The Hermeneutics of Facticity*, translated by John van Buren (Bloomington: Indiana University Press, 1999).

————, "The Origin of the Work of Art," in *Basic Writings*, edited by David Farrell Krell (San Francisco, CA: Harper San Francisco, 1993), 143–212.

————, *Phenomenological Interpretations of Aristotle: Initiation into Phenomenological Research*, translated by Richard Rojcewicz (Bloomington: Indiana University Press, 2001).

————, *Plato's Sophist*, translated by Richard Rojcewicz and André Schuwer (Bloomington: Indiana University Press, 1997).

————, *Zollikon Seminars*, edited by Medard Boss (Evanston, IL: Northwestern University Press, 2001).

Bennett W. Helm, *Emotional Reason* (Cambridge: Cambridge University Press, 2001).

————, "Emotions as Evaluative Feelings," *Emotion Review* 1 (2009): 248–255.

————, *Love, Friendship, and the Self* (New York: Oxford University Press, 2010).

————, "Love, Identification, and the Emotions," *American Philosophical Quarterly* 46 (2009): 39–59.

Kathleen Marie Higgins, review of *Deeper Than Reason* by Jenefer Robinson, *Mind* 116 (2007): 209–212.

Stefan G. Hofmann, "Cognitive Processes during Fear Acquisition and Extinction in Animals and Humans," *Clinical Psychology Review* 28 (2008): 199–210.

Per Holth, "The Persistence of Category Mistakes in Psychology," *Behavior and Philosophy* 29 (2001): 203–219.

Karen Horney, *Self-Analysis* (New York: Norton, 1942).

Rebekka Hufendiek, *Embodied Emotions: A Naturalist Approach to a Normative Phenomenon* (New York: Routledge, 2016).

David Hume, *A Treatise of Human Nature*, 2nd edition, edited by L. A. Selby-Bigge and revised by P. H. Nidditch (Oxford: Oxford University Press, 1978).

Lester Hunt, "Martha Nussbaum on the Emotions," *Ethics* 116 (2006): 552–577.

Edmund Husserl, *Analyses Concerning Passive and Active Synthesis*, translated by Anthony J. Steinbock (Dordrecht: Kluwer Academic Publishers, 2001).

————, *The Crisis of European Sciences and Transcendental Phenomenology*, translated by David Carr (Evanston, IL: Northwestern University Press, 1970).

————, *Experience and Judgment: Investigations in a Genealogy of Logic*, translated by James S. Churchill and Karl Ameriks (Evanston, IL: Northwestern University Press, 1973).

————, *Logical Investigations*, translated by J. N. Findlay (Amherst, NY: Humanity Books, 2000).

————, *Phenomenology and the Foundations of the Sciences*, translated by Ted E. Klein and William E. Pohl (The Hague: Martinus Nijhoff, 1980).

Luce Irigaray, *I Love to You*, translated by Alison Martin (London: Routledge, 1996).

Carroll E. Izard, *Human Emotions* (New York: Plenum Press, 1977).

Alison M. Jaggar, "Love and Knowledge: Emotion in Feminist Epistemology," *Inquiry* 32 (1989): 151–176.

William James, "Are We Automata?," *Mind* 4 (1879): 1–22.

———, *Essays in Philosophy*, edited by Frederick Burkhardt et al. (Cambridge, MA: Harvard University Press, 1978).

———, *Essays in Radical Empiricism* (Cambridge, MA: Harvard University Press, 1976).

———, *A Pluralistic Universe* (Lincoln: University of Nebraska Press, 1996).

———, *Pragmatism* (New York: Meridian Books, 1955).

———, *Psychology: The Briefer Course*, edited by Gordon Allport (Notre Dame, IN: University of Notre Dame Press, 1985).

———, "The Psychology of Belief," *Mind* 14 (1889): 321–352.

———, *The Varieties of Religious Experience* (New York: Vintage Books, 1990).

———, "What Is an Emotion?," *Mind* 9 (1884): 188–205.

Kay Redfield Jamison, *An Unquiet Mind* (New York: Alfred A. Knopf, 1996).

William R. Jankowiak and Edward F. Fischer, "A Cross-Cultural Perspective on Romantic Love," *Ethnology* 31 (1992): 149–155.

Mark Jefferson, "What Is Wrong with Sentimentality?," *Mind* 92 (1983): 519–529.

Gregory Johnson, "LeDoux's Fear Circuit and the Status of Emotion as a Non-cognitive Process," *Philosophical Psychology* 21 (2008): 739–757.

Mark Johnson, *The Meaning of the Body: Aesthetics of Human Understanding* (Chicago: University of Chicago Press, 2007).

Rolf M. Johnson, *Three Faces of Love* (DeKalb: Northern Illinois University Press, 2001).

Adrian Johnston and Catherine Malabou, *Self and Emotional Life: Philosophy, Psychoanalysis, and Neuroscience* (New York: Columbia University Press, 2013).

Mark Johnston, "The Authority of Affect," *Philosophy and Phenomenological Research* 63 (2001): 181–214.

Troy Jollimore, "Love: The Vision View," in *Love, Reason and Morality*, edited by Esther Engels Kroeker and Katrien Schaubroek (London: Routledge, 2017), 1–19.

———, *Love's Vision* (Princeton, NJ: Princeton University Press, 2011).

———, "Meaningless Happiness and Meaningful Suffering," *Southern Journal of Philosophy* 42 (2004): 333–347.

Mairwen K. Jones and Ross G. Menzies, "Danger Expectancies, Self-Efficacy, and Insight in Spider Phobia," *Behaviour Research and Therapy* 38 (2000): 585–600.

Jerome Kagan, "Temperament," in *The Oxford Companion to Emotion and the Affective Sciences*, edited by David Sander and Klaus R. Scherer (Oxford: Oxford University Press, 2009), 389–390.

———, *What Is Emotion?* (New Haven, CT: Yale University Press, 2007).

Jerome Kagan and Nancy Snidman, *The Long Shadow of Temperament* (Cambridge, MA: Harvard University Press, 2004).

Jerome Kagan, Nancy Snidman, and Doreen M. Arcus, "Initial Reactions to Unfamiliarity," *Current Directions in Psychological Science* 1.6 (1992): 171–174.

Immanuel Kant, *Anthropology from a Pragmatic Point of View*, translated by Victor Lyle Dowdell (Carbondale: Southern Illinois University Press, 1996).

Jack Kelly, "Reason and Emotion," *Southern Journal of Philosophy* 10 (1972): 379–382.

Anthony Kenny, *Action, Emotion and Will* (London: Routledge & Kegan Paul, 1963).

George C. Kerner, "Emotions Are Judgments of Value," *Topoi* 1 (1982): 52–56.

Søren Kierkegaard, *Christian Discourses*, translated by Howard V. Hong and Edna Hong (Princeton, NJ: Princeton University Press, 1997).

———, *Journals and Papers*, edited by Howard V. Hong and Edna Hong, 7 vols.,(Bloomington: Indiana University Press, 1967–1978).

———, *Papers and Journals: A Selection*, translated by Alastair Hannay (New York: Penguin, 1996).

———, *Works of Love*, translated by Howard V. Hong and Edna Hong (Princeton, NJ: Princeton University Press, 1995).

Aurel Kolnai, "The Standard Modes of Aversion: Fear, Disgust, and Hatred," *Mind* 107 (1998): 581–595.

Sylvia D. Kreibig, "Autonomic Nervous System Activity in Emotion: A Review," *Biological Psychology* 84 (2010): 394–421.

Sharon Krishek, *Kierkegaard on Faith and Love* (Cambridge: Cambridge University Press, 2009).

———, "Kierkegaard on Impartiality and Love," forthcoming in *European Journal of Philosophy* (published online 2016).

Vaishnav Krishnan and Eric J. Nestler, "The Molecular Neurobiology of Depression," *Nature* 455 (2008): 894–902.

Kristján Kristjánsson, "Some Remaining Problems in Cognitive Theories of Emotion," *International Philosophical Quarterly* 41 (2001): 393–410.

Joel Krueger, "Empathy and the Extended Mind," *Zygon* 44 (2009): 675–698.

Milan Kundera, *Identity: A Novel*, translated by Linda Asher (New York: Harper Perennial, 1999).

———, *The Unbearable Lightness of Being*, translated by Michael Henry Heim (New York: Harper Perennial, 1991).

Joshua Landy, *Philosophy as Fiction: Self, Deception, and Knowledge in Proust* (Oxford: Oxford University Press, 2004).

Peter J. Lang, "The Three-System Approach to Emotion," in *The Structure of Emotion*, edited by Niels Birbaumer and Arne Öhman (Seattle: Hogrefe & Huber, 1993), 18–30.

Richard S. Lazarus, "Appraisal: The Long and the Short of It," in *The Nature of Emotion*, edited by Paul Ekman and Richard J. Davidson (New York: Oxford University Press, 1994), 208–215.

———, *Psychological Stress and the Coping Process* (New York: McGraw-Hill, 1966).

———, "Emotions and Adaptation," *Nebraska Symposium on Motivation* 16 (1968): 175–266.

———, *Emotion and Adaptation* (New York: Oxford University Press, 1991).

Richard S. Lazarus and Elizabeth Alfert, "Short-Circuiting of Threat by Experimentally Altering Cognitive Appraisal," *Journal of Abnormal and Social Psychology* 69 (1964): 195–205.

Jonathan Lear, *Happiness, Death, and the Remainder of Life* (Cambridge, MA: Harvard University Press, 2000).

———, *Love and Its Place in Nature: A Philosophical Interpretation of Freudian Psychoanalysis* (New Haven, CT: Yale University Press, 1998).

Joseph LeDoux, *Anxious: Using the Brain to Understand and Treat Fear and Anxiety* (New York: Viking, 2015).

———, "Coming to Terms with Fear," *Proceedings of the National Academy of Sciences of the United States of America* 111 (2014): 2871–2878.

———, "Comment: What's Basic about the Brain Mechanisms of Emotion?," *Emotion Review* 6 (2014): 318–320.

———, "Emotion, Memory, and the Brain," *Scientific American* 270.6 (1994): 50–57.

———, *The Emotional Brain* (New York: Simon and Schuster, 1996).

———, "Low Roads and Higher Order Thoughts in Emotion," *Cortex* 59 (2014): 214–215.

———, "Rethinking the Emotional Brain," *Neuron* 73 (2012): 653–676.

———, *Synaptic Self* (New York: Viking, 2002).

Brian Leiter, "Moralities Are a Sign-Language of the Affects," *Social Philosophy and Policy* 30 (2013): 237–258.

Oliver Letwin, *Ethics, Emotion, and the Unity of the Self* (London: Croom Helm, 1987).

Robert W. Levenson, "Autonomic Nervous System Differences among Emotions," *Psychological Science* 3 (1992): 23–27.

———, "The Search for Autonomic Specificity," in *The Nature of Emotion*, edited by Paul Ekman and Richard J. Davidson (New York: Oxford University Press, 1994), 252–257.

Robert W. Levenson, Paul Ekman, and Wallace V. Friesen, "Voluntary Facial Action Generates Emotion-Specific Autonomic Nervous System Activity," *Psychophysiology* 27 (1990): 363–384.

David Michael Levin, *The Body's Recollection of Being: Phenomenological Psychology and the Deconstruction of Nihilism* (London: Routledge & Kegan Paul, 1985).

Alphonso Lingis, *Dangerous Emotions* (Berkeley: University of California Press, 2000).

———, *The Imperative* (Bloomington: Indiana University Press, 1998).

Margaret Olivia Little, "Seeing and Caring: The Role of Affect in Feminist Epistemology," *Hypatia* 10 (1995): 117–137.

Eric Lormand, "Toward a Theory of Moods," *Philosophical Studies* 47 (1985): 385–407.

William A. Luijpen, *Existential Phenomenology* (Pittsburgh: Duquesne University Press, 1960).

William E. Lyons, *Emotion* (Cambridge: Cambridge University Press, 1980).

Kym Maclaren, "Emotional Clichés and Authentic Passions," *Phenomenology and the Cognitive Sciences* 10 (2011): 45–65.

———, "Emotional Metamorphoses," in *Embodiment and Agency*, edited by Sue Campbell, Letitia Maynell, and Susan Sherwin (University Park: Pennsylvania State University Press, 2009), 25–45.

Michelle Maiese, *Embodiment, Emotion, and Cognition* (New York: Palgrave Macmillan, 2011).

———, "How Can Emotions Be Both Cognitive and Bodily?," *Phenomenology and the Cognitive Sciences* 13 (2014): 513–531.

Norman Malcolm, "Thoughtless Brutes," *Proceedings and Addresses of the American Philosophical Association* 46 (1973): 5–20.

Jean-Luc Marion, *The Erotic Phenomenon*, translated by Stephen Lewis (Chicago: University of Chicago Press, 2007).

———, *God without Being*, translated by Thomas A. Carlson (Chicago: University of Chicago Press, 1991).

———, *In Excess: Studies of Saturated Phenomena*, translated by Robyn Horner and Vincent Berraud (New York: Fordham University Press, 2002).

———, "What Love Knows," in *Prolegomena to Charity*, translated by Stephen Lewis (New York: Fordham University Press, 2002), 153–168.

Joel Marks, "A Theory of Emotion," *Philosophical Studies* 42 (1982): 227–242.

David Matsumoto, "The Role of Facial Response in the Experience of Emotion," *Journal of Personality and Social Psychology* 52 (1987): 769–774.

Iris B. Mauss, Maya Tamir, Craig L. Anderson, and Nicole Savino, "Can Seeking Happiness Make People Unhappy?," *Emotion* 11 (2011): 807–815.

Glen Mazis, *Emotion and Embodiment* (New York: Peter Lang, 1993).

John McDowell, "The Content of Perceptual Experience," *Philosophical Quarterly* 44 (1994): 190–205.

———, "Functionalism and Anomalous Monism," in *Actions and Events*, edited by Ernest LePore and Brian McLaughlin (Oxford: Blackwell, 1985), 387–398.

———, *Mind and World* (Cambridge, MA: Harvard University Press, 1994).

———, *Mind, Value, and Reality* (Cambridge, MA: Harvard University Press, 1998).

———, *Perception as a Capacity for Knowledge* (Milwaukee: Marquette University Press, 2011).

Colin McGinn, *The Problem of Consciousness* (Oxford: Blackwell, 1991).

Jennifer McWeeny, "Freedom in Feeling: The Emotions and Their Expansion of Human Knowledge" (Senior Thesis, Colorado College, 1998).

Nick Medford, Mauricio Sierra, Dawn Baker, and Anthony S. David, "Understanding and Treating Depersonalisation Disorder," *Advances in Psychiatric Treatment* 11 (2005): 92–100.

Alexius Meinong, *On Emotional Presentation*, translated by Marie-Luise Schubert Kalsi (Evanston, IL: Northwestern University Press, 1972).

Maurice Merleau-Ponty, "Eye and Mind," translated by Carleton Dallery, in *The Primacy of Perception*, edited by James M. Edie (Evanston, IL: Northwestern University Press, 1964), 159–190.

———, *Phenomenology of Perception*, translated by Colin Smith (New York: Routledge, 2002).

———, *The Visible and the Invisible*, translated by Alphonso Lingis (Evanston, IL: Northwestern University Press, 1968).

———, *The World of Perception*, translated by Oliver Davis (New York: Routledge, 2004).

André T. Miller, Charl Nortje, and Shaun B. Helders, "Irrational Cognitions and the Fear of Flying," *Journal of Rational-Emotive and Cognitive-Behavior Therapy* 16 (1998): 135–148.

Agnes Moors, "Automatic Constructive Appraisal as a Candidate Cause of Emotion," *Emotion Review* 2 (2010): 139–156.

Agnes Moors, Phoebe C. Ellsworth, Klaus R. Scherer, and Nico H. Frijda, "Appraisal Theories of Emotion: State of the Art and Future Development," *Emotion Review* 5 (2013): 119–124.

John Morreall, "Fear without Belief," *Journal of Philosophy* 90 (1993): 359–366.

Stephen Mulhall, "Can There Be an Epistemology of Moods?," *Royal Institute of Philosophy Supplement* 41 (1996): 191–210.

———, *Inheritance and Originality* (New York: Oxford University Press, 2001).

———, *On Being in the World* (London: Routledge, 1990).

Iris Murdoch, *Existentialists and Mystics: Writings on Philosophy and Literature*, edited by Peter Conradi (London: Penguin, 1997).

———, "*Sein und Zeit*: Pursuit of Being," in *Iris Murdoch, Philosopher*, edited by Justin Broackes (New York: Oxford University Press, 2012), 93–109.

———, *The Sovereignty of Good* (London: Routledge, 1991).

Vladimir Nabokov, *Lolita* (New York: Vintage Books, 1997).

Thomas Nagel, *Mortal Questions* (Cambridge: Cambridge University Press, 1979).

———, *The View from Nowhere* (Oxford: Oxford University Press, 1986).

Ronald Alan Nash, "Cognitive Theories of Emotion," *Noûs* 23 (1989): 481–504.

Alexander Nehamas, *Nietzsche: Life as Literature* (Cambridge, MA: Harvard University Press, 1985).

———, *On Friendship* (New York: Basic Books, 2016).

———, *Only a Promise of Happiness* (Princeton, NJ: Princeton University Press, 2007).

———, "Only in the Contemplation of Beauty Is Human Life Worth Living," *European Journal of Philosophy* 15 (2007): 1–18.

Alex Neill, "Fear and Belief," *Philosophy and Literature* 19 (1995): 94–101.

Jerome Neu, *Emotion, Thought, and Therapy* (Berkeley: University of California Press, 1977).

———, *A Tear is an Intellectual Thing: The Meanings of Emotion* (New York: Oxford University Press, 2000).

Friedrich Nietzsche, *The Antichrist*, translated by Anthony M. Ludovici (Amherst, NY: Prometheus Books, 2000).

———, *The Gay Science*, translated by Josefine Nauckhoff (Cambridge: Cambridge University Press, 2001).

———, *Human, All Too Human*, translated by R. J. Hollingdale (Cambridge: Cambridge University Press, 1986).

———, *On Truth and Untruth: Selected Writings*, translated by Taylor Carman (New York: Harper Perennial, 2010).

———, "Schopenhauer as Educator," in *Unfashionable Observations*, translated by Richard T. Gray (Stanford, CA: Stanford University Press, 1995), 169–255.

———, *The Will to Power*, edited by Walter Kaufmann (New York: Vintage Books, 1968).

Alva Noë, *Action in Perception* (Cambridge, MA: MIT Press, 2004).

John H. Nota, *Max Scheler: The Man and His Work* (Chicago: Franciscan Herald Press, 1983).

Martha C. Nussbaum, "Emotions as Judgments of Value and Importance," in *Thinking about Feeling*, edited by Robert C. Solomon (New York: Oxford University Press, 2004), 183–199.

———, *The Fragility of Goodness* (Cambridge: Cambridge University Press, 1986).

———, *Hiding from Humanity: Disgust, Shame, and the Law* (Princeton, NJ: Princeton University Press, 2004).

———, *Political Emotions: Why Love Matters for Justice* (Cambridge, MA: Harvard University Press, 2013).

———, *The Therapy of Desire* (Princeton, NJ: Princeton University Press, 1994).

———, *Upheavals of Thought: The Intelligence of Emotions* (Cambridge: Cambridge University Press, 2001).

Keith Oatley, *Best Laid Schemes: The Psychology of Emotions* (Cambridge: Cambridge University Press, 1992).

Keith Oatley and Elaine Duncan, "Incidents of Emotion in Daily Life," in *International Review of Studies on Emotion* 2 (1992): 249–293.

Graham Oddie, *Value, Reality, and Desire* (New York: Oxford University Press, 2005).

Arne Öhman and Joaquim J. F. Soares, "Emotional Conditioning to Masked Stimuli: Expectancies for Aversive Outcomes Following Nonrecognized Fear-Relevant Stimuli," *Journal of Experimental Psychology* 127 (1998): 69–82.

———, "'Unconscious Anxiety': Phobic Responses to Masked Stimuli." *Journal of Abnormal Psychology* 103 (1994): 231–240.

Donna M. Orange, *Emotional Understanding* (New York: Guilford Press, 1995).

José Ortega y Gasset, *On Love: Aspects of a Single Theme*, translated by Tony Talbot (New York: Meridian Books, 1957).

Elisabeth Pacherie, "Perception, Emotions, and Delusions," in *Delusion and Self-Deception*, edited by Tim Bayne and Jordi Fernandez (New York: Psychology Press, 2009), 105–123.

Jaak Panksepp, *Affective Neuroscience* (New York: Oxford University Press, 1998).

————, "On the Embodied Neural Nature of Core Emotional Affects," *Journal of Consciousness Studies* 12.8–10 (2005): 158–184.

Jaak Panksepp and Lucy Biven, *The Archaeology of Mind: Neuroevolutionary Origins of Human Emotions* (New York: Norton, 2012).

Murray C. Parkes and Richard J. Brown, "Health after Bereavement: A Controlled Study of Young Boston Widows and Widowers," *Psychosomatic Medicine* 34 (1972): 449–461.

Brian Parkinson, Peter Totterdell, Rob B. Briner, and Shirley Reynolds, *Changing Moods: The Psychology of Mood and Mood Regulation* (London: Longman, 1996).

Blaise Pascal, *Pensées*, translated by Roger Ariew (Indianapolis: Hackett, 2005).

Christopher Peacocke, "Scenarios, Concepts, and Perception," in *The Contents of Experience*, edited by Tim Crane (Cambridge: Cambridge University Press, 1992), 105–135.

Sarah Pessin, *Ibn Gabirol's Theology of Desire* (Cambridge: Cambridge University Press, 2013).

Luiz Pessoa, "On the Relationship between Emotion and Cognition," *Nature Reviews Neuroscience* 9 (2008): 148–158.

Luiz Pessoa and Ralph Adolphs, "Emotion Processing and the Amygdala: From a 'Low Road' to 'Many Roads' of Evaluating Biological Significance," *Nature Reviews Neuroscience* 11 (2010): 773–783.

Elizabeth A. Phelps and Joseph E. LeDoux, "Contributions of the Amygdala to Emotion Processing," *Neuron* 48 (2005): 175–187.

Pierre Philippot, Gaëtane Chapelle, and Sylvie Blairy, "Respiratory Feedback in the Generation of Emotion," *Cognition and Emotion* 16 (2002): 605–627.

Hanna Pickard, "Emotions and the Problem of Other Minds," *Royal Institute of Philosophy Supplement* 52 (2003): 87–103.

Henry Pietersma, *Phenomenological Epistemology* (New York: Oxford University Press, 2000).

Steven Pinker, *How the Mind Works* (New York: Norton, 2009).

Peter Poellner, *Nietzsche and Metaphysics* (Oxford: Oxford University Press, 2000).

Michael Polanyi, *Personal Knowledge* (Chicago: University of Chicago Press, 1962).

Carolyn Price, *Emotion* (Cambridge: Polity Press, 2015).

Jesse J. Prinz, *Beyond Human Nature: How Culture and Experience Shape the Human Mind* (New York: Norton, 2014).

————, "Embodied Emotions," in *Thinking about Feeling*, edited by Robert C. Solomon (New York: Oxford University Press, 2004), 44–58.

————, "The Emotional Basis of Moral Judgments," *Philosophical Explorations* 9 (2006): 29–43.

————, *The Emotional Construction of Morals* (New York: Oxford University Press, 2007).

————, *Gut Reactions: A Perceptual Theory of Emotion* (Oxford: Oxford University Press, 2004).

———, "Response to D'Arms and Hills," *Philosophy and Phenomenological Research* 76 (2008): 729–732.

———, "Sensational Judgmentalism: Reconciling Solomon and James," in *Passion, Death, and Spirituality: The Philosophy of Robert C. Solomon*, edited by Kathleen Higgins and David Sherman (Dordrecht: Springer, 2012), 3–14.

Marcel Proust, *The Captive*, in one volume with *The Fugitive*, translated by C. K. Scott Moncrieff, Terence Kilmartin, and D. J. Enright (New York: Modern Library, 2003).

———, *Cities of the Plain*, in one volume with *The Guermantes Way*, translated by C. K. Scott Moncrieff and Terence Kilmartin (New York: Vintage Books, 1982).

———, *Time Regained*, translated by Andreas Mayor and Terence Kilmartin, revised by D. J. Enright (New York: Modern Library, 1993).

David Pugmire, *Rediscovering Emotion* (Edinburgh: Edinburgh University Press, 1998).

———, *Sound Sentiments: Integrity in the Emotions* (New York: Oxford University Press, 2005).

Hilary Putnam, *Reason, Truth, and History* (Cambridge: Cambridge University Press, 1981).

———, *The Threefold Cord: Mind, Body, and World* (New York: Columbia University Press, 1999).

Filip Radovic and Susanna Radovic, "Feelings of Unreality: A Conceptual and Phenomenological Analysis of the Language of Depersonalization," *Philosophy, Psychiatry, and Psychology* 9 (2002): 271–279.

Matthew Ratcliffe, *Experiences of Depression: A Study in Phenomenology* (Oxford: Oxford University Press, 2015).

———, "The Feeling of Being," *Journal of Consciousness Studies* 12.8–10 (2005): 43–60.

———, *Feelings of Being: Phenomenology, Psychiatry, and the Sense of Reality* (Oxford: Oxford University Press, 2008).

———, "The Phenomenological Role of Affect in the Capgras Delusion," *Continental Philosophy Review* 41 (2008): 195–216.

———, "The Phenomenology of Mood and the Meaning of Life," in *The Oxford Handbook of Philosophy of Emotion*, edited by Peter Goldie (Oxford: Oxford University Press, 2010), 349–371.

———, *Rethinking Commonsense Psychology* (New York: Palgrave Macmillan, 2007).

———, "Why Mood Matters," in *The Cambridge Companion to Heidegger's "Being and Time"*, edited by Mark A. Wrathall (Cambridge: Cambridge University Press, 2013): 157–176.

Paul Redding, *The Logic of Affect* (Ithaca, NY: Cornell University Press, 1999).

C. D. C. Reeve, *Love's Confusions* (Cambridge, MA: Harvard University Press, 2005).

James D. Reid, *Being Here Is Glorious* (Evanston, IL: Northwestern University Press, 2015).

————, "Ethical Criticism in Heidegger's Early Freiburg Lectures," *Review of Metaphysics* 59 (2005): 33–71.

Rainer Reisenzein, "Arnold's Theory of Emotion in Historical Perspective," *Cognition and Emotion* 20 (2006): 920–951.

————, "Emotional Experience in the Computational Belief-Desire Theory of Emotion," *Emotion Review* 1 (2009): 214–222.

Rainer Reisenzein and Sabine A. Döring, "Ten Perspectives on Emotional Experience," *Emotional Review* 1 (2009): 195–205.

Henry S. Richardson, "Desire and the Good in *De Anima*," in *Essays on Aristotle's "De Anima"*, edited by Martha C. Nussbaum and Amélie O. Rorty (New York: Oxford University Press, 1992), 381–399.

Robert C. Roberts, *Emotions: An Essay in Aid of Moral Psychology* (Cambridge: Cambridge University Press, 2003).

————, *Emotions in the Moral Life* (Cambridge: Cambridge University Press, 2013).

————, "Existence, Emotion, and Virtue," in *The Cambridge Companion to Kierkegaard*, edited by Alastair Hannay and Gordon D. Marino (Cambridge: Cambridge University Press, 1998), 177–206.

————, Review of *Wisdom in Love* by Rick Anthony Furtak, *Faith and Philosophy* 26 (2009): 98–104.

————, "What an Emotion Is: A Sketch," *Philosophical Review* 97 (1988): 183–209.

Tomi-Ann Roberts and Yousef Arefi-Afshar, "Not All Who Stand Tall Are Proud: Gender Differences in the Proprioceptive Effects of Upright Posture," *Cognition and Emotion* 21 (2007): 714–727.

Jenefer Robinson, *Deeper Than Reason: Emotion and Its Role in Literature, Music, and Art* (New York: Oxford University Press, 2005).

————, "Emotion: Biological Fact or Social Construction?," in *Thinking about Feeling*, edited by Robert C. Solomon (New York: Oxford University Press, 2004), 28–43.

————, "Startle," *Journal of Philosophy* 92 (1995): 53–74.

Marilynne Robinson, *The Givenness of Things* (New York: Farrar, Straus and Giroux, 2015).

Edmund T. Rolls, *The Brain and Emotion* (Oxford: Oxford University Press, 1999).

————, *Emotion and Decision-Making Explained* (Oxford: Oxford University Press, 2014).

————, *Emotion Explained* (Oxford: Oxford University Press, 2005).

————, *Memory, Attention, and Decision-Making* (Oxford: Oxford University Press, 2008).

————, *Neuroculture: On the Implications of Brain Science* (Oxford: Oxford University Press, 2012).

Edmund T. Rolls and Fabian Grabenhorst, "The Orbitofrontal Cortex and Beyond: From Affect to Decision-Making," *Progress in Neurobiology* 86 (2008): 216–244.

Amélie O. Rorty, "Explaining Emotions," in *Explaining Emotions*, edited by Amélie O. Rorty (Berkeley: University of California Press, 1980), 103–127.

Ira J. Roseman, "Appraisal Determinants of Discrete Emotions," *Cognition and Emotion* 5 (1991): 161–200.

———, "Cognitive Determinants of Emotion," *Review of Personality and Social Psychology* 5 (1984): 11–36.

René Rosfort and Giovanni Stanghellini, "The Person in between Moods and Affects," *Philosophy, Psychiatry, and Psychology* 16 (2009): 251–266.

Adina Roskies, "Are Ethical Judgments Intrinsically Motivational?," *Philosophical Psychology* 16 (2003): 51–66.

Philip Roth, *Everyman* (New York: Vintage Books, 2007).

Mary K. Rothbart, *Becoming Who We Are: Temperament and Personality in Development* (New York: Guilford Press, 2011).

Barbara O. Rothbaum et al., "Effectiveness of Computer-Generated (Virtual Reality) Graded Exposure in the Treatment of Acrophobia," *American Journal of Psychiatry* 152 (1995): 626–628.

Paul Rozin and April E. Fallon, "A Perspective on Disgust," *Psychological Review* 94 (1987): 23–41.

Anthony Rudd, *Expressing the World* (Chicago: Open Court, 2003).

———, *Self, Value, and Narrative* (Oxford: Oxford University Press, 2012).

James A. Russell and Ghyslaine Lemay, "Emotion Concepts," in *Handbook of Emotions*, 2nd edition, edited by Michael Lewis and Jeannette M. Haviland-Jones (New York: Guilford Press, 2000), 491–503.

John E. Russon, *Human Experience: Philosophy, Neurosis, and the Elements of Everyday Life* (Albany: SUNY Press, 2003).

Gilbert Ryle, *The Concept of Mind* (Chicago: University of Chicago Press, 1984).

Mikko Salmela, "True Emotions," *Philosophical Quarterly* 56 (2006): 382–405.

———, *True Emotions* (Amsterdam: John Benjamins, 2014).

Eric L. Santner, *On the Psychotheology of Everyday Life* (Chicago: University of Chicago Press, 2001).

Jean-Paul Sartre, *Being and Nothingness*, translated by Hazel Barnes (New York: Washington Square Press, 1966).

———, *The Emotions: Outline of a Theory*, translated by Bernard Frechtman (New York: Citadel Press, 1993).

———, *The Imaginary: A Phenomenological Psychology of the Imagination*, translated by Jonathan Webber (London: Routledge, 2004).

Sally L. Satel and Scott O. Lilienfeld, *Brainwashed: The Seductive Appeal of Mindless Neuroscience* (New York: Basic Books, 2013).

Jennifer Saul, "Implicit Bias, Stereotype Threat, and Women in Philosophy," in *Women in Philosophy: What Needs to Change?*, edited by Katrina Hutchison and Fiona Jenkins (Oxford: Oxford University Press, 2013), 39–60.

Andrea Scarantino, "Insights and Blindspots of the Cognitivist Theory of Emotions," *British Journal for the Philosophy of Science* 61 (2010): 729–768.

Max Scheler, *The Constitution of the Human Being*, translated by John Cutting (Milwaukee: Marquette University Press, 2008).

———, *Formalism in Ethics and Non-formal Ethics of Values*, translated by Manfred S. Frings and Roger L. Funk (Evanston, IL: Northwestern University Press, 1973).

————, *The Nature of Sympathy*, translated by Peter Heath (New Haven, CT: Yale University Press, 1954).

————, *On Feeling, Knowing, and Valuing*, edited by Harold J. Bershady (Chicago: University of Chicago Press, 1992).

————, "Ordo Amoris," in *Selected Philosophical Essays*, translated by David R. Lachterman (Evanston, IL: Northwestern University Press, 1973), 98–135.

————, *Ressentiment*, translated by L. B. Coser and W. W. Holdheim (Milwaukee: Marquette University Press, 1994).

Klaus R. Scherer, "The Nature and Study of Appraisal," in *Appraisal Processes in Emotion: Theory, Methods, Research*, edited by Klaus R. Scherer, Angela Schorr, and Tom Johnstone (New York: Oxford University Press, 2001), 369–391.

————, "Studying the Emotion-Antecedent Appraisal Process," *Cognition and Emotion* 7 (1993): 325–355.

Klaus R. Scherer and Grazia Ceschi, "Lost Luggage: A Field Study of Emotion-Antecedent Appraisal," *Motivation and Emotion* 21 (1997): 211–235.

Robin May Schott, *Cognition and Eros* (University Park: Pennsylvania State University Press, 1993).

Timothy Schroeder, *Three Faces of Desire* (New York: Oxford University Press, 2004).

Norbert Schwarz and Gerald L. Clore, "Feelings and Phenomenal Experiences," in *Social Psychology: Handbook of Basic Principles*, edited by E. Tory Higgins and Arie Kruglanski (New York: Guilford Press, 1996), 385–407.

Eric Schwitzgebel, "In-Between Believing," *Philosophical Quarterly* 51 (2001): 76–82.

Roger Scruton, *Sexual Desire: A Moral Philosophy of the Erotic* (New York: Free Press, 1986).

John R. Searle, *Intentionality: An Essay in the Philosophy of Mind* (Cambridge: Cambridge University Press, 1983).

Marguerite Sechehaye, *Autobiography of a Schizophrenic Girl*, translated by Grace Rubin-Rabson (New York: Meridian, 1994).

Alexander F. Shand, *The Foundations of Character: Being a Study of the Tendencies of the Emotions and Sentiments* (London: Macmillan, 1914).

Phillip R. Shaver, Hillary J. Morgan, and Shelley Wu, "Is Love a 'Basic' Emotion?," *Personal Relationships* 3 (1996): 81–96.

Richard Shusterman, *Body Consciousness* (Cambridge: Cambridge University Press, 2008).

Matthias Siemer, "Mood Experience: Implications of a Dispositional Theory of Moods," *Emotion Review* 1 (2009): 256–263.

————, "Mood-Congruent Cognitions Constitute Mood Experience," *Emotion* 5 (2005): 296–308.

Matthias Siemer, Iris Mauss, and James J. Gross, "Same Situation—Different Emotions: How Appraisals Shape Our Emotions," *Emotion* 7 (2007): 592–600.

Paul J. Silvia, *Exploring the Psychology of Interest* (New York: Oxford University Press, 2006).

Daphne Simeon and Jeffrey Abugel, *Feeling Unreal: Depersonalization Disorder and the Loss of the Self* (Oxford: Oxford University Press, 2006).

Irving Singer, *The Nature of Love*, 3 vols. (Chicago: University of Chicago Press, 1984–1987).

Jan Slaby, "Emotional Rationality and Feelings of Being," in *Feelings of Being Alive*, edited by Joerg Fingerhut and Sabine Marienberg (Berlin: Walter de Gruyter, 2012), 55–77.

Michael Slote, *A Sentimentalist Theory of the Mind* (New York: Oxford University Press, 2014).

Craig A. Smith and Phoebe C. Ellsworth, "Patterns of Cognitive Appraisal in Emotion," *Journal of Personality and Social Psychology* 48 (1985): 813–838.

Quentin Smith, *The Felt Meanings of the World: A Metaphysics of Feeling* (West Lafayette, IN: Purdue University Press, 1986).

———, "On Heidegger's Theory of Moods," *Modern Schoolman* 58 (1981): 211–235.

Robert Sokolowski, *Phenomenology of the Human Person* (Cambridge: Cambridge University Press, 2008).

Robert C. Solomon, "Emotions and Choice," *Review of Metaphysics* 27 (1973): 20–41.

———, "Emotions, Thoughts, and Feelings: What Is a 'Cognitive Theory' of the Emotions and Does it Neglect Affectivity?," *Royal Institute of Philosophy Supplement* 52 (2003): 1–18.

———, *Not Passion's Slave* (New York: Oxford University Press, 2003).

———, *The Passions* (Garden City, NY: Anchor Press, 1976).

———, *True to Our Feelings* (New York: Oxford University Press, 2007).

Richard Sorabji, *Emotion and Peace of Mind* (New York: Oxford University Press, 2000).

———, "Emotions and the Psychotherapy of the Ancients," in *Philosophical Psychology: Psychology, Emotions, and Freedom*, edited by Craig Steven Titus (Arlington, VA: Institute for the Psychological Sciences Press / Washington, DC: Catholic University of America Press, 2009), 176–195.

Peter H. Spader, *Scheler's Ethical Personalism* (New York: Fordham University Press, 2002).

Giovanni Stanghellini and René Rosfort, *Emotions and Personhood: Exploring Fragility—Making Sense of Vulnerability* (Oxford: Oxford University Press, 2013).

Charles Starkey, "Emotion and Full Understanding," *Ethical Theory and Moral Practice* 11 (2008): 425–454.

Anthony J. Steinbock, *Moral Emotions: Reclaiming the Evidence of the Heart* (Evanston, IL: Northwestern University Press, 2014).

Sabine Stepper and Fritz Strack, "Proprioceptive Determinants of Emotional and Nonemotional Feelings," *Journal of Personality and Social Psychology* 64 (1993): 211–220.

Bryan Stevenson, *Just Mercy: A Story of Justice and Redemption* (New York: Spiegel & Grau, 2014).

Stephen P. Stich, "Beliefs and Subdoxastic States," *Philosophy of Science* 45 (1978): 499–518.

Michael Stocker, "Emotional Thoughts," *American Philosophical Quarterly* 24 (1987): 59–69.

———, "Intellectual and Other Nonstandard Emotions," in *The Oxford Handbook of Philosophy of Emotion*, edited by Peter Goldie (Oxford: Oxford University Press, 2010), 401–423.

———, "Some Considerations about Intellectual Desire and Emotions," in *Thinking about Feeling*, edited by Robert C. Solomon (New York: Oxford University Press, 2004), 135–148.

———, *Valuing Emotions* (Cambridge: Cambridge University Press, 1996).

Patrick Stokes, *Kierkegaard's Mirrors: Interest, Self, and Moral Vision* (New York: Palgrave Macmillan, 2010).

Robert Stolorow, *Trauma and Human Existence: Autobiographical, Psychoanalytic, and Philosophical Reflections* (New York: Analytic Press, 2007).

———, *World, Affectivity, Trauma* (New York: Routledge, 2011).

Tony Stone and Andrew W. Young, "Delusions and Brain Injury: The Philosophy and Psychology of Belief," *Mind and Language* 12 (1997): 327–364.

Fritz Strack, Leonard Martin, and Sabine Stepper, "Inhibiting and Facilitating Conditions of the Human Smile: A Nonobtrusive Test of the Facial Feedback Hypothesis," *Journal of Personality and Social Psychology* 54 (1988): 768–777.

Stephan Strasser, *Phenomenology of Feeling: An Essay on the Phenomena of the Heart*, translated by Robert E. Wood (Pittsburgh: Duquesne University Press, 1977).

P. F. Strawson, *Skepticism and Naturalism* (New York: Columbia University Press, 1985).

Fredrik Svenaeus, "Depression and the Self: Bodily Resonance and Attuned Being-in-the-World," in *Depression, Emotion, and the Self*, edited by Matthew Ratcliffe and Achim Stephan (Exeter: Imprint Academic, 2014), 1–16.

Christine Tappolet, "Ambivalent Emotions and the Perceptual Account of Emotions," *Analysis* 65.3 (2005): 229–233.

———, *Emotions, Value, and Agency* (New York: Oxford University Press, 2016).

———, "Emotions and the Intelligibility of Akratic Action," in *Weakness of Will and Practical Irrationality*, edited by Sarah Stroud and Christine Tappolet (New York: Oxford University Press, 2003), 97–120.

———, "Values and Emotions," in *Morality and the Emotions*, edited by Carla Bagnoli (Oxford: Clarendon Press, 2011), 117–134.

Charles Taylor, "Merleau-Ponty and the Epistemological Picture," in *The Cambridge Companion to Merleau-Ponty*, edited by Taylor Carman and Mark B. N. Hansen (Cambridge: Cambridge University Press, 2005), 26–49.

Gabriele Taylor, *Pride, Shame, and Guilt* (Oxford: Clarendon Press, 1985).

Bethany A. Teachman et al., "A New Mode of Fear Expression: Perceptual Bias in Height Fear," *Emotion* 8 (2008): 296–301.

Paul Thagard, *Hot Thought: Mechanisms and Applications of Emotional Cognition* (Cambridge, MA: MIT Press, 2006).

M. Guy Thompson, *The Truth about Freud's Technique: The Encounter with the Real* (New York: New York University Press, 1994).

Iain D. Thomson, *Heidegger, Art, and Postmodernity* (Cambridge: Cambridge University Press, 2011).

———, "Ontotheology," in *Interpreting Heidegger: Critical Essays*, edited by Daniel O. Dahlstrom (Cambridge: Cambridge University Press, 2010), 106–131.

———, "Thinking Love: Heidegger and Arendt," forthcoming in *Continental Philosophy Review*.

Henry David Thoreau, *Journal*, edited by Bradford Torrey and Francis H. Allen, 14 vols. (New York: Dover Publications, 1962).

Susan J. Thorpe and Paul M. Salkovskis, "Phobic Beliefs: Do Cognitive Factors Play a Role in Specific Phobias?," *Behaviour Research and Therapy* 33 (1995): 805–816.

Samuel Todes, *Body and World* (Cambridge, MA: MIT Press, 2001).

Leo Tolstoy, *The Death of Ivan Ilyich*, translated by Lynn Solotaroff (New York: Bantam Classics, 1981).

Maura Tumulty, "Managing Mismatch between Belief and Behavior," *Pacific Philosophical Quarterly* 95 (2014): 261–292.

Michael Tye, *Ten Problems of Consciousness* (Cambridge, MA: MIT Press, 1995).

Eric Luis Uhlmann and Geoffrey L. Cohen, "I Think It, Therefore It's True: Effects of Self-Perceived Objectivity on Hiring Discrimination," *Organizational Behavior and Human Decision Processes* 104 (2007): 207–233.

Daniela Vallega-Neu, *The Bodily Dimension in Thinking* (Albany: SUNY Press, 2005).

David C. Van Essen and Jack L. Gallant, "Neural Mechanisms of Form and Motion Processing in the Primate Visual System," *Neuron* 13 (1994): 1–10.

Theo Van Willigenburg, "Reason and Love," *Ethical Theory and Moral Practice* 8 (2005): 45–62.

Francisco J. Varela, "Neurophenomenology: A Methodological Remedy for the Hard Problem," *Journal of Consciousness Studies* 3 (1996): 330–349.

Paul Voice, "The Authority of Love as Sentimental Contract," *Essays in Philosophy* 12 (2011): 93–111.

Eric-Jan Wagenmakers et al., "Registered Replication Report: Strack, Martin, & Stepper (1988)," *Perspectives on Psychological Science* 11 (2016): 917–928.

William J. Wainwright, *Reason and the Heart* (Ithaca, NY: Cornell University Press, 1995).

Paul J. Whalen et al., "Masked Presentations of Emotional Facial Expressions Modulate Amygdala Activity without Explicit Knowledge," *Journal of Neuroscience* 18 (1998): 411–418.

Richard J. White, *Love's Philosophy* (Lanham, MD: Rowman & Littlefield, 2001).

Demian Whiting, "The Feeling Theory of Emotion and Object-Directed Emotions," *European Journal of Philosophy* 19 (2009): 281–303.

David Wiggins, *Needs, Values, Truth* (New York: Oxford University Press, 1998).

Bernard Williams, *Ethics and the Limits of Philosophy* (Cambridge, MA: Harvard University Press, 1985).

———, *Truth and Truthfulness* (Princeton, NJ: Princeton University Press, 2002).

Lawrence E. Williams and John A. Bargh, "Experiencing Physical Warmth Promotes Interpersonal Warmth," *Science* 322 (2008): 606–607.

Katherine Withy, "Owned Emotions," in *Heidegger, Authenticity, and the Self*, edited by Denis McManus (London: Routledge, 2014), 21–36.

Ludwig Wittgenstein, *Philosophical Investigations*, 4th edition, translated by G. E. M. Anscombe, P. M. S. Hacker, and Joachim Schulte (Oxford: Blackwell, 2009).

———, *Tractatus Logico-Philosophicus*, translated by C. K. Ogden (London: Routledge & Kegan Paul, 1955).

Susan Wolf, "The Good, the True, and the Lovable," in *Contours of Agency*, edited by Sarah Buss and Lee Overton (Cambridge, MA: MIT Press, 2002), 227–244.

Richard Wollheim, *On the Emotions* (New Haven, CT: Yale University Press, 1999).

Mark R. Wynn, *Emotional Experience and Religious Understanding* (Cambridge: Cambridge University Press, 2005).

———, *Renewing the Senses* (Oxford: Oxford University Press, 2013).

Jenny Yiend, Kirsten Barnicot, and Ernst H. W. Koster, "Attention and Emotion," in *Handbook of Cognition and Emotion*, edited by Michael D. Robinson, Edward R. Watkins, and Eddie Harmon-Jones (New York: Guilford Press, 2013), 97–116.

Larry J. Young, "Love: Neuroscience Reveals All," *Nature* 457 (2009): 148.

Linda T. Zagzebski, "Emotion and Moral Judgment," *Philosophy and Phenomenological Research* 66 (2003): 104–124.

Dan Zahavi, *Husserl's Phenomenology* (Stanford, CA: Stanford University Press, 2003).

———, *Self-Awareness and Alterity: A Phenomenological Investigation* (Evanston, IL: Northwestern University Press, 1999).

Robert B. Zajonc, "Feeling and Thinking: Preferences Need No Inferences," *American Psychologist* 35 (1980): 151–175.

———, "Mere Exposure," *Current Directions in Psychological Science* 10 (2001): 224–228.

———, "On the Primacy of Affect," *American Psychologist* 39.2 (1984): 117–123.

Robert B. Zajonc, Sheila T. Murphy, and Marita Inglehart, "Feeling and Facial Efference: Implications of the Vascular Theory of Emotion," *Psychological Review* 96 (1989): 395–416.

Adam Zeman, *Consciousness: A User's Guide* (New Haven, CT: Yale University Press, 2002).

Dolf Zillmann, "Sequential Dependencies in Emotional Experience and Behavior," in *Emotion: Interdisciplinary Perspectives*, edited by Robert Kavanaugh, Betty Zimmerberg, and Steven Fein (Mahwah, NJ: Lawrence Erlbaum Associates, 1996), 243–272.

INDEX

abnormal states. *See* impairment, emotional
"accidents of circumstance," 182
action, 8, 12, 35–36, 116, 132, 168
Adams, E. M., 65n31
affect. *See* emotion
"affective blindsight," 56n14
affective cognition. *See* emotions: cognitive
    aspects of
affective-cognitive divide, ostensible, 23–32,
    47n77, 73
affirmation, 69, 79–80, 88–91, 127–131,
    135–136, 145–150, 183, 192–195
Alfert, Elizabeth, 43n68
Altieri, Charles, 15n25
ambiguity. *See* uncertainty
amygdala, 25–35, 55n12, 56n14, 75
Anderson, R. Lanier, 186n57
anger, 7, 33–34, 41–44, 67, 88, 106, 124–125,
    161–162, 173–175
anxiety, 36, 58, 124–125, 166,
    180–181, 194n77
apathy, 80, 99, 150, 161, 168
appraisal, 6–14, 16, 18, 30–35, 43, 47n77,
    58, 67, 70–72, 83, 85, 89–90, 95–97,
    161–162
appreciation, 71–73, 79–80, 109, 118, 126–
    127, 131–138, 146, 152–153, 180–187,
    192–194. *See also* gratitude

apprehension, 9, 14, 19, 46–47, 62–74, 91–93,
    95–99, 111–112, 127, 132–134, 146,
    155–156, 166, 172–175, 178–180, 183,
    185–187, 189–190. *See also* recognition
a priori, emotional, 107–108, 110–120,
    149, 154n83. *See also* dispositional
    emotions
arachnophobia, 55–57, 61–64
Arendt, Hannah, 192–193
Aristotle, 34, 42, 62n25, 77n6, 94–95, 115,
    140n44, 155
Armon-Jones, Claire, 46n76, 87n28
Armstrong, John, 146
Arnold, Magda, 9n13, 10n14, 11,
    15n25, 92n40
Aron, Arthur P., 41, 108n12
attention, 9, 61–62, 55, 67, 89, 96–97, 108–111,
    115–116, 125–128, 133–136, 147–157,
    159–165, 169–170, 185, 190. *See also*
    intentionality
attraction, 40–41, 142n48, 149–152, 182
attunement, 128, 139, 160–180, 183–185,
    187–188, 191, 195
authenticity, 151, 192–197
awareness, 8, 19, 23n1, 24, 27–28, 39, 41,
    56–57, 69, 72–73, 78–81, 83, 89, 91–93,
    97–98, 103, 109–111, 115–119, 126–128,
    136, 166, 170–171, 174, 177

Ax, Albert F., 42n63
axiology, 11, 52, 70–72, 75–76, 84,
    109–111, 128–131, 138–139, 159, 165,
    171–172, 175–176, 185, 187. *See also*
    significance; value

background emotions. *See* dispositional
    emotions
background versus situational emotions,
    104–106
"bad moods," 167
Bahlul, Raja, 67n37
Baier, Annette C., 114, 193n74
Barber, Michael D., 151n77
Barlassina, Luca, 65n31
beauty, 62, 85, 93, 139–141, 151n76
Bechara, Antoine, 38n49
Beckett, Samuel, 70, 181
belief(s), 7, 10–12, 43, 56–63, 68, 79–81, 91.
    See also appraisal; judgment
    conflicting, 62–63, 85–91
    conviction, 56–57, 63, 69, 79–80,
        86–87, 91
    dispassionate, 79, 97–98
    unreasonable, 56–62
Ben-Ze'ev, Aaron, 19n36, 45n73
Binswanger, Ludwig, 190–191
biographical factors, 95–96, 133–134, 151–152,
    156, 178–181, 183–184, 186–191
"blindfright," 56n14
bodily illness, 165–167
Bollas, Christopher, 88n31
boredom, 125–126, 166–168
Brady, Michael S., 30n26, 75n1, 184n54
Brakel, Linda A. W., 89n32
Brennan, Tad, 81n15
Bretano, Franz, 7
Broad, C. D., 92n40
Brogaard, Berit, 26, 160n1
Brothers, Leslie, 29n20
Brown, Robert, 152

Calhoun, Cheshire, 57n16, 60, 61n23,
    65n31, 86, 95n46, 170, 179n42,
    184n53, 188n62
Capgras delusion, 38n48, 154n83

care, 75–76, 79, 95, 104–121, 123–155, 164,
    170, 181–184, 195
    spectrum of, 113–116, 126–127,
        132–133
Cataldi, Sue L., 74, 192n71
category mistakes, 34–35, 55n12
causality, 13–14, 19n35, 20, 46, 60, 67n36,
    71, 83–84, 137
Cavell, Stanley, 156n86, 171–172
cerebral cortex, 23–28, 55n13
Churchland, Patricia S., 75n1
Churchland, Paul M., 39n51
Clark, Stephen R. L., 146
Clore, Gerald L., 81n16, 89–90n35,
    162–163
cognition, 4–21, 23, 27–28, 34, 37–38,
    51–53, 56–70, 73–74, 75–92, 94–95,
    97–99, 120, 169
    affective, 7–14, 51, 84–86, 88–90, 109,
        152–153, 134–136, 160–163
    embodied, 20, 46–47, 72–73, 82–86, 89,
        92, 95–96, 159, 166–167, 179
    coherence, 150–151, 155, 191–192
Coleridge, Samuel Taylor, 93
Colombetti, Giovanna, 32n32, 85n24,
    98n53, 105n5, 114n22, 166n16,
    169n22, 175n33
commitment. *See* dedication
concern. *See* care
construals, emotions as, 59, 92, 137
"corporeal" *a priori*, 109n13

Damasio, Antonio, 4n3, 16, 23–28,
    35–36, 37–38, 63n27, 75n1, 77n7,
    93n42, 94n45
Dante, 133–134
"dark" cognitions, 60
Davidson, Richard J., 27n14, 42n65
death. *See* mortality
dedication, 115, 135, 194–195
Deigh, John, 20
delusion(s), 38n48, 119, 139, 145,
    154–156, 171
denial, 55n12, 59, 65–66, 195–197
Dennett, Daniel C., 33n34
Deonna, Julien A., 55, 57n16, 96n48

depression, 162–165, 168–169
de Sousa, Ronald, 15n26, 51n2, 64n29, 82n17, 156, 165n13, 179n44, 187
Dewey, John, 68n38
Dillon, M. C., 87
disclosure, 11, 70, 83, 95–96, 136, 149, 166, 194–195. *See also* revelatory, emotions as
discrimination. *See* moral consequence, emotions with; social inequality
"disembodied," emotions as allegedly, 12n18, 16n29, 51–52, 83
disgust, 42, 113n20, 189
dispositional emotions, 104–106, 119, 127–128, 173–175. *See also* care
dissatisfaction, 162n9
distrust, 17, 62–63, 134, 168
dopamine, 176
Döring, Sabine A., 33n34, 59–60n20, 61n23
Dreyfus, Hubert L., 115n25
Dufrenne, Mikel, 109n13
"dumb view" of emotions, 6. *See also* noncognitive theories
Dunston, Susan L., 80n14
Düringer, Eva-Maria, 19n36, 160n1
Dutton, Donald G., 41

Ekman, Paul, 33n33, 108n12
Ellis, Ralph, 149, 155
Elster, Jon, 39n53, 89n35
embodied (Jamesian) account of emotions, summarized, 15–18
embodied feeling. *See* somatic agitation
embodied knowledge, 63–64, 68–72, 92. *See also* cognition: embodied
Emerson, Ralph Waldo, 161, 170
emotional knowing, 70, 81–82, 84–85, 95–97, 103, 145, 185. *See also* emotions: logic of
emotions
　cognitive aspects of, 7–14, 51, 84–86, 88–90, 109, 152–153, 134–136, 160–163, 179
　distinguishing among, 7, 13–14, 96–98, 105
　enabling conditions for, 10, 70, 81, 85–101, 106, 154

epistemic reliability of, 4–5, 8–9, 11, 13–14, 53, 121, 160, 167–168
　felt quality of, 21, 44–45, 51–52, 88, 103 (*see also* somatic agitation)
　logic of, 3–4, 13–14, 33–34, 43, 53–54, 68, 83, 98–99, 128, 150–151, 144, 172, 182
　relational qualities of, 36–37, 52–53, 76–77, 92, 176–177, 187–188
empathy, 186–190
epistemology, 4–5, 11, 14, 20, 58, 63–64, 70, 72–73, 85, 89, 103, 126, 140–141, 156, 171–173
ethical relevance, emotions with. *See* moral consequence, emotions with
evaluation, emotional. *See* appraisal
Evans, Dylan, 26n13
experience, 15–16, 28, 30, 34, 39–40, 68, 74, 82, 86–87, 90, 99, 106, 109–114, 129, 143–144, 147, 152, 162–165, 167, 172–173, 176–179, 181, 185
"eye of the beholder," 93, 128, 146, 161, 165

facial expressions, 16–17, 27, 39–42, 51, 98–99, 153
familiarity, 15, 27–28, 119, 154n83, 188–189
"fast track" hypothesis. *See* "low road" hypothesis
fear, 7, 13, 36, 42–43, 53–55, 60–66, 68, 70, 74, 75–78, 81, 88–90, 96, 103–105, 107, 111–112, 164
　neuroscience of, 25–34
Ferreira, M. Jamie, 133n27
Fiedler, Klaus, 111n18
Fisher, Phillip, 4n2
Fiumara, Gemma Corradi, 73n48
Flanagan, Owen J., 37
Forgas, Joseph P., 111, 169
formal objects. *See* intentionality
"for us," 180
Frankfurt, Harry G., 83, 107, 111n17, 112, 113–114n21, 118n30, 123, 125n6, 125–128, 130–132, 142n48, 144–149, 165
Frankish, Keith, 80n13

Freud, Sigmund, 89n33, 114n21, 184n54, 195n77
friendship, 90, 95–96, 150–151, 153, 155, 184–188
Frijda, Nico H., 15n25, 56n14, 105n4
"full blooded believing," 62
Furtak, Rick Anthony, 12n18, 20n36, 82, 104n2, 136n33, 165n14, 193n75

Gadamer, Hans-Georg, 14, 46
Gardner, Sebastian, 95n46, 96n48
Gendler, Tamar Szabó, 69
Gendlin, Eugene T., 62n24, 88–89, 99n54, 184
Gibson, James J., 113n20
Gilbert, Paul, 45n73
"God is love," 145
Goldie, Peter, 4n2, 40, 45n73, 54, 72n46, 91n39
Goleman, Daniel, 31n30, 35
"good moods," 169
Gordon, Robert M., 42n61
gratitude, 82–83, 104
Greenspan, Patricia, 25–26, 35, 56–57, 79n10
grief, 68, 69–70, 74, 79–80, 103–106, 164–165, 181–182
Griffiths, Paul E., 26n10, 87–88n29, 176n37
Griskevicius, Vladas, 162
Guignon, Charles, 113n20
guilt, 39n53, 52

Haidt, Jonathan, 28n19
Hansen, Jennifer, 21n38, 169
happiness. *See* joy
Hass, Lawrence, 88n31
"heart has its reasons," 4, 74, 123
Heidegger, Martin, 14, 28n17, 77n8, 83n18, 92n40, 93, 112–113, 117, 120n33, 128–129, 137n37, 147, 149n71, 166–167, 169, 178–179, 180n46, 192
Helm, Bennett W., 53n6, 63n27, 76n4, 125, 161
honesty, 61, 65, 133, 149, 195–196. *See also* authenticity
hope, 11–13, 141

Horney, Karen, 194n77
Hufendiek, Rebekka, 97n49
Hume, David, 17n32, 54
Husserl, Edmund, 7n8, 8n11, 46n75, 68, 80n13, 83, 93, 97n49, 120, 167, 176, 183n51
"hybrid theories," 20n37

illusion. *See* perception: illusory
imagination, 87n28, 132–133, 139–140
impairment, emotional, 25, 38n49, 51, 119, 154n83, 164–165
indifference, 114–116, 125–126, 142, 148, 177–178
individual differences, 150, 179, 188–190
individuality, 130–132, 135–136, 140, 144, 149, 151–152, 156, 164, 181–182, 186–187
intentionality, 5–10, 12–14, 19, 23, 36, 45–46, 52–53, 61, 63–64, 67, 71–72, 75–78, 90–92, 94–95, 96–98, 110, 137, 147, 162–163, 170, 176–177, 185
interest, 113–115, 130–131
interpretation, 32, 86, 134, 137–138, 146, 153, 170n27, 185n55
intrinsic value, 126–127, 130–132, 135, 145, 147–149, 154
Irigaray, Luce, 136, 149n72
irrational emotions, 54–56, 60–62, 160, 165
Izard, Carroll E., 115

Jaggar, Alison M., 6, 170n27
James, William, 15–18, 33, 39n53, 45, 54, 77, 106n6, 114, 141, 145, 187n61, 191
Jamison, Kay Redfield, 191n68
jealousy, 67n36, 89, 107, 183–184
Johnson, Gregory, 28, 32n32, 55n13
Johnson, Mark, 36–37, 76n3
Jollimore, Troy, 78n9, 138n41, 147, 151, 152–153, 155n85
joy, 83, 106–107, 137, 149–150, 161–162, 174–175
judgment, 10, 12, 63–64, 78, 98, 129n18, 162. *See also* appraisal; belief(s)
justice, 109, 148, 175

Kant, Immanuel, 97
Kenny, Anthony, 12
Kierkegaard, Søren, 110–111, 117n29, 123, 126, 129, 130n19, 131–133, 143, 151, 153n80, 188, 196
knee-jerk reactions, 28–29. *See also* "startle" response
Kolnai, Aurel, 76n5
Krishek, Sharon, 117n29, 132–133, 150, 188
Kundera, Milan, 150, 189–190

Lazarus, Richard S., 43n68, 67n36, 77n8, 92n40, 148, 162
Lear, Jonathan, 117n28, 192n71
LeDoux, Joseph, 23–40, 55n13, 66n34, 75, 84n22, 170n27
Lemay, Ghyslaine, 107
Lennon, Kathleen, 45n73
Levenson, Robert W., 40, 42nn63–64, 43n65
Little, Margaret Olivia, 177
love, v, 7n8, 8n11, 18, 20, 35, 63n26, 67, 71, 73, 77n6, 79–81, 96, 104–105, 107–120, 123–127, 129–136, 137–156, 164, 176, 181–182, 183–184, 186, 192–196. *See also* care
of neighbor, 129–131, 134–136
unrequited, 150n75
"low road" hypothesis, 24–28, 30–32, 37, 84, 160n1
Lyons, William E., 10n14, 67n36

Maclaren, Kym, 79n12, 94n44, 192n72
Malcolm, Norman, 69n40
Marion, Jean-Luc, 123, 125–126, 127, 136n34, 139n43, 144n54, 146, 151n76, 187n59
Martin, Leonard, 40–41
Matsumoto, David, 41
"matters of concern." *See* care; "world of concern"
McDowell, John, 34n37, 97n50, 142, 172n29, 186
McGinn, Colin, 39
McWeeny, Jennifer, 82n16
"me and mine," 148

meaning, 28, 82, 109, 116, 128–129, 139, 154, 176–179. *See also* value
mechanistic viewpoint, 35–36, 129n16, 138–139, 177
Meinong, Alexius, 14n23, 53n7
melancholy. *See* sadness
Merleau-Ponty, Maurice, 33n34, 36–37, 45–46, 77n6, 83n18, 88n31, 89n34, 105–106, 109, 128, 135, 168–169, 179n42, 180–181, 182n49, 183, 187–188, 196
mind-body problem, 4–6, 18–20, 53–54, 71–72, 87, 167
mixed emotions, 65, 90–91, 173–175
mood, 159–178. *See also* dispositional emotions
Moors, Agnes, 90n35
moral consequence, emotions with, 36, 58–60, 62–63, 81n15, 86
mortality, 69–70, 79–81, 150, 155, 181–182, 188–189, 193, 194n77
Mulhall, Stephen, 78n10, 129n16, 145, 160n2
Murdoch, Iris, 111n17, 134, 139, 149n71, 182, 188n63

Nabokov, Vladimir, 153–154
Nagel, Thomas, 44n70, 143, 193n76
Nash, Ronald A., 20
Nehamas, Alexander, 150–151, 155n85, 182n49, 186n57, 197
Neu, Jerome, 14, 107
neuroscience, 23–40, 55–56, 63, 84, 160n1
amygdala, 25–35, 55n12, 56n14, 75
cerebral cortex, 23–28, 55n13
"low road" hypothesis, 24–28, 30–32, 37, 84, 160n1
prefrontal cortex, 24–26
subcortical and cortical division, 23–32
ventromedial cortex, 63n27
Newen, Albert, 65n31
Nietzsche, Friedrich, 120, 125, 138n39, 141n47, 173, 178n40, 179, 185, 193
nihilism, 35–36, 129n16, 139, 159, 172, 177, 193n75
noncognitive theories, 6–20, 32, 56, 58–60, 67, 78–79, 84, 87–88, 97–98

Nussbaum, Martha C., 6n6, 7, 13n21, 16n29, 17, 31, 33n33, 45n72, 46n76, 60n21, 63n26, 68n39, 77n6, 78n9, 80n14, 92n40, 96, 104, 106n7, 134

Oatley, Keith, 33n33
objects of emotion. *See* intentionality
Ortega y Gasset, José, 126, 132
Ortony, Andrew, 90n35, 162
oxytocin, 35–36, 176

Panksepp, Jaak, 25n5, 30n25
partiality, 142, 144, 152–155, 179, 186
Pascal, Blaise, 4, 123
Peacocke, Christopher, 95n46
perception, 7, 14–15, 23, 27–28, 45–47, 67–68, 71–72, 82, 86, 88–89, 90, 92, 111, 115, 129, 140, 143, 163, 172, 183, 190, 197
illusory, 66, 139, 141–142, 161, 172
"perceptions of significance," 82, 90
personality, 178–180, 187–190, 191–195
Pessoa, Luiz, 24n4, 28, 30
phobias, 54–68, 195n77
physiological disturbance. *See* somatic agitation
Pickard, Hanna, 75
Pietersma, Henry, 85
plasticity, neural, 38
Plato, 17, 113n21, 149n71
Poellner, Peter, 120
Polanyi, Michael, 11n16, 164n11
positive emotions, 12–13, 40–41, 83, 95, 104–107, 114–118, 137, 149–150, 162–163, 174–175
possibilities, 103, 111, 124–125, 134, 136, 168, 192
prefrontal cortex, 24–26
prejudice, 152–153, 180n46. *See also* racism; sexism
Price, Carolyn, 87n28, 91n39
pride, 20, 41, 95, 105
Prinz, Jesse J., 19n35, 26n10, 35, 39n53, 39n55, 47n77, 52n5, 55, 67, 71n45, 77n7, 81n15, 84, 97–98, 154n83
propositional thought, 24, 62n25, 63–65, 68–69, 81–82, 85. *See also* belief(s)

Proust, Marcel, 69–70, 151n77, 181–184, 187n59, 197
Pugmire, David, 39, 53n6, 191n70, 195
"pure beholding," 77n8
Putnam, Hilary, 142n49, 180

qualitative properties. *See* value
"quasi-judgmentalist" accounts, 20n37

racism, 58, 173–175
Ratcliffe, Matthew, 38n48, 45n73, 59n19, 62n25, 71–72, 73n50, 78, 80, 86n25, 95n46, 119, 163, 148–149, 166–167, 177
reality, sense of, 93, 98, 103, 106n6, 110–111, 130–131, 134, 142n49, 145, 155, 167, 171–172, 189–190
recalcitrant emotions, 54–70. *See also* irrational emotions
recognition, 11, 18, 19–21, 28, 33, 64–68, 84, 80–81, 94–96, 119–120, 127–129, 133–134, 148, 174
Redding, Paul, 5, 176n37
Reeve, C. D. C., 146n61
regret, 106, 184
Reid, James D., 88n30, 193n75
Reisenzein, Rainer, 10n14, 19–20n36, 66
relief, 53, 98–99, 104
revelatory, emotions as, 11, 103, 108–110, 135–136, 138, 144–145, 167–169, 174–176, 178–184, 192. *See also* disclosure
Roberts, Robert C., 13n20, 16n29, 46n75, 54–55, 58–59, 72, 92n40, 106, 125n5, 137n38, 160n2
Roberts, Tomi-Ann, 41n59
Robinson, Jenefer, 25n8, 30–31, 33n33, 34n38, 35n41, 37n47, 44n70, 54, 58–59, 61n22, 67n36, 81, 87, 89n35, 97–98
Rolls, Edmund T., 24n4, 27, 29n20, 30, 42n64, 84n22, 162n8
Rorty, Amélie O., 55n13
"rose-colored glasses," 163
Rosfort, René, 152n79, 165–166, 184n52
Roskies, Adina, 63n27

Roth, Philip, 91
Russell, James A., 107
Russon, John E., 168
Ryle, Gilbert, 34n39

sadness, 41, 68–70, 78–79, 95–96, 150, 162–164, 186
Salmela, Mikko, 32, 84, 86, 90, 98, 192
Santner, Eric L., 144n56
Sartre, Jean-Paul, 7–8, 15n25, 73, 88n31, 103n1
Scarantino, Andrea, 56n14, 87–88n29
Scheler, Max, 85, 102, 108–109, 112n19, 115, 124, 127–128, 131, 134, 138, 142n49, 144, 147, 164, 176, 180, 190n66
Scherer, Klaus R., 43n68, 184n53
Schott, Robin May, 72n46
Schroeder, Timothy, 35
Scruton, Roger, 150n75, 153n80
Searle, John R., 7n9
Sechehaye, Marguerite, 119
self, 21, 36–37, 44, 53, 86, 91–92, 95–96, 99, 112, 131
    awareness, 39, 45–46, 62–63, 89, 164, 178–179, 184, 190, 192–196
    consciousness, 34, 72–73, 96–97
    deception, 60n20, 194–195
selflessness, 128, 134–135
sexism, 58–59, 81n15
Shakespeare, William, 44, 65
shame, 13–14, 105, 186
Shusterman, Richard, 64n28
Siemer, Matthias, 161n5
significance, 14, 21, 33–36, 38, 62–64, 70–72, 74, 77–80, 82, 91–96, 103, 110–111, 132–133, 148, 171, 176, 152–153, 181–182. See also value
Silvia, Paul J., 115n25
Singer, Irving, 176
social inequality, 58–60, 62–63, 81n15, 186
social justice, 148, 173–176, 178, 186, 194
Socrates, 17, 113, 135
Sokolowski, Robert, 34–35
Solomon, Robert C., 11, 23n1, 35n40, 44n70, 46–47n76, 92n40, 137n36, 161n3

somatic agitation, 4–6, 15–18, 38–47, 42, 51–52, 93, 166–167
Sorabji, Richard, 10, 26n10, 55n12, 162n9
Stanghellini, Giovanni, 152n79, 165–166, 184n52
"startle" response, 23–25, 27n14, 28–29, 32
Stepper, Sabine, 40–41
Stevenson, Bryan, 173–175
Stocker, Michael, 46n76, 62–63, 98n52, 114n21, 132n24
Stoicism, 81n15
Stokes, Patrick, 114n23, 153n80
Stolorow, Robert, 85n23
Strack, Fritz, 40–41
Strawson, P. F., 77n8

Tappolet, Christine, 6, 15n27, 26, 31, 61n23, 87n29
Taylor, Charles, 89
temperament, 95, 157, 172, 187–188, 190–191, 195–196
Teroni, Fabrice, 55, 57n16, 96n48
Thompson, M. Guy, 149n72, 195
Thomson, Iain D., 192
Thoreau, Henry David, 93, 171–172
Todes, Samuel, 73, 92n40, 162n9
Tolstoy, Leo, 80
tragedy, 150n75, 151, 154–155, 186, 195
trust, 4, 35–36, 62–65, 150, 185, 187–188

uncertainty, 62–63, 85–87, 90–92, 175, 188, 196
unconscious, 56n14, 59–60, 80, 89, 96n48, 160n1
unity, phenomenal, 30, 33–34, 53–54, 67–68, 73–74, 85–86, 92–93, 96–97, 185
upheaval, 4, 39–40, 51–52, 64, 69–72, 95–96, 184, 193–194. See also somatic agitation

value, 11, 14, 19–21, 33, 38, 51–52, 69–72, 74, 63–67, 75–80, 87–88, 91, 93–99, 106, 108–109, 111–112, 118, 125, 133, 137–138, 141, 145, 152–155, 164, 172–173, 188, 192–193, 197
Vargas, Patrick T., 111

ventromedial cortex, 63n27
"view from nowhere," 143, 154, 186, 188
Voice, Paul, 151n77
vulnerability, 73, 112, 130–131, 150, 183, 191–192

Wagenmakers, Eric-Jan, 41n57
White, Richard J., 187
Whiting, Demian, 98n52
Wiggins, David, 129
Williams, Bernard, 143, 183n51, 197
Williams, Lawrence, 41
Wittgenstein, Ludwig, 68n39, 97n49

Wollheim, Richard, 104
"world of concern," 103, 164
worry, 44, 105, 107, 112, 142
Wynn, Mark R., 52n4, 68n39, 98n53

Yiend, Jenny, 30

Zagzebski, Linda T., 53n6, 87n27
Zahavi, Dan, 8n11, 37n46, 46n74, 83n18, 166
Zajonc, Robert B., 15n27, 37n47, 40n57, 51n1, 87n29
Zeman, Adam, 28n19

CPSIA information can be obtained
at www.ICGtesting.com
Printed in the USA
BVHW030238080221
599338BV00002B/90